I0821352

THE MASSES OF
Seán and Peadar Ó Riada

EXPLORATIONS IN VERNACULAR CHANT

Dedicated to

Vincent O'Keeffe

(1933–2017)

Singer of Tales

THE MASSES OF
Seán and Peadar Ó Riada

EXPLORATIONS IN VERNACULAR CHANT

JOHN O'KEEFFE

First published in 2017 by
Cork University Press
Youngline Industrial Estate
Pouladuff Road, Togher
Cork T12 HT6V, Ireland

© Text John O'Keeffe 2017
© Music The Ó Riada Estate

All rights reserved. No part of this book may be reprinted or reproduced or utilised in any electronic, mechanical or other means, now known or hereafter invented, including photocopying and recording or otherwise, without either the prior written permission of the publisher or a licence permitting restricted copying in Ireland issued by the Irish Copyright Licensing Agency Ltd, 25 Denzille Lane, Dublin 2.

The right of the author to be identified as originator of this work has been asserted by him in accordance with Copyright and Related Rights Acts 2000 to 2007.

British Library Cataloguing in Publication Data
A CIP catalogue record for this book is available from the British Library.

ISBN 978-1-782052-35-7

Typeset by Studio 10 Design
Printed and bound by CPI Group (UK) Ltd, Croydon, CR0 4YY

Published with the support of the National University of Ireland and Maynooth Scholastic Trust.

CONTENTS

FOREWORD

This book is a very important contribution to liturgical musicology in the Catholic tradition and it achieves a number of tasks admirably. The study examines three settings of the mass ordinary by the two Cúil Aodha composers, father and son, Seán and Peadar Ó Riada. The principal focus is on compositional process and the primacy and integrity of the liturgical text, in this case the Irish vernacular. It is the first time that Seán Ó Riada's mass settings have been the focus of a study in their own right. Given that Peadar Ó Riada inherited the direction of Cór Chúil Aodha from his father and that he too has contributed significantly to the corpus of vernacular liturgical chant, it is entirely appropriate that the compositions of father and son be treated together.

Those who work at the pastoral coalface of Catholic liturgical music in Ireland know and respect the work of Dr John O'Keeffe through his patient and devoted service as Director of Sacred Music at St Patrick's College, Maynooth for over twenty-five years. This wealth of liturgical experience and reflection on music and liturgy is evident in his own liturgical compositions and his teaching. As a lecturer and choral director at Maynooth he has influenced countless students and seminarians. The present work distils those many years of experience and thinking about liturgical music, and introduces these insights to a wider audience in Ireland and beyond. While the focus of this study is Irish, the message is universal: the pre-eminence of the text in the compositional process in the masses of Seán and Peadar Ó Riada should be the aim of all liturgical music worthy of the name.

I cannot think of anyone else who could do full justice to the Ó Riada mass settings: John O'Keeffe has the range of skills and competence for this task. He draws on his knowledge of western medieval chant, the contemporary vernacular Catholic tradition, Irish traditional music, liturgical studies and ethnomusicology to inform his analysis and discussion. O'Keeffe's deep knowledge and experience of Gregorian chant is especially evident in his analysis of the Ó Riada compositions. The examination of modality in all three mass settings reflects recent researches in medieval chant scholarship and it is refreshing to see Jean Claire's concept of 'archaic modality' used in this Irish context. The analysis of Peadar Ó Riada's *Aifreann Eoin na Croise* is very rich with its emphasis on motivic structure and text-motif relationships in this work. These central chapters on the three mass settings are also enriched by the author's deep awareness of the importance of debates on orality and oral transmission in ethnomusicological studies and in recent chant scholarship. The analysis of the mass settings is infused with insights from the work of Treitler, Jeffery, Dobszay, Nowacki, Cowdery and other eminent scholars.

The mass settings of Seán Ó Riada emerge out of a milieu where religious faith and culture were inextricably united. They have stood the test of time very well. They retain a place in the Irish psyche which is probably due to the continuing reverence for the role of Seán Ó Riada in the re-vitalisation of Irish traditional music in the 1960s and '70s. When the young composer, Seán Ó Riada, moved with his family to the Irish-speaking village of Cúil Aodha in the Múscraí Gaeltacht of west Cork, he immersed himself in the rich tradition of ornamented Irish song. There he established a choir of men and boys, known as 'Cór Chúil Aodha', now under the direction of his son, Peadar. Seán Ó Riada's intellectual and spiritual contacts with the Benedictine monks of Glenstal Abbey and his rootedness in the traditions of Múscraí, provided the inspiration and focus for his two settings of the mass ordinary in Irish, *Ceol an aifrinn and Aifreann 2*. These mass settings have not always travelled well beyond the Múscraí Gaeltacht, often sounding banal and unremarkable when sung by choirs and congregations who lack feeling for the Irish song tradition and real proficiency in Irish. Within the context of Cúil Aodha itself, these mass settings are anything but banal: they are electrifying, deceptively simple and authentic, as evidenced by the recordings of Cór Chúil Aodha. Peadar Ó Riada's more recent *Aifreann Eoin na Croise* exemplifies his work. He has had the opportunity to continue his father's work within the Cúil Aodha tradition, while developing a distinctive and, as this study reveals, equally significant voice of his own.

In the *Confessio*, St Patrick speaks of hearing the 'voice of the Irish'. Of course, there are several voices of the Irish today using diverse languages in worship. Much contemporary vernacular liturgical music in English is unrooted and has a mid-Atlantic quality. It is driven by large publishing houses and appeals to a consumer mentality. At the heart of the Christian vocation lie concepts of truth, beauty and holiness, and one could add authenticity as an all-encompassing concept. The individual Christian and the Christian community are called to live authentic lives according to the Gospel. Authenticity in worship is paramount: if the voice and face presented to God is not real and true, what is? The authentic voice of the Christian is one coloured by origin, identity, culture and life experience grounded in truth. Finding one's voice is an intrinsic part of growth as a human being and growth in holiness. The challenge for the composer of liturgical music is twofold: to speak with his or her own voice, and to speak with the voice of the community, the particular *ecclesia*, the *vox populi*. This latter task is best achieved by sinking roots deep into the soil of place and tradition. Without doubt, the Ó Riada voice from Cúil Aodha is the voice of place and community, an authentic voice of the Christian Irish in the post-Vatican II era.

Much has been written in recent decades on the relationships between music and culture, liturgy and ritual, but almost no attention has been devoted to the foundational relationship between music and the liturgical text. Indeed, many composers appear to have become insensitive to the integrity of liturgical texts and this study challenges composers and liturgical musicians anew to be keenly aware of its paramount importance. The central concern of the study is the musical setting of prose texts associated with the liturgy: in other words – chant composition. It proposes a fresh and liberating definition of chant and redeems the concept of 'vernacular chant' from existing limited understandings. Above all, it does this by means of music which is exceptional in its quality and in its cultural and liturgical integrity.

FRANK LAWRENCE
University College Dublin
October 2017

ACKNOWLEDGEMENTS

My thanks to Peadar Ó Riada, for allowing me full access to his own music and that of his father, Seán Ó Riada. The knowledge that such vernacular church music not only exists, but continues to be developed in an Irish liturgical context, provides an ongoing source of inspiration. The expertise of Dr Ann Buckley (TCD) in both medieval musicology and ethnomusicology proved decisive in the initial framing of this study, and I acknowledge with gratitude her guidance and encouragement along an exploratory pathway. My thanks to Cork University Press for its assistance as the manuscript was being prepared for publication. Sincere thanks to Dr Darina McCarthy for her expert preparation of the musical examples and for her overall assistance in the editing process.

I owe a debt of gratitude to Fr Frank McNamara, founder of the Schola Cantorum at St Finian's College, Mullingar, who introduced me to the riches of western plainchant, and to Mícheál Ua Duinnín, who first brought me in contact with the song tradition of Cúil Aodha, and fostered throughout his lifetime the cultural links between the ancient baronies of Múscraí (West Cork) and Uíbh Ráthach (South Kerry). Thanks are due to Dr Katarina Livljanic (Sorbonne and University of Limerick) whose teaching and performing of chant as an orally-grounded musical tradition has been a significant influence. My thanks also to Professor Gerard Gillen, for his foresight in instituting at Maynooth University a pioneering PhD programme for professional performers, helping in this significant way to span the ancient chasm between cantor and musicus.

I am grateful also to many others who contributed in various ways and at various crucial times in my research: Professor László Dobszay of the Liszt Ferenc Academy of Church Music, Budapest, and Professor Edward Nowacki of the University of Cincinnati; Professor Pádraig Ó Fiannachta of St Patrick's College, Maynooth; Fr Placid Murray and Fr Senan Furlong of Glenstal Abbey; Dr Tomás Ó Canainn and Mr Ronan Mc Donagh; Fr Paul Kenny and Dr David Wright.

I acknowledge with thanks the help provided by the staff of the Irish Traditional Music Archive, the National Centre for Liturgy and the library staff at Maynooth University. All Ó Riada music excerpts are here reproduced under license with Real World Works Ltd., and the accompanying recording was mastered by Paul Keegan of Retreat Studios. Thanks are due to The Board of Trinity College for the illustration featured on the front cover, also to Aoife Dowling (AIRO), Professor Jim Cowdery and the Estate of Tomás Ó Canainn for images reproduced in the body of the study.

Such a labour could not have been undertaken without institutional encouragement and a recent period of sabbatical leave from St Patrick's College and Maynooth University. It could not have been sustained, however, without the unwavering support of family, in particular that of my wife, Gráinne, whose generosity of spirit has, from the very beginning, animated and blessed the project.

JOHN O'KEEFFE
Maynooth
October 2017

Cór Chúil Aodha at the Dublin *Oireachtas*, 1969. Seán Ó Riada is seated in the second row from back (on left), his son Peadar in front row (centre).
© PEADAR Ó RIADA ARCHIVES

Peadar Ó Riada with Cór Chúil Aodha in the parish church at Coolea, 2008.
© PEADAR Ó RIADA ARCHIVES

Introduction

This book presents an investigation into the liturgical music of Seán and Peadar Ó Riada through an examination of three Roman rite mass settings composed in the Irish vernacular, from within the cultural context of the West Cork Gaeltacht of Múscraí (Muskerry).[1] The main part of the work, running from chapters three to six, consists of a detailed analysis of the contents of the mass settings, a body of material which is considered from the following perspectives: as emanating from a living oral culture of native traditional song; as part of a historical continuum of monophonic liturgical composition for the Roman rite, having at its origins the orally-derived compositional traditions of plainchant; as part of a broader aesthetic context of text/music relationships found in the repertoires of plainchant, medieval song and 'folk' or traditional song; and finally, as part of the new liturgical reality existing since the Second Vatican Council which requires viable and sustainable musical approaches to the setting of vernacular texts.

Proceeding in the context of an understanding of Christian liturgical music as 'a combination of music and words', the study is situated within a framework best summarised under the categories of models, modes and motifs. Although these concepts relate to specific questions arising from each of the three mass settings, they will be seen to apply in various ways to the totality of material being investigated.

The broadest umbrella is that provided by the term model, understood as 'an existing framework' which is interpreted from a variety of perspectives, ranging from liturgical to textual to musical. The framework of the Roman rite, with its yearly, weekly and daily unfolding of liturgical celebrations, themselves governed by given ritual models, provides the broader context within which liturgical composers work. A particular aspect of this context, discussed in chapter one, is provided by the documents associated with the liturgical reforms of the Second Vatican Council (henceforth described as Vatican II). The rites of the markedly word-based Roman liturgy, in particular that of the mass, are themselves comprised of given song-oriented texts, generally categorised under the headings of 'proper' (variable) and 'ordinary' (fixed), of which the latter may more easily be recognised as models. Existing, through-composed, monophonic settings of these fixed, ordinary texts, as expressed in the Latin-language tradition of Gregorian chant, provide specific musical models against which to compare the corresponding Irish vernacular versions of the combined Ó Riada corpus (taking into consideration similarities and dissimilarities in textual form, expression and, as we shall see, 'number').

The composition of the original Latin and subsequent Irish-language versions of these ordinary texts may in themselves be seen at a deeper level to emerge from a model of textual orality which expresses itself through characteristic 'adding' forms such as the litany, and through the employment of textual couplets governed by the oral device of 'parallelism'. The versions of both languages are linked above all, however, in their adherence to the formally asymmetrical and numerically indiscriminate patterns of prose, and this study will proceed on the basis of an essential definition of Roman rite liturgical music: sung prose. Prose and orality combine in a particular way in the body of ancillary Irish devotional prayer texts selected by both Ó Riadas to serve as native propers. The implications of the musical engagement of Peadar Ó Riada with this type of textual material for the until now largely unexplored area of official Roman rite vernacular propers will be considered in the final part of this study.

The orally based song tradition of Cúil Aodha (situated in the heart of the Múscraí Gaeltacht) out of which this liturgical corpus emanates provides a specific musico-cultural framework, the nature of which will be examined in chapter one, and the compositional models of which will, as the study progresses, be seen to influence in various ways, and to various degrees, the work of the two composers. In Peadar Ó Riada's case, this will be seen to express itself through the instinctive incorporation of musical fragments and phrases from within that tradition. In the work of his father Seán Ó Riada, on the other hand, we will observe in his dealings with selected symmetrical, poetically-regulated texts, examples of wholesale adoption of pre-existing song models. The compositional challenge of sung liturgical prose, however, provides the main focus of the analysis of the three mass settings. This challenge, new to the Irish song tradition, was first met by Seán Ó Riada in his setting *Ceol an aifrinn*. At the end of the analysis of the more liturgically significant prose elements from the mass – characterised, as we shall see, by the use of sung recitative – I will explore, from within the cultural matrix of Cúil Aodha, the possibility of a specific local model as a potential starting point for the composer. Towards the end of the study, the significance of the mass ordinary settings of Seán Ó Riada as compositional models for vernacular liturgical composers will be considered.

The specific model of the diatonic scale, with its fixed pattern of tones and semitones, provides the given context for the concept of mode which is considered throughout this study. Medieval understandings of mode, which acknowledge the governing influence of tetrachords and include questions of *ambitus*, final note and reciting note, provide useful points of reference in considering the diatonic Ó Riada corpus of unison melody. These are presented towards the end of chapter two, together with more recent reflections on modality in oral traditions, including that of chant. In Seán Ó Riada's *Aifreann 2*, where tonality emerges as the central compositional question, traditional modal theory combines with the more recent concept of 'archaic modality' and tonal evidence from within the native tradition to form a composite lens through which the music may be viewed.

In attempting to identify processes governing the generation of the vast monophonic repertoires of traditional and medieval song, musicologists have traditionally utilised paradigms spanning the distance from the artificial, closed system of modes, on the one hand, to the more musically derived, yet similarly limiting concept of melodic models, on the other. Recent scholarship on the 'how' of orally derived repertoires, including those of chant, medieval song and Irish traditional music, has mapped a more useful and satisfying middle way, through consideration of the concept of motifs.

Derived from a literary concept known as the 'oral-formulaic theory', this motif-based approach suggests specific ways in which oral musicians operate, and by which the traditions they serve continue to expand and develop in an organic and sustainable fashion. The availability of such processes to oral composers, which has historically enabled the emergence of the various liturgical repertoires of western plainchant, has obvious implications in our own time, as musicians consider the implications of the arrival of the third edition of the *Roman Missal* (2011), containing hundreds of newly translated vernacular prose propers intended for song. Motivic construction, while detectable in Seán Ó Riada's *Ceol an aifrinn* and *Aifreann 2*, will be seen to be all-pervasive in the third and, arguably, the most 'oral' of the three mass settings considered in this study, Peadar Ó Riada's *Aifreann Eoin na Croise.* The textual make-up of this large-scale composition, with its extremely long opening chant and substantial psalm and communion settings, is more readily identifiable with the Roman tradition of sung propers, and the separate motivic analysis contained in chapter six considers some of the generative, aesthetic, cultural and liturgical implications of the work.

Musical models, modes and motifs exist, of course, to serve the delivery of the liturgical and scriptural texts, expressed in the Roman rite through a multiplicity of sung forms. Woven through the whole tapestry of the work is the question of the relationship between text and music – the 'combination of music and words' mentioned at the outset of the Vatican II Liturgy Constitution's deliberations on sacred music – a question which has fascinated musicians and composers from all periods and genres. In our context it may be reduced to the stylistic arena where melody meets text and to the decisions taken by composers from within the monophonic traditions of chant, medieval song and Irish traditional song, as they strive to craft artistically satisfying and liturgically viable solutions. Chapter two explores some common artistic and aesthetic ground between these traditions, and considers in ascending order of importance the influence of referential, rhetorical and numerical factors in the encounter between text and monophonic song. From this, helpful pointers are identified which are then brought forward into the analysis proper. In the second part of the chapter, a section entitled 'Liturgical Composition and Orality – Models, Modes and Motifs' brings together the figures of Roman cantor, medieval troubadour and contemporary Gaelic songmaker, and reflects on some of the strengths and limitations of the various traditions in relation to the large-scale project of liturgical composition. It also explores, in some detail, traditional and emerging orally derived understandings of modality, and a concluding sub-section briefly introduces the concept of motivic composition, a phenomenon observable in medieval and traditional song repertoires. A more comprehensive treatment of this last question is reserved for the final part of the work. This has been prompted by the analysis of *Aifreann Eoin na Croise*, arguably the most significant of the three masses considered in this study in terms of pointers favourable to the emergence of a new Roman rite vernacular chant.

Let us now sing the praises of famous men ... who spoke in prophetic oracles ... who composed musical tunes ... their wealth will remain with their descendants ... the assembly declares their wisdom and the congregation proclaims their praise.

(Ecclesiasticus 44: 1–15, from Mass for the Feast of All the Saints of Ireland, 6 November)

1

Tradition and Context

Vatican II: Towards a Vernacular Church Music

In the spring of 1968, Seán Ó Riada[1] attended a presentation in Glenstal Abbey[2] by Fr Charles O'Callaghan, professor of sacred music at Maynooth, on the recently issued Vatican II instruction, *Musicam sacram*.[3] This document, which set out to define more clearly the role of music in the light of the newly established liturgical norms, explored in greater pastoral and practical detail the principles set forth some years earlier in *Sacrosanctum concilium*, the foundational document on the liturgy.[4] The new norms included those governing the use of vernacular languages in liturgical celebrations, and, between them, these two documents would form a central platform on which the future of Catholic church music would be built.

The translation of the Roman rite into vernacular languages following on from Vatican II was a hugely significant event in the history of Catholic Church music and it presented composers with an immense volume and variety of 'new' liturgical texts. The translated texts followed very closely their original models, retaining the overall structures, forms and general characteristics of their Latin precursors. Thus was produced another huge body of largely prose-based texts for which musical solutions would have to be provided. Because of the sheer size of the task, it began to be realised that elemental musical approaches would have to be sought, languages receptive enough and flexible enough to accommodate scriptural and liturgical words in the way Gregorian chant had so successfully done. Ten years after the beginning of the Council, Pope Paul VI addressed an international association of church musicians in the following terms: 'One hopes for a new flowering of the art of religious music in our time. Since the vernacular is admitted to worship in every country it ought not to be denied the beauty and power of religious music and *appropriate chant*' [my italics].[5] Paul VI's adoption of a concept of a vernacular 'chant', then, is indicative of a musico-liturgical vision eager to embrace the new order of things, but directed by the awareness of an already-existing tradition.

The nature and indispensability of the Roman chant tradition to the liturgical practice of the universal Church had already been defined at the outset of the Council's deliberations in its acknowledgement of liturgical music as 'a combination of sacred music and words',[6] words 'drawn chiefly from the sacred scripture and from liturgical sources'.[7] As to the nature of the relationship between text and music, the words of Pope Pius X, whose seminal *Motu proprio* (1903) on sacred music informs much of Vatican II's deliberations, decree that the 'chief duty' of sacred music of any kind is 'to clothe the liturgical text ... with suitable melody'.[8] For Pius X, this duty is most perfectly accomplished in the tradition of Gregorian chant, the primacy of which is upheld in Vatican II's description of it as the chant 'proper to the Roman liturgy',[9] and, more crucially for our topic, as a basis for future developments in vernacular music. As *Musicam sacram* states: 'Above all, the study and practice of Gregorian chant is to be promoted, because, with its special characteristics, it is a basis of great importance for the development of sacred music.'[10]

Composers of vernacular church music were asked to be aware of the Church's rich heritage of liturgical music and also to 'increase its store'.[11] Under the heading 'Preparing Melodies for Vernacular Texts', the Council Fathers had the following to say:

> Musicians will enter on this new work with the desire to continue that tradition which has furnished the Church, in her divine worship, with a truly abundant heritage. Let them examine the works of the past, their types and characteristics, but let them also pay careful attention to the new laws and requirements of the liturgy, so that 'new forms may in some way grow organically from forms that already exist', and the new work will form a new part in the musical heritage of the Church, not unworthy of its past.[12]

The accumulated wisdom and richness of inherited musico-liturgical forms, then, were to inform the contemporary composer's efforts to find 'new forms' of expression for vernacular liturgical texts.

In keeping with the Second Vatican Council's spirit of *aggiornamento* and openness to the world, attention had also been focused from the outset on the cultural and musical heritage of individual peoples, with a view to identifying elements of worship which could be adapted to their 'native genius'.[13] The determining role of the composer is again implicit in the following passage concerning the question of liturgical enculturation:

> Adapting sacred music for those regions which possess a musical tradition of their own ... will require a very specialized preparation ... It will be a question in fact of how to harmonize the sense of the sacred with the spirit, traditions and characteristic expressions proper to each of these peoples. Those who work in this field should have a sufficient knowledge both of the liturgy and musical tradition of the Church, and of the language, popular songs and other characteristic expressions of the people for whose benefit they are working.[14]

As one of the panellists of the Glenstal symposium on *Musicam sacram*, having been invited in the hope that he would have something to say on the subject of traditional Irish music, Seán Ó Riada would have noted this paragraph with particular interest. In 1963, the year of the Liturgy Constitution, he had obtained a music lectureship at University College Cork and taken the decision to embrace fully all aspects of native Irish culture by moving his family to the west Cork Gaeltacht area of Cúil Aodha (Coolea). The following year he had formed a church choir of local men, many of them accomplished traditional singers, and together they had been working on a combination of traditional Latin chants and a growing body of native vernacular religious texts for which Ó Riada provided musical settings.[15]

In his essay, 'Ó Riada at Glenstal Abbey', the Benedictine monk Dom Paul McDonnell recounts how, later that year, for Christmas 1968, he sent a greeting card to Seán Ó Riada, the main illustration of which was a plainchant melody of a Gospel acclamation for long in use in the monastic liturgy.[16] 'By return of post,' he recalls, 'he sent a plain postcard on which he had scribbled the Our Father in Irish, set to his own music.'[17] The hand-written setting, also sent to Tomás Ó Canainn and reproduced later in his Harris and Freyer article, is marked 'go mall, oscailte, sean-nósach' ('slowly, openly, in the old [traditional] manner') and is quite clearly in a traditional Irish sean-nós style.[18]

The significance for our topic of this exchange of cards (or was it musical positions?) between the monk and the musician is difficult to overstate. McDonnell sends, from the heart of the Latin tradition, a hallowed chant from the Church's universal canon, while in response Ó Riada sends, from the heart of the Gaeltacht, his own musical setting of the Lord's Prayer

1.1 Glenstal to Cúil Aodha, December 1968

1.2 Cúil Aodha to Glenstal, December 1968

('Ár nAthair') as realised in the distinctive rhythms of Irish prose. The nature of Ó Riada's reply certainly bespeaks a confidence, perhaps not so much in his own abilities as in the artistic richness and potential of the native tradition. The validity of the composer's response, however, could not be gauged through an assessment of the merits of one piece, however well written: such an assessment would ultimately have to take place within the context of a more comprehensive musico-liturgical output. As things turned out, this 'Ár nAthair' setting, which McDonnell reckoned to be the composer's first essay in liturgical music, was to mark the beginning of a process, initiated by the composer and continued to this day in the work of his son Peadar Ó Riada. This process has produced a significant body of Irish vernacular compositions for the Roman rite, a corpus of music which this book intends to explore through the lenses of three mass settings.

During the April seminar in Glenstal, Seán Ó Riada had signalled his intention to develop a 'sung mass' in the parish church at Cúil Aodha and indicated that he would write the music for it.[19] In the summer of that year, according to McDonnell, some Glenstal colleagues attending an Irish-language summer school in Ballyvourney met with Ó Riada, and during the course of their visit 'he was persuaded to write some settings for parts of the mass (Kyrie, etc.). From this he developed the "Ó Riada Mass".'[20] This mass, which included his 'Ár nAthair' setting, was eventually published in 1971 as *Ceol an aifrinn* ('The music of the mass'). The Benedictines had an even more direct influence on Ó Riada's second mass, commissioned through Dom Paul McDonnell for a congress of religious held at Glenstal in 1970 and published posthumously in 1979 as *Aifreann 2*. Some twenty years after the writing of *Aifreann 2*, Peadar Ó Riada,[21] who had succeeded his father at the parish church of Cúil Aodha following on the latter's untimely death in 1971, was commissioned by the Carmelite Community of Clarendon Street, Dublin, to compose an Irish mass for a celebration in December 1990 marking the 400th anniversary of the death of St John of the Cross. This large-scale composition, *Aifreann Eoin na Croise* (Mass of John of the Cross), completes our trinity of mass settings.

Cúil Aodha and Traditional Song

In general musical terms it may be stated that the three mass settings emerged from within a native traditional context characterised by a particularly vibrant song tradition. In a 1978 article from *Ceol tíre* (Newsletter of the Folk Music Society of Ireland) on the songs of Múscraí (the area surrounding Cúil Aodha), Nicholas Carolan identifies some relevant aspects of this tradition:

> Muskerry – Múscraí Uí Fhloinn – is an isolated largely Gaeltacht region of west Cork comprising two baronies adjacent to the Kerry border. Protected by its mountains from cultural buffetings, it has preserved and

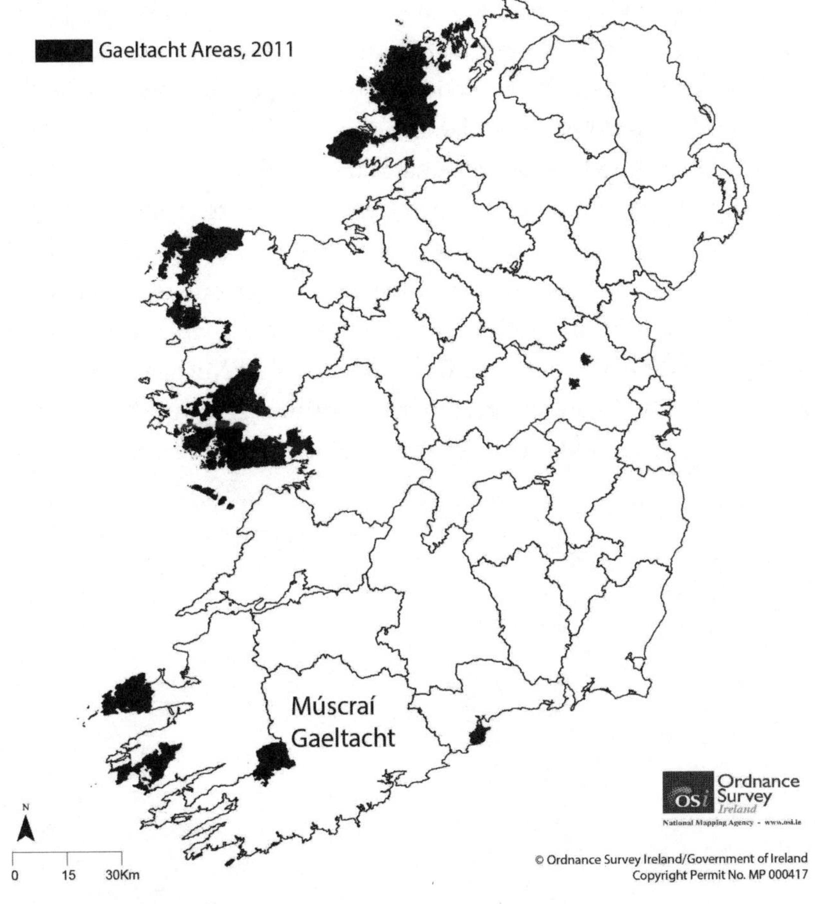

1.3 Múscraí Gaeltacht

> developed a distinctive song repertory and singing style … The big songs, both those in Irish and English, are sung slowly, employ a very large range, and are melodically elaborate and complex … The composing of songs is also more widespread here than is usual in the Gaeltacht. The annual *dámhscoil* or school of poetry has been meeting since the 1920s and produces songs in both languages.[22]

The historical importance of Múscraí as a rich repository of traditional song is documented by a series of significant song collections from the area, beginning with the 1901 *Múscraighe Fileata* of Cúil Aodha native Seán Ó Cuill.[23] During 1913 and 1914 the English-born scholar Martin Freeman based himself in nearby Baile Mhúirne and began work on a major collection which would later be published in the *Journal of the Folk Song Society*.[24] Dáibhí Ó Cróinín, who describes it as 'perhaps the most famous of all collections of Irish song', details and contextualises the collection in the following passage: 'Before even the great English collector Cecil Sharpe undertook his well-known collecting trips to the Southern Appalachian region of the United States, Freeman had noted down and published the words and airs of 172 songs ('filling seven notebooks of music and five of words') from a variety of Baile Mhúirne singers …'.[25] Ó Cróinín details a number of significant but mainly unpublished collections associated with Baile Mhúirne from the 1920s, 1930s and 1940s which preceded the next major publication associated with the area, *Ceol ón Mumhain* (de Noraidh, 1965), a collection significant, among other things, for the editor's attempts to notate the tonal and ornamental intricacies of the local singing style:[26]

1.4 'Bruach na Carraige Báine' (Ceol ón Mumhain)

From the mid-1940s onwards, visiting collectors including Séamus Ennis and the Americans Alan Lomax and Jean Ritchie began to take an interest in Baile Mhic Íre singer, Elisabeth ('Bess') Cronin who commanded a rich repertoire of local songs, light and 'heavy', in both Irish and English. *The Songs of Elisabeth Cronin, Traditional Singer* (Ó Cróinín, 2000) is the most significant recent publication of material from Múscraí and it documents the life, context and musical legacy of this remarkable singer, described by Séamus Ennis as 'The Muskerry Queen of Song'.[27]

Carolan's 1978 *Ceol tíre* summary of the music of Múscraí makes reference to a cultural tradition marked out by its readiness to create something new.[28] From the beginnings of the *Oireachtas* competition in 1897, Baile Mhúirne participants in storytelling and in songmaking, in particular the genre of the *agallamh beirte* or dialogue song, have been consistently prominent. Such was Baile Mhúirne's success in the early days of the festival that it was jokingly referred to as *Príomh-Chathair na Gaeltachta* ('the capital of the Gaeltacht'). The local *Dámhscoil* or Bardic School which emerged in the 1920s as a result of the activities of the Irish-language movement, and which continues to meet annually, has a particular significance for this study in that it represents a ritual forum for the performance and assessment of newly composed words and music. Here poetry and song naturally intermingle (as Peadar Ó Riada suggests: 'The distance between music and language here is very short.')[29] and young and old members of the community readily and generously contribute to the proceedings. Baile Mhúirne singer and composer Mícheál Ua Duinnín describes the manner of poetry presentation as follows: 'The poems were sung to local well-known airs of their own choice and those that couldn't sing recited their poems.'[30] In such a cultural environment, composition in words and music is experienced as a worthwhile and natural occupation. Thus Ua Duinnín, referring to a local acquaintance, could casually remark, 'Peaití was always composing ...'.[31] A cultural context where creativity is expressed in terms of an ongoing, consistent process of *productivity* has obvious implications for the enterprise of vernacular liturgical music. And the explicit valuing of this type of creativity as an essential ingredient in such an enterprise is inherent in the following assessment by Ua Duinnín of the distinctive contribution of Cór Chúil Aodha, as compared with other liturgical choirs: 'they are moving forward all the time, producing something *new*'.[32]

The largely unaccompanied unison song tradition of Múscraí, characterised, as already indicated, by a significant body of elaborate melodies 'which employ a very large range', provides a clear artistic framework and, more importantly, a working, living 'language' for the combined Ó Riada output in the area of liturgical music.[33] In the detailed study of the material which forms the main body of this study, attention will be directed to the 'characteristic expressions' (to return to the relevant phrase from *Musicam sacram*)[34] of that musico-textual language and to how they are harnessed to serve the delivery of a wide range of liturgical texts. The melodic richness of that expression encompasses the full gamut of musical elements, from scalar patterns to melodic phrases, through considerations of melodic architecture and tonality, to the broader dynamics governing orally derived material and the generative processes of traditional Irish music.

The Roman Liturgy – Rites, Texts, Chant and Orality

The music of the three Ó Riada masses is, of course, destined for use in the celebration of the Roman liturgy, which simultaneously provides both composers with a 'fount' and 'summit' for their compositional efforts.[35] A source is provided in the first instance by the structured regularity of weekly and yearly celebration of the Church's rites but, more specifically, by the *texts* which both comprise and individualise those rites.[36] A defining characteristic of the Roman musico-textual inheritance is its almost exclusively *prose*-based nature, a question which will be central to our reflections. The extent to which the two composers and their inherited musical language successfully engage with this overall textual 'given' will, in fact, ultimately indicate the measure of the material's success as 'vernacular chant'.

While the concept of chant as 'sung prose' forms a central plank of this study, broadening conceptions of chant beyond purely musical or even religious considerations, what is inescapable, however, is the specifically liturgical expression of it in the various plainchant traditions of the western Church. The immensely rich tradition of western liturgical chant forms a consistent backdrop in the investigation of these three Ó Riada masses, not only from the perspective of the Roman tradition of prose-based mass propers, but more particularly as a point of reference for the composers' settings of the mass ordinary texts, where comparisons may more easily be drawn across language boundaries.

MASS ORDINARY

The textual forms of the classic mass ordinary range from the shorter litanic Kyrie and Agnus Dei, through the more fully developed form of the Gloria, described by Willi Apel as 'an extended series of short and ever varying sentences',[37] to the similarly cast but more extended Credo structure. Many of the defining textual characteristics of the mass ordinary come together in a concentrated way in the more modestly proportioned Sanctus, an asymmetrical form featuring elements of both repetition and development.

The scriptural basis of the Roman mass ordinary is distilled also in the textual content of the Sanctus, described by Lucien Deiss as 'a chain of individual biblical acclamations', drawn from the Old and New Testaments:

> The *Sanctus* is a chain of individual biblical acclamations linked together. In using them in the celebration, the liturgy does not strip them of their original biblical 'density' but enriches them by placing them in the context of the Eucharist and its light. There are four acclamations, one of which is repeated:
>
> Holy, holy, holy Lord, God of power and might.
> Heaven and earth are filled with [full of] your glory.
> Hosanna in the highest.
> Blessed is he who comes in the name of the Lord.
> Hosanna in the highest.[38]

The five-line form of the 1974 *Roman Missal* version, referenced above by Deiss, might be further defined in terms of the more detailed, equally fixed numerical sequence, 7, 4, 2, 5, 2, representing the number of naturally stressed accents in each line of text. The fixed numerical proportions of official mass ordinary translations represent inescapable realities for liturgical composers, and we shall see as the work progresses how both Ó Riadas, but especially Seán who was the first to engage with them, responded to the particular metrical givens of the corresponding Irish versions of these texts.

MASS PROPER

If the texts of the mass ordinary might be described as liturgical texts with a scriptural basis, then those of the mass proper might conversely merit the description of 'scriptural texts within a liturgical frame'. The seeds of the Roman tradition of 'proper' (i.e. specifically appropriate) antiphons and psalms may be traced back at least as far as fifth-century Jerusalem and the pilgrim Egeria's account of the liturgical practice she observed there: 'Now it is this which stands out in all of this ... that they see to it that the psalms and antiphons are always ... so suitable and so appropriate that they pertain to the very thing that is being done.'[39]

The popular definition of Gregorian chant as 'sung bible' is largely derived from the musical weaving of hundreds of what Richard Crocker significantly terms biblical 'sentences' into the fabric of the annual liturgical cycle of feasts and seasons.[40] The prose-based nature of these sentences, commonly described as 'antiphons', which make up the vast bulk of the Roman rite chant tradition, may be seen in the following typical examples:

> 'The Lord said to me: You are my Son; this day have I begotten you.' (Midnight Mass of the Nativity)
>
> 'The Lord and ruler is coming; kingship is his, and government and power.' (Feast of the Epiphany)
>
> 'Your merciful love, O God, we have received in the midst of your temple. Your praise, O God, like your name, reaches the ends of the earth; your right hand is filled with saving justice.' (Feast of the Presentation)[41]

As can be seen, antiphons are assigned to or are 'proper to' certain celebrations, hence the description of these continually changing texts as 'sung propers'. The ability to musically render on a large scale texts of such metrically indiscriminate pattern, which historically produced the rich inheritance of plainchant, has been explained, through more recent chant scholarship, by the fact that this music was produced within a living, orally based tradition of song.

CHANT AND ORALITY

In searching for connections between the musical traditions of plainchant and that from which the music examined here has emanated, i.e. Irish traditional song, the phenomenon of *orality* constitutes a fundamentally valuable point of contact. Regina Randhofer places the concept in context for us:

> The term 'orality' (coined by Walter J. Ong [1982] on the analogy of 'literacy') describes a condition of society in which ... communication is conducted through speech, knowledge is kept in memory, thinking and expression are one single process. Oral societies, therefore, have to deal with the question of how to preserve and pass on their knowledge.

> The demands of oral noetic economy influence the structure, style and content of oral composition: it is organised in mnemonic patterns, e.g. additive style rather than subordinative style, various forms of repetition ... redundancy etc.[42]

Recent decades have witnessed the emergence of orality as a primary frame of reference within plainchant scholarship. In the following passage from a review of Peter Jeffery's 1992 study,[43] David Hiley outlines the nature and origins of what has become known as 'the new historical view' of the repertoire. The opening sentence is particularly relevant to this study, presenting as it does the notion of *continuity of process* between historical and contemporary orally derived repertoires:

> Ethnomusicology is concerned with musical repertoires which were *and are* [my italics] transmitted orally. That was also the case with plainchant right up to Carolingian times ... The best-known rethinking of chant history in order to take proper account of its oral transmission is that carried through by Leo Treitler and Helmut Hucke. As one of the many striking challenges to our pre-conceived notions Treitler put forward the analogy of the transmission of Serbo-Croatian epic poetry. This had been investigated by Milman Parry and Albert B. Lord for the similarities it offered to the way in which Homeric poetry might have been transmitted. The analogy was brilliantly successful ... mostly because it did indeed appear to explain so many features of strongly formulaic chants such as tracts. This and other ideas – about the musical make-up of chants, the role of notation in their later transmission, and the nature and origin of notation itself – have come to form a complex in our minds which has been identified by the catch-phrase 'the new historical view'.[44]

The Roman chant inheritance of scriptural and liturgical texts is itself strongly marked by orally derived patterns of expression.[45] Clearly evident in the parallelisms of the textual couplets of psalmody, the oral influence may also be seen in the litanic elements which appear regularly throughout the textual tapestry of the mass ordinary. Referring implicitly to the category of proper antiphons which grew around the liturgy, Peter Jeffery suggests that 'chant texts often give indications that they were not merely excerpted from a book, but rather developed from the way texts were quoted from memory during sermons and other oral renditions'.[46] Oral devices such as the litany and the textual couplet frequently feature in the otherwise prose-based structures of the various Irish prayer texts drawn on by the Ó Riadas to serve as native propers.

My characterisation of such texts as propers, both here and later on in the study, may need some explanation at this point, given the fact that the imposing repertoire of Roman propers emerged from within a distinctive cultural environment and represents the fruits of a living theological, patristic liturgical tradition. Taking the word in its broadest sense (i.e. 'appropriate to'), we shall see that, within the Ó Riada corpus being studied, distinctly proper leanings will be observed in the entrance antiphons of *Ceol an aifrinn* and *Aifreann Eoin na Croise*, indeed throughout the content of the latter (e.g. the psalm is of the feast, and supplementary texts of the saint's spirituality). However, this concept of native propers is even more broadly based, following Dobszay's description of Roman rite propers, which may be summarised as 'prayer-oriented prose texts set to music' (see p. 243). This definition places the focus more usefully on textual *structure* rather than *content*, and highlights the central concern of this study: chant composition – the musical setting of prose texts associated with the liturgy.

2
Words and Music

Introduction

This chapter will focus on certain aspects of the relationship between words and music. In addition to reflection from within the Irish song tradition itself, the study needs to draw from the experience of other monophonic traditions. A primary context is, of course, the chant of the Christian liturgy, which will form a consistent backdrop to our reflections. The surviving corpus of medieval monophonic song, including both sacred and secular sung forms, provides (both in terms of the size and variety of its repertoire, and the richness of scholarly reflection on the manner of its expression) a natural and potentially illuminating framework against which to judge the traditional, essentially monophonic material under investigation. A key resource on the question of medieval text/music aesthetics is John Stevens' study, *Words and Music in the Middle Ages*.[1]

Stevens' book deals with the full gamut of textual forms from the prose-based recitational texts of Gregorian chant through to the more consciously poetic art of the troubadours and trouvères. While the plainchant lens is a natural one to employ in considering the Ó Riada corpus, a body of material comprised principally of official, largely asymmetrical liturgical texts, his reflections on later medieval chant and on the more secular art of song-making have much to offer that is relevant.[2]

Traditional Irish and Medieval Song

Studies of the orally derived repertoires of medieval song and 'folk' or traditional song attest to the close structural relationship which exists between music and text.[3] In her classic study on the medieval tradition, Elisabeth Aubrey observes that music 'relied on the poetry for its structure and was wedded to the text in its delivery',[4] while an introduction to the subject of 'sean-nós' ('old-style') singing in the closely allied traditions of Ireland and Scotland, notes that 'the style is deeply rooted in the rhythms of the Gaelic language and in the metres and rhythms of Gaelic poetry'.[5] In both monodic traditions, a phrase-based compositional approach predominates, with the music marking off the textual sense-units by means of discrete, musically self-contained gestures, set within the broader architectural unfolding of the melody, as may be seen from the following examples:

2.1.1 'In Rama sonat gemitus' (twelfth-century *cantio*)[6]

2.1.2 'Bean dubh a' ghleanna' (from the Munster tradition)[7]

Despite such structurally close connections, however, Aubrey is at pains to point out that 'the music of the troubadours was not dependent on poetry for all of its coherence or meaning'.[8] Her noting within specific compositions of a 'discrepancy between poetic and musical graphs' is confirmed, for instance, by an observation that 'poetic rhyme is rarely mirrored by musical repetition'.[9] Hugh Shields, observing a similar process at work in a representative example from the Irish narrative song tradition, sees this mutual independence within the music/text union as a positive thing for the overall composition, noting that the musical structure 'contrasts agreeably' with that of the text: 'The melody is organized symmetrically in its phrases (ABBA) so that musical repetition contrasts agreeably with the repetition of couplet rhymes (*aabb*).'[10]

Broader markers identified by Aubrey, underscoring the relative independence of both music and text in the troubadour repertoire, might just as easily apply to the Irish song tradition:

> Given the common practice of sharing melodies among poems, as well as the presence of phrase repetition within a song and the reuse of the melody for several stanzas, it is obvious that the words of a particular text and the notes of a particular melody were not exclusively and inextricably linked.[11]

An Irish-based practice of 'sharing melodies among poems' is referred to in Seán Ó Riada's observation that 'Gaelic poets usually wrote their poems to fit an existing tune',[12] a statement attested to by the numerous tune-references contained in various collections of Irish poetry, both sacred and secular, published from the fourteenth through to the nineteenth century.[13] That these tunes were not always exclusively Irish in origin, however, is evidenced by the following quote from Aubrey Gwynn concerning the content and purpose of the fourteenth-century *Red Book of Ossory*, which interestingly refers to the influence of English and French models on one local populace:

> That the streets of Kilkenny were often enlivened by songs that were too worldly for Bishop Ledrede's pious ears (*cantilenae teatralibus turpibus et secularibus*) is plain from the fact that the bishop went to the trouble of composing some sixty cantilenae in Latin, which were of a more edifying character but could be sung to tunes which less edifying English and French words had made popular in the city.[14]

A relevant, near-contemporary continental insight into the practice of fitting words to pre-existing music comes to us from the troubadour Bernart de Ventadorn, who refers to the difficulties of 'seating' words into a melody which he himself had composed: 'I have been so worried as to how I might best "seat" words in this melody which I have constructed in pedes.'[15]

From the above we are conscious of a process involving two distinct elements (text and melody) which come together in close relationship, without loss of their identity or independence, to produce 'song'. This spousal relationship, inherent in the phrase often used by traditional singers that 'the words and melody lie well together', is inferred by John Stevens from a passage of Dante's *Paradiso* where the poet, in gazing at his beloved Beatrice, feels that it is as if he is looking at a mirror image of himself:

> a sé rivolge, per veder se'l vetro
> li dice il vero, e vede ch'el s'accorda
> con esso come note con suo metro. (*Par.* XXVIII.4)
> ('He turns back to himself to see if the mirror tells him the truth, and he sees the reality agreeing with the image as music to its verse.')[16]

Stevens reflects on an aesthetic understanding of song where 'the music is as intimately and sensitively bound up with words as an object to its reflection in a mirror, or as a shadow to the body that casts it. The sounds of the music and the sounds of the words are not indivisible; but when they are together, they are closely analogous, or parallel.'[17]

When the ideals of such an aesthetic are not fully met, the effects are keenly felt by those from within the tradition, as is evidenced by the following passage from Seán Ó Baoill's *The Irish Song Tradition*, which maintains the spousal analogy:

> William Carleton, the Tyrone novelist, records that his mother, when asked to sing the English version of 'Bean an Fhir Rua', said: 'I'll sing it for you, but the English words and the air are like a quarrelling man and wife – the Irish melts into the tune, but the English doesn't.[18]

Relational qualities such as agreement, give-and-take and compromise seem to form the bedrock of the continually fruitful relationship between words and music which lies at the heart of traditional song, and which, according to the pioneering scholar Annie Gilchrist, can lead to the generation of new musical forms:

> The contact of tune and words results in the adaptation of one to the other. Sometimes, one, sometimes each, insensibly yields something of its rhythm, or stretches or contracts its line or melody, and before long the pair settle as it were into place and the old tune may then be half-way towards a new one.[19]

Gilchrist's statement, in attesting to traditional melody's inherent and inherited flexibility and its ability to accommodate itself to varying textual requirements, broadens out the concept of traditional song beyond understandings which might give undue weight to the fixed nature of pre-existing melodic models.

Speech and Melody

> Singing a song is like telling a story. Know what I mean? What they say at home: abair amhrán, inis scéal. Say a song, tell a story. They don't tell you to sing a song … Abair, Abair. That means you're telling a story – in a nice way. And without the story, the song is lost; and without putting the story over in the song, the song is lost on an audience, or whoever is listening to you. That's the whole thing, to 'put the song over', as they say. (Traditional singer Seosamh Ó hÉanaí.)[20]

Ó hÉanaí's inherited understanding of the meaning of 'abair amhrán' interestingly echoes the medieval phrase 'hymnum dicere' (lit. 'to say a hymn').[21] A pertinent parallel may be found on the front cover of Seán Ó Riada's *Ceol an aifrinn*, which quotes the following verse from the Gospels of Matthew and Mark concerning the institution of the Eucharist: 'samo dicto exierunt in monte oliveti' ('a psalm having been said, they went out to the Mount of Olives').[22]

The twin concepts of speech and melody form the backdrop to John Stevens' reflections on the repertoire of Gregorian chant. His interesting overview is framed in the context of his understanding of the repertoire as: 'simply the most magnificent monument of western monophonic art, pervasive, enduring, inescapable. Its particular usefulness … in the present study is that it enables us to examine the relations of words and notes without the distracting complications of metre.'[23] Stevens points to the phenomenon of written liquescent neumes, present from the earliest neumatically notated Gregorian manuscripts, as being evidence that 'chant … was closer to speech in its flexibility, fluidity, nuance of sound (and "un-notability") than the singing styles to which we are more accustomed'.[24] The liquescent phenomenon, notable for its written attention to details of pronunciation, in particular to the clear separation of vowels and the practice of singing on the consonant, when applied in practice to the delivery of a text, produces a performance aesthetic which concurs very closely with that of traditional Irish singing.[25] Sean-nós singer Mícheál Ua Duinnín, in criticising singers who do not take enough care in their pronunciation of texts, refers specifically to the treatment of vowels and consonants in both Irish- and English-language song traditions: '... the last consonant of a word like 'Irelan-*d*', for instance. Singers tend not to take care with them ... 'Chris-*t*', for example ... That couldn't happen in sean-nós ... 'B*ua*chaill na gr*ua*ige breá buí' … the *double*-vowel is very important.'[26] Ó Duinnín's criticisms come from an understanding of song in which words and their meaning are prioritised:

> The words really set the tone, or the mood, or the *rhythm* of a song ... because, I suppose the words really are the important factor ... There is no point in teaching a song to somebody unless you explain exactly – 'tis like maths, really – you have to explain every *phrase* really; you have to get down to it and explain the words. If you go out and don't know what you're singing, you might as well not sing at all.[27]

Applying this to the liturgical context of Gregorian chant, where salvific words are to be, in the words of Pius X, 'presented to the understanding of the faithful',[28] it is hardly surprising that musicians should be equally, if not more, concerned with 'putting the song over' to their listeners.[29] What is required of the singer by both traditions may be applied with even greater seriousness to the work of the composer, the person responsible for combining textual and musical patterns into an intelligible unity.

Prose and Recitative

'Chant: A kind of church music in which prose is sung.'[30] Stevens establishes from the outset that the characteristic form of Roman rite sung texts is, in fact, prose, not poetry. He defines his terms in the following manner:

> 'Prose' may seem an inappropriate term, to say the least, with which to characterise some of the greatest poetry in the Western inheritance – the Psalms, the Lamentations, the Canticles, for instance. In the present context I mean, simply, writing which does not conform to any of the main traditions of medieval verse – syllable-counting, accentual or quantitative.[31]

The challenges posed by such a textual reality to the compositional skills or inheritance of the musician are given a context in the following quote from the Rev. J. Chapman, included in Virginia S. Blankenhorn's 2003 *Irish Song-Craft and Metrical Practice since 1600*, which also defines prose in terms of contrast with its more musically congenial relative, verse:

> Prose differs from verse, not in the proportions, or in the individual character of its cadences, but in the indiscriminate variety of the feet that occupy the cadences; and in the irregularity of its clausular divisions. It is composed of all sorts of cadences, arranged without attention to obvious rule, and divided into clauses that have no obviously ascertainable proportion, and present no responses to the ear, at any legitimate or determined intervals.[32]

One of the fundamental ways in which prose texts have traditionally been approached by musicians of all idioms has been through the use of '*recitative*'. The natural rhythms of 'ordinary speech' (another definition of 'prose') and melody come together in a second definition of chant provided by the *Chambers Dictionary*: 'to recite in a singing manner'.[33] In the Irish secular heritage, as in other European folk traditions, sung recitative is associated with the prose-based genres of the lament (*caoine*) and the epic form of the lay (*laoi*).[34] Referring to the musical style typifying the Ossianic tradition of epic poetry, Gerard Murphy states: 'Ossianic ballads [*sic*] were originally sung to airs with a wandering rhythm, reminiscent of plainchant and suited to the rhythms of their syllabic metre. These comparatively free rhythms differ greatly from the fixed rhythms of present-day song-metres.'[35] Hugh Shields notes in many examples of the genre the presence of textual couplets mirrored by a repeated two-part musical formula. Most clearly evident in the melodic structure of 'Laoi na mná móire', as recorded from the singing of Séamus Ó hIghne,[36] the universality of this phenomenon across national boundaries may be seen from the use of the term 'psalmodic style' as a descriptor for recitative-based material in a recent large-scale survey of Hungarian folksong.[37]

2.2 'Laoi na mná móire', melodic structure

In their major studies of the liturgical chant repertoire, both Willi Apel and David Hiley begin their stylistic analyses by focusing on the foundational, all-pervasive layer of 'liturgical recitative', as expressed in prayer tones, reading tones and in particular, psalmody.[38] Stevens traces the influence of the principle of recitation on important 'structural notes' through to the melismatic category of the repertoire in an analysis of the Palm Sunday responsory 'Ingrediente Domino', and concludes:

> It is in fact psalmody which gives the clue to an understanding of the way words (as sounds) relate to the notes. In the respond alone, a dozen verbal accents come on one of the two structural notes (cf. Ingredi*en*te, *Do*mino, *san*ctam, civi*ta*tem, etc.). The most important relationship turns out to be basic and simple; it is essentially that of recitation, at least in those chants – and they are legion – which have developed from the psalms.[39]

The intelligible delivery of scriptural prose by means of music demands the connection of both at the most basic structural level, a given summarised in the following terms by chant scholar Helmut Hucke, who states that 'the basic principle of composition in Gregorian chant is the division of the text into units defined by sense: the melodic phrases correspond to these sense units'.[40] Leo Treitler takes this concept further, looking at it from a more individualised artistic standpoint: 'The melody is a record of its maker's response to the relationships among word-order, syntax and phrasing ... [it] sets commas, underscores syntax, it associates words and clauses, it places emphasis. It is a means for the clear articulation and elucidation of texts in their oral delivery.'[41]

The chant maker's orally grounded combination of words and music takes place within the context, already noted in the case of Irish traditional and European medieval song, of a complex and finely balanced text/music relationship. This context is one in which music remains free to follow its own laws of articulation and composition, supremely sensitive to the textual structure, certainly, but not, as we shall see, enslaved by or ensnared in, every detail of its content, rhetoric or 'meaning'.

The 'Non-Relationship' of Words and Music

There are several reasons why the diverse and changing relations of music and poetry never cease to fascinate and have seemed to justify expenditure of time and labour. But the principal reason is that they compel one to ask the central question about what might, for want of a better term, be called the 'aesthetic' of the age. To consider the relationship – or what in some cases seems like a non-relationship – between a poem and its melody is to find oneself meditating on the 'meaning', for contemporaries, of the sounds they heard ... (John Stevens)[42]

> Often when the strain is most pathetic or dignified, the sense of the poetry bears little relation to the expression of the air. (Edward Bunting)[43]

> For 'heaven' and 'earth', you might use a high note and a low note, or a bright note and a dark note, or you might go the opposite way ... (Peadar Ó Riada)[44]

In the event, Peadar Ó Riada, the author of the final quote, follows none of the above approaches, choosing in his *Aifreann Eoin na Croise* to set the relevant Sanctus passage in the context of a formulaic melodic phrase which features no clearly contrasting aesthetically 'referential' gestures. Ó Riada's statement, taken in conjunction with Edward Bunting's observation from two centuries earlier, signals a certain conceptual freedom in the interplay between words and music in the Irish song tradition, a tradition which relies on unaccompanied melody to carry the text.

A constant point of reference for the author of the opening quotation, John Stevens, in his survey of medieval chant and song, is the following key passage from Guido d'Arezzo's eleventh-century chant treatise, *Micrologus*, which signals the close unity, certainly, but more crucially, the relative independence in the medieval composer's mind of the concepts of words and music: 'Thus, in verse we often see such concordant and mutually congruous lines that you wonder, as it were, at a certain harmony of language. And if music be added to this, with a similar interrelationship, you will be doubly charmed by a two-fold melody.'[45] This point is developed elsewhere in the treatise where Guido draws a parallel between the art of the musician and that of the poet:

> I speak of chants as metrical because we often sing in such a way that we appear almost to scan verses by feet, as happens when we sing actual meters – in which one must take care lest neumes of two syllables persist excessively without an admixture of some of three or four syllables. For just as lyric poets join now one kind of foot, now another, so composers reasonably juxtapose different and various neumes. Diversity is reasonable if it creates a measured variety of neumes and phrases, yet in such a way that neumes answer harmoniously to neumes and phrases to phrases, with always a certain resemblance. That is, let the likeness be incomplete, in the manner of the outstandingly lovely chant of St Ambrose.[46]

In his analysis of *D'amourous cuer* by the troubadour Adam de la Halle, Stevens perceives the Guidonian understanding as being carried through into later medieval song composition. He concludes his analysis as follows:

> . . . the musician was free to exercise his own fine invention. He does not have to echo the rhyme-schemes in his melody; he does not have to (and apparently never does) reproduce the sounds of individual words or phrases or their stresses – which vary continuously in any case from stanza to stanza. Still less is he concerned with the meaning of the words, individually or as a totality. His sole business is to create an *armonia* which will run alongside the verse, self-sufficient, a beautiful object in its own right.[47]

In trying to get at the heart of the problem of melody/text relationships in medieval music, Stevens is forced to consider and ultimately reject the prospect of any significant influence being wielded on musical expression by considerations of textual imagery, emotion (poetic or personal), or rhetoric.

IMAGERY AND EMOTION

Following his survey of text and melody in early medieval prose sequences, Stevens states: 'I must stress the total absence (as it seems to me) in the sequences so far discussed of any relationship which might in my definition be called … referential (that is, involving reference, intellectual, imaginative, emotional, to things outside the music itself) …'.[48] This echoes the earlier findings of Willi Apel in his 1958 study of the overall repertoire of Gregorian chant. In a section entitled 'Expression, Mood, Word-Painting', Apel states: 'Deliberate expression of the text, of its general mood or of single words, is, it seems to me … contrary to the basic premises of the chant …'.[49] In his exploration of various genres of later, secular monophonic song, Stevens finds nothing to change his views. Drawing on the reflections contained in Dante's *De vulgari eloquentia* on poetry and song, he notes:

> Dante never mentions, and I am sure did not have in mind, either a 'conceptual' relationship between the poem and the melody (the musician is not concerned with intellectual ideas as Renaissance composers so intensely were) or an emotional one (the musician is not concerned with real or imagined feelings).[50]

RHETORIC

On the subject of rhetoric (which he defines as 'the art of persuasion'), Stevens considers the chant repertoire to find an example of a 'live and practical connection between words and music'.[51] He focuses on the melisma in the context of the rhetorical device of *amplificatio*, the way in which an orator might emphasise or give weight to a particular word. The apparent freedom of the melisma from considerations of text emphasis or even accent is well documented in chant studies,[52] a fact that is adverted to in the following passage from an address given by Dom Jean Prou, Abbot of Solesmes:

> It looks, occasionally, as if a composer has not really made a word sing, or at least not as much as he usually does. A closer examination almost always reveals, however, that in such cases the composer has simply, with deliberate intention, sacrificed a detail in the interest of the whole; the apparent neglect of a word was in reality an integral and necessary element in the construction of the phrase. All of the pretended 'conflicts' between text and melody in Gregorian composition which, in the past, were claimed to exist, have now vanished in the light of a fuller knowledge of the text, melody, the rhythm and modality.[53]

Concluding a survey of largely chant-based music and musical theorising from the early Middle Ages, Stevens suggests that 'a theory of expressive sound closely related to subject-matter, a theory apparently derived from antique rhetoric, has only a limited place in "the medieval experience of music"'.[54] This point is broadened and taken chronologically further by Timothy McGee in a statement covering the period from the late Middle Ages through to the Renaissance: '... prior to the very late sixteenth century, the typical direct relationship between rhetoric and musical composition was rather general, consisting mostly of the observance of the syntax of the text by reflecting the textual phrase structure in the musical phrases that set it ...'.[55]

In the course of McGee's article, however, the author considers not a 'direct' but rather a broader *parallel* relationship between music and rhetoric, in their use of a similar repertoire of compositional devices. Under the rhetorical heading of *Elocutio*, he lists amongst these the devices of *anaphora* (repetition of the same word at the beginning of successive clauses), *antithesis* (the use of opposite or contradictory words or phrases) and *synonymia* (the use of different words to mean the same thing), all of which he says have their equivalents in the motifs or phrases of musical composition.[56] Later on, in our analysis of the Ó Riada material, we will observe these parallel concepts at work in the way in which both composers deal with textual structures such as, for example, the litany and the textual couplet.

In the working out of the text/music relationship in the unaccompanied monophonic traditions under discussion, since specific text-based pictorial, emotional or rhetorical considerations seem to play little or no part, attention is directed to the search for other perhaps deeper and more elemental points of mutual contact. The parallel yet relatively independent movement of text and melody 'through time' is a key concept put forward by Elizabeth Aubrey in *The Music of the Troubadours*: 'The melody of this *canso* inhabits a layer superimposed over the poem, both developing from a point, to a distant point, and a return ... The melody moves through time at a pace different from that of the poem, and ... its effect changes with the changing text.'[57] In searching for possible connections between music and text, Aubrey thus identifies a common governing factor to which both phenomena may be answerable, without loss of their respective independence.

Words, Music and Number

> The first generalization to emerge is that they [medieval musicians] are often working with a definition of *musica* which is broad enough to include them both and which indeed does not always distinguish between them, since music and speech are both arts which measure sounds in time. (John Stevens)[58]

In striving to find a basis for the connection between speech and melody, both of which 'measure sounds in time', Stevens finds himself inevitably drawn to a pre-existing concept which precedes words and music, and 'is broad enough to include them both': number. He quotes the following passage from Plotinus (AD 205–270) who says: 'Number exists before objects which are described by number. The variety of sense objects merely recalls to the soul the notion of number.'[59] In terms of the metaphorical connection between words and music, Stevens' own elegant definition of 'number' is worth quoting: '... number is a term to describe all relationships of harmony and proportion *between moving bodies* ...' [my italics].[60]

Stevens first of all considers the role of number in the crafting of troubadour verse, noting the 'metrical ingenuity' of the poets who were responsible for a corpus which, on the basis of István Fránk's *Répertoire métrique*,[61] 'contains approximately 1,575 separate and distinguishable metrical schemes, of which some 1,200 were only used once'.[62] He then goes on to explore the existence of number in melody. Having considered in some detail the purely melodic make-up of the earlier-mentioned chanson, *D'amourous cuer*, he says:

> It is again not easy to put this kind of analysis into words – into words, at least, that will convey the imaginative and intricate design which this melody so patently has. In the last resort we have to feel it *as music*. It is a flowing pattern in which various kinds of 'numbers' are musically realized – in actual numbers of notes and note-groups, and in proportions, balances, echoes; it is, to repeat, an *armonia*.[63]

At the heart of the art of the composer who would fit melody to a text structure, Stevens suggests, is the ability to create such a numerically satisfying *armonia*, 'a beautiful object in its own right ... which will run alongside' the numbers of the verse.[64]

Stevens' survey of word/music relationships covers a range of textual forms from the syllabic prose sequence,[65] to the asymmetrical *chanson*,[66] to the more melismatic and consciously poetic *cantio*.[67] The results of his detailed investigation of the medieval corpus of chant and song provide little evidence of any significant influence being wielded by either rhetoric or extra-musical 'reference'. However, they strongly support his theory that 'Behind both words and notes lies "number". A numerical Idea waiting to be incarnated ...'.[68]

Questions of rhetoric, reference and number all come together in the following passage, which bears a remarkable aesthetic affinity with John Stevens' above assessment of melody and text in medieval song:

> … those airs are not, like so many modern melodies, mere *ad libitum* arrangements of a pleasing succession of tones, unshackled by a rigid obedience to metrical laws; they are arrangements of tones, *in a general way expressive of the sentiments of* [my italics] the songs for which they were composed, *but always strictly coincident with, and subservient to, the laws of rhythm and metre which govern the construction of those songs, and to which they consequently owe their peculiarities of structure* [my italics]. And hence it obviously follows that the entire body of our vocal melodies may be easily divided into, and arranged under, as many classes as there are metrical forms of construction in our native lyrics …[69]

The author, writing more than a century earlier than Stevens, is George Petrie, and the body of material to which he is referring, that of Irish traditional song. Edward Bunting's earlier observation of this material that 'often … the sense of the poetry bears little relation to the expression of the air' has been superseded by a more perceptive and all-encompassing assessment in which melodies are said to be 'in a general way expressive of' the text,[70] to which, however, they are absolutely bound by the laws of number.

A more recent, more conclusive twinning of the concepts of music and number in the context of Irish traditional song may be observed in the following passage, pronounced at a ceremony inducting Múscraí traditional singer Máire Ní Cheócháin into the *Acadamh Fódhla*,[71] in which 'music' and 'metre' are described in biblical terms as the singer's 'crook' and 'staff':

> Mise scoláire léinn is eagna/ Sean-nós mo shlí/ Is í an ceol mo bhacall/ Is é an meadaracht mo shlat/ Gach focal 'na choiligh sheasamh/ Gach scéal go h-eirbeall siar …
>
> (I am a scholar of learning and knowledge/ 'Sean-nós' my path/ Music is my crook/ Metre is my staff/ Every word standing like a cock/ Every story tailing away back …)[72]

The heritage of Irish traditional song has its roots, then, in the relationship between music and number. The idea of 'pre-existent number' and its implications for music hold an even greater significance for a corpus of liturgical music such as will be examined in this book, a corpus characterised by 'peculiarities of structure' (Petrie) and one which has arisen directly in response to the numerical givenness (syllabic, accentual, linear etc.) of prescribed liturgical and devotional texts.

Liturgical Composition and Orality: Models, Modes and Motifs

MODELS

> I have been so worried as to how I might best 'seat' words in this melody which I have constructed in pedes.[73] (Bernart de Ventadorn, troubador)

> I just [had] a tune that would suit myself according to the rhythm of the words ... you know, *corresponding in sound*.[74] (Iain MacNeacail, Hebridean song-maker)

Number and rhythm provide the interface for the meeting between melody and text in the art of both the medieval troubadour and the Gaelic song-maker. In the case of Bernart de Ventadorn, music, in the form of a melodic 'model', would seem to have led the way, while the quote from Iain MacNeacail places more emphasis on the leading nature of the textual model. In his portrait of MacNeacail, Thomas McKean takes issue with ethnomusicologist Ives' assertion that 'a traditional song-maker creates new words to old tunes': 'This is too extreme: Iain does not select a tune beforehand. Instead he has a song text in mind which serves as a rhythmic – and by extension melodic – model.'[75] The concept of pre-existent number lies at the heart of the *Weise* or *Ton*, 'a term used in medieval and Renaissance German literature to describe a verse form together with its melody'.[76] A kind of melodic-type or stock melody, the history of the *Weise* stretches back to the beginnings of the thirteenth century, and the model was to prove extremely productive in the hands of the Meistersingers, for whom it was common practice to write poems on a received *Ton*. In the following passage Edward Nowacki contrasts the compositional skills required by the medieval Meistersinger (and with him, by inference, the Gaelic poet/song-maker) with those needed by the Old

Roman cantor, as he notes the limited musical potential of the overall *Weise* concept, particularly as measured against the challenges of the vast and, numerically speaking, extremely varied antiphon repertories associated with the traditions of western plainchant:

> We must now reconsider the concept of the traditional tune or *Weise* as a model of chant composition. In the German tradition the *Weise* belongs to a body of traditional folk tunes that are adapted to newly written poetry. In the Old Roman antiphon repertory, it is the texts that are the more fixed part of the tradition, since they constitute a protected canon that is transmitted in writing. To be sure, the Old Roman cantor could set texts newly added to the canon to one of the highly profiled song types … in the manner of a Meistersinger combining *Wort und Weise*. But he need not have done so, and could not have done so unless the length of the text fitted the details of the melodic stereotype in question. However, his command of tonal syntax was so pliable that he could always declaim a text in a manner that was at once unique and idiomatic, innovative and traditional.[77]

This passage places in perspective the potential challenge facing a traditional orally based song-maker (with an inheritance of a presumably limited number of pre-existing musico-textual models), who would engage with a 'protected canon' of metrically random liturgical texts (such as, for instance, the mass ordinary or proper of the Roman rite). We must be careful, however, not to create too great a conceptual chasm between the song-maker and the liturgical composer, remembering instead that Nowacki's 'cantor' was in fact working from within what most scholars accept as being the most demonstrably oral of all the western plainchant traditions, Old Roman Chant, and that the office antiphon repertory of this and other chant traditions is itself characterised by the use of 'model' melodies.

The orality of the liturgical composer, this direct and ongoing contact with a living tradition of text-melody relationships, must have been a crucial factor in rendering the Roman cantor's 'command of tonal syntax … so pliable that he could always declaim a text in a manner that was at once unique and idiomatic, innovative and traditional'. We are reminded here of ethnomusicologist Annie Gilchrist's observation of the historical adaptability of folk melodic models to 'stretch or contract' as required: 'Sometimes, one, sometimes each, insensibly yields something of its rhythm, or stretches or contracts its line or melody, and before long the pair settle as it were into place and the old tune may then be half-way towards a new one.'[78] Gilchrist's final phrase adverts to the organic nature of folk music and the generative processes at work in gradually creating and developing vast repertories of western monophonic music.

MODES

> I will not assert that the tonalities of this melody are exactly those found in either of the so-called Dorian or Eolian [*sic*] modes, nor even of that Phrygian, to which Selden tells us 'the Irish were wholly inclined'; but I may venture to say that their affinity with the tones of the *Canto Fermo*, or old modes of the church ... must be at once apparent to, and arrest the attention of, all those who have made themselves acquainted with the peculiar characteristics of the old ecclesiastical or Gregorian music. (George Petrie, *Ancient Music of Ireland*, Vol. II)[79]

The musical identity of a melody is governed by the physical make-up of the broader modal or scalar context of which it forms a part. Both western chant and Irish traditional song operate basically out of the diatonic model of tones and semitones, though of course there is evidence in the theory of the former, and in the practice of the latter, of the use of microtonal degrees.[80] The recorded and written versions of the three Ó Riada masses, however, clearly indicate a diatonic musical context, and on this basis certain comparisons may be drawn with the more explicitly scientific heritage of reflection on medieval modality.

Gregorian Modal Theory

An early treatise on the elements of the diatonic scale, the ninth-century *De harmonica* attributed to Hucbald, defines the two-octave scale model (*a'*-A), inherited from Boethius, as a descending series of *tetrachords* (a tone-tone-semitone structure spanning the interval of a perfect fourth). By the eleventh century, the structural importance of the fourth (*diatessaron*) has been matched in theoretical writings by an acknowledgement of the intervals of the fifth (*diapente*) and octave (*diapason*):

> You should remember that these three intervals are called 'symphonies', that is, smooth unions of notes, because in the diapason the different notes sound as one and because the diapente and the diapason are the basis of diaphony, that is, organum, and produce notes similar in every case. (*Micrologus*)[81]

The elemental power of the first, fourth and fifth degrees of the diatonic scale is noted by Edward Bunting in his third and final collection, *The Ancient Music of Ireland*.[82] In the opening chapter, 'Characteristics of Irish Melody', he observes that three-quarters of major-key, triple-time harp and song airs that he has collected are governed by the following phrasal dynamic:

> tonic-tonic // tonic-dominant // tonic-subdominant // tonic-tonic

The governing power of these scalar degrees may not easily be escaped by any composer working within a diatonic medium, irrespective of musical genre.[83] Intervals of octave and fifth above the tonic will be seen to assume major structural importance in Seán Ó Riada's wide-range, major-mode *Ceol an aifrinn*. At the other end of the mass series we will encounter in *Aifreann Eoin na Croise* a melodic fabric largely derived from tetrachordally based motifs. The distinctive tonal energies of the degrees of the fourth and fifth are crystallised in a particular way in the structural make-up of melodies occupying the Gregorian chant category of mode 7, which will be considered later as a conceptual lens through which the more elusive tonality of Seán Ó Riada's *Aifreann 2* may be viewed.

Finals, Tenors, Contours

> A tone or mode is a rule which distinguishes every chant in its final. (*Dialogus de musica*)[84]

> To attribute mode to a musical item implies some hierarchy of pitch relationships … it is more than merely a scale. (Harold Powers)[85]

> A modal system may be a rational construction, devised or revised by the learned; or it may be a traditional assemblage of musical entities used and retained by the working musician. And further, the possession

> of modality may be construed as a natural musical property, inevitably inherent in all music of the culture . . . (Harold Powers)[86]

The opening classic definition of tonality, which appears in the late tenth-/early eleventh-century Italian treatise *Dialogus de musica*, lies at the basis of the Gregorian *oktoechos* or eight-mode system. In the words of Harold Powers, it 'recurs in dozens of theoretical works over the next six or seven centuries; it is indeed part of the ultimate origin of the conventional notion of the "tonic", current since the 18th century, which is almost inseparable in textbooks from the notion of "finishing"'.[87] The *Dialogus de musica* treatise was matched in terms of subsequent influence and wideness of circulation only by the early eleventh-century *Micrologus* of Guido d'Arezzo, which clearly confirmed the 'final note' rule:

> Though any chant is made up of all the notes and intervals, the note that ends it holds the chief place, for it sounds both longer and more lasting. The previous notes, as is evident to trained musicians only, are so adjusted to the last one that in an amazing way they seem to draw a certain semblance of colour from it.[88]

Along with considerations of final note (which in the case of any chant may ultimately be situated within the tetrachordal series *D*, *E*, *F*, *G*), Guido, in chapter twelve ('On the division of four modes into eight') and chapter thirteen ('On the recognition of the eight modes by their height and depth'), includes the question of melodic ambitus. He also draws attention in chapter thirteen to the structural significance of pitches governing initial and medial phrasal cadences. By the end of the eleventh century, such structurally significant pitches were being associated with the tenors of the accompanying psalmody,[89] thus providing a further reference point, that of reciting tone:

> The addition of the tenor to the final and the initials further refines the hierarchy of single pitch modal functions, for it implies that one among the secondary strong points has a certain limiting power and governance over the others: it is the one which in fact is the upper limit of the theoretical possibilities for a resting point, and it is to be established by reference to the psalm-tone tenor. (Harold Powers)[90]

2.3 Modal Table

The *oktoechos* modal theory, however, as Powers notes, was an attempt, *after the event*, to systematise and regularise (frequently for practical liturgical usage) a massive repertoire of chants characterised by a 'natural melodic modality'. This attempt to organise the repertoire within a 'closed and symmetrical system' inevitably involved compromise:

> The consistencies … are the result of medieval classification, adaptation and adjustment, which took full advantage of the existing modalities of the chant repertory, and brought the borrowed eightfold system into as much harmony as possible with existing melodies, melody types and psalmodic practices. The result was on the whole successful but there were numerous discrepancies … there were many cases in Latin liturgical song where a satisfactory fit was never really achieved.[91]

In his 1962 article 'L'évolution modale dans les répertoires liturgiques occidentaux', Dom Jean Claire of Solesmes began a series of scholarly reflections on the modal character of plainchant prior to the adoption of the *oktoechos*.[92] His resulting theory of 'archaic modality' suggests, in chant scholarship terms, a fundamental shift of analytical focus away from the final note, turning instead towards the question of the principal structural or reciting note. In support of his theory is the evidence provided by examples of early office antiphons, sharing the same melody but concluding at different pitches, thus weakening the case for the notion of the absolute dominance of the final in the mind of the composers who generated the music. This freedom with regard to final note that may be observed in early composition is matched by a similar tonal freedom, evident throughout the repertoire, in chants which clearly exhibit melodic characteristics from more than one mode. As Theodore Karp notes: 'One of the ways in which Gregorian chant achieves variety is through the use of formulaic motives characteristic of one mode within the framework of melodies whose broader structures are founded in some other mode. The vocabularies of the several modes interpenetrate one another.'[93] Questions concerning shared melodic material and varying finals crop up regularly in attempts since the late nineteenth century to systematically investigate various national and international repertoires of folk music. Breandán Breathnach's 1980 *New Grove* entry on Irish traditional music conceives of mode in terms of final note, as he broadly categorises the melodic material in the following terms: C (*doh*): 60%; G (*soh*): 20%; A (*lah*): 12%; D (*ray*): 8%. Breathnach acknowledges, however, that 'different parts of an air can be related to different tonics'.[94] A recognition of modal fluidity in folk music of the broader Gaelic tradition is evident in Annie Gilchrist's contribution to an early edition of the *Journal of the Folk-song Society*: 'No doubt there will be differences of opinion regarding classification in some of these tunes, especially those in which the modes are mixed, and certain others in which it is difficult to believe that the last note of the tune is the true tonic ...'.[95]

Questions concerning final note and mode in Irish traditional music are subsumed within a larger conceptual framework by contemporary musicologist James Cowdery, whose 1990 book *The Melodic Tradition of Ireland* explores the generative processes of the tradition in terms of freely migrating melodic motifs or phrases which are shown to transcend modal boundaries. In addition to building on twentieth-century frameworks of folk tune analysis, Cowdery also adverts to scholarship drawn from other world-music traditions and from plainchant. In attempting to define inherent processes governing tune relationships, development and transmission within the Irish melodic tradition, Cowdery attests to the primacy of melodic contour over other musical considerations, elevating it to the status of a principle, which he terms the 'outlining principle'. He states the results of his findings as follows, stressing: '... an important point about the outlining principle: contour will out, cadence and final notwithstanding'.[96] The primacy, within another oral tradition, of contour over any pre-fixed notions of tonality is upheld in the following statement by chant scholar Theodore Karp concerning the process of transferring orally derived chants into written form: 'When notating chants employing more than the one variable degree allowed within the Guidonian system, scribes tended to sacrifice the overall tonal gestalt in favour of the shape of individual gestures rather than the opposite.'[97]

In considering the melodic make-up and modal behaviour of Seán Ó Riada's orally derived, tonally unified mass settings, in particular *Aifreann 2* (the only one of the three mass settings to be presented in purely monophonic form), we will observe the freedom with which the composer operates with respect to questions of final note and the 'mixing of modes' within individual pieces, as noted by Gilchrist in her assessment of Gaelic melody in general.

MOTIFS

> The formulaic character of medieval chant is the feature that has most often been linked, in recent writing, to the oral processes of transmission.[98]

The common framework of orality which lies behind the repertoires of folk music and liturgical chant provides the context for Peter Jeffery's *Re-Envisioning Past Musical Cultures: ethnomusicology in the study of Gregorian chant*, a book which critically examines questions relating to chant transmission and generation, arising out of chant scholar Leo Treitler's revolutionary and highly influential application of the Parry-Lord oral-formulaic theory. This theory, which arose from detailed study of oral epics, including those of Homer, was crystallised in Albert Lord's classic work *The Singer of Tales*,[99] on the surviving Yugoslavian tradition, and it was taken up subsequently by scholars in a range of disciplines, including literature, chant and folk music. In his book *Folk Music in the Modern World*, Philip Bohlman summarises key aspects of the theory, and considers their significance from a broad ethnomusicological perspective:

> This theory recognizes tremendous stability in formulae, with wide-ranging variation and creativity in the performance of the entire epic ... The long Yugoslav epics ... illustrate the dual role formula plays as a mnemonic device and a catalyst for creativity. So important is this role that some scholars measure the extent of orality in folk music by the prevalence of formulaic structures.[100]

The 'creative', or generative, potential of the formula/motif in the Irish melodic context is attested to in James Cowdery's study of the Irish melodic tradition, where he concludes in relation to both the song tradition and the instrumental tradition that 'the actual *process* of composition is suggested by complex permutations based on melodic pools'.[101] A similar view is expressed by Edward Nowacki in his study of the Old Roman antiphon repertoire where, leaving aside for a moment the skill of the cantor-composers in adapting material in a 'unique and innovative' way,[102] he acknowledges in general terms that 'the Office antiphons give the impression of a limited amount of material that is simply used over and over again'.[103]

The artistic use of repeated and varied melodic formulae or motifs as a unifying device within specific chant compositions is implicit in the following fascinating passage from a medieval chant composer, Guido d'Arezzo:

> The musician should also plan that the phrases be of the same length, like lines of verse, and be sometimes repeated, either the same or modified by some change, even though slight, and, if they are particularly beautiful, be duplicated, with their 'parts' not too diverse; and let those occasional phrases that are the same be varied as to intervals [*per modos*], or, if they retain the same intervals, let them be heard transposed higher or lower.

> Also a neume, turning back on itself, may return the same way it came and by the same steps.[104]

In his analysis of the Irish song-melody 'An raibh tú ag an gcarraig?' Seán Ó Riada observes a similar motivic process at work:

> Perhaps the best example of internal logic, fully developed, is in the song skeleton of 'An raibh tú ag an gcarraig'. It begins with three notes in a certain relationship, and this relationship is the hub of the whole song, the three notes being inverted, permuted and combined right through.[105]

2.4 'An raibh tú ag an gcarraig?' (*Our Musical Heritage*)

In his recent major survey of the Gregorian mass propers, *Aspects of Orality and Formularity in Gregorian Chant*, Theodore Karp draws on the work of Parry and Lord and of Treitler, also on the insights of literature scholar Ruth Finnegan, whose work *Oral Poetry* represents a significant contribution to the debate on orality.[106] Karp summarizes his topic in the following terms:

> Formulas are nearly indispensable vehicles for oral cultures. Thus it is only natural that Gregorian chant, which arose in an oral culture and which for centuries hung in a balance between oral-aural and written traditions, should be heavily formulaic ... Formulas that occur in more than one genre or in more than one mode provide essential threads of unity to the language of chant.[107]

One of the central tenets of the oral-formulaic theory is Lord's insistence on the adaptability of the formula: 'We shall see that the formulas are not the ossified clichés which they have the reputation of being, but that they are capable of change and are indeed frequently highly productive of other and new formulas.'[108] In discussing the inherently flexible nature of the melodic formula/motif within an orally based chant tradition, Peter Jeffery considers such factors as distribution, frequency of repetition, ranges of variability and freedom of association with textual structures: 'One type of flexibility, of course, is seen when the "same" formula is applied to different texts, with different numbers of syllables or patterns of accentuation; this type has been examined in parts of the Gregorian repertory.'[109] The generative potential of the formulaic technique within the context of an 'epic' textual canvas, the appearance of melodic formulae across different liturgical genres and melodic modes, and their adaptation to varying textual conditions, will be explored in a specific ethnomusicological context towards the end of this study in the *Aifreann Eoin na Croise* of Peadar Ó Riada, a work which is, as we shall see, highly formulaic in its design.

3

Ceol an aifrinn: Seán Ó Riada

Introduction

With this mass setting, we are introduced for the first time to the prose-based translations of the Irish vernacular mass ordinary, which represent an inescapable reality of textual content, form and number for any composer attempting the genre. Ó Riada's setting of these texts will be viewed as part of a continuum of Roman rite monophonic settings from the Gregorian tradition, specific examples of which will combine to form a composite frame of reference against which to consider the new material. In accordance with the aims of this study, priority will be given in the analysis to discussion of the prose settings, with the hymns, which will be discussed separately, accorded a secondary position. Discussion of the subsidiary musical aspect of the keyboard accompaniment will take place towards the end of the analysis. The important question of prose propers, which will feature more prominently later on in the study, is signalled at the very outset of the mass.

A distinctive framework is supplied by the religious and musical heritage of Múscraí which provides the cultural context for *Ceol an aifrinn*,[1] and the final section of this chapter considers the composer's assimilation of local musical culture together with the musical challenges associated with its liturgico-textual integration. Bridging the gap between the official Roman liturgical texts and the more devotional native compositions (prose-based and strophic) is the consistent appearance in both contexts of litanic textual passages which present Ó Riada with very particular compositional challenges.

Regarding the challenge of the overall textual canvas of the mass, telling use of the liturgically associated medium of sung recitative, in combination with specific tonal elements from the native song tradition, will be seen to provide a liturgically viable and culturally grounded vehicle for the words. As we encounter for the first time also the union of these liturgical words with the music of traditional Irish song, particular attention will be focused on the aesthetic implications of the interplay between the two entities, with its attendant referential, rhetorical and numerical considerations.

Contents

1. *Iontróid (Is beannaithe Tigh Dé)*
2. *Kyrie eleison*
3. *An ghlóir*
4. *Ofráil (hymn: Ag Críost an síol)*
5. *An phréafáid*
6. *Sanctus*
7. *An phaidir*
8. *Agnus Dei*
9. *Iomann comaoineach (hymn: Gile mo chroí)*
10. *Iomann iargomaoineach (hymn: Réir Dé go ndeineam)*
11. *Bí, a Íosa*[2]
12. *A Rí an Domhnaigh*

Ó Riada's choice of titles for the various pieces is not an insignificant feature. For the ordinary elements of the mass he uses a mixture of Irish and Gregorian titles, avoiding, for instance, 'Gloria', 'Praefatio' and 'Pater noster' in favour of their Irish versions (nos 3, 5 and 7). From the proper elements we note his selection of symmetrical hymn forms for the offertory, communion and recession (nos 4, 9, 10, 11 and 12), in contrast to his retention of the concept of a traditional 'introit', reflected both in the choice of title and in his selection of a non-metrical entrance chant.

IONTRÓID: IS BEANNAITHE TIGH DÉ

Is beannaithe Tigh Dé,	*God's house is blessed,*
is beannaímid féin dó,	*and we ourselves salute it,*
mar a bhfuil sé leis an dá aspal déag.	*where he is with the twelve apostles.*
Go mbeannaí Mac Dé dhúinn.	*May the Son of God bless us.*
Is beannaithe Thú, a Athair bheannaithe.	*You are blessed, O blessed Father.*
Is beannaithe Thú, a Mhic an Athar bheannaithe.	*You are blessed, O Son of the blessed Father.*
Is beannaithe Thú, a Theampaill an Sprid Naoimh.	*You are blessed, Temple of the Holy Spirit.*
Is beannaithe Thú, a Eaglais na Tríonóide.	*You are blessed, O Church of the Trinity.*[3]

3.1 Seán Ó Riada: *Ceol an aifrinn, Iontróid* (bars 1–12)

The *Iontróid* succinctly encapsulates for us many of the issues relating not just to this particular mass setting, but to the study as a whole. The first and critical decision taken by Ó Riada was his selection of a prose-based text to open up the celebration. In choosing this approach, he was, it may confidently be asserted, actively avoiding (and this pattern will be repeated in his second mass) the utilisation of metrical strophic forms, of which there are many later on in the mass setting. By deciding in favour of asymmetrical prose, Ó Riada aligns himself very closely with one of the foundational principles of Roman rite liturgical music, and his adoption of what may be described as an appropriate Introit antiphon signals from the outset a continuity with the Roman tradition of chanted propers, a question which will assume greater importance towards the end of this study.

The musical expression of the text, a traditional prayer of blessing associated with entry into a church,[4] is couched in the *doh* mode and occupies a range of a tenth (features which are common enough in the Munster song tradition), and the overall melodic composition balances recitational elements with more lyrically mobile passages. It is through-composed, with the numerical qualities of the textual form clearly dictating the nature of the musical expression. The opening section (bars /1–4) is set in the middle/upper register, oscillating structurally between high *b-flat*' (*doh*'), on which the opening is hung, and *f*' (*soh*), which concludes the section. The second litanic section (bars 5–13), however, is dominated by a series of rising recitations (on *c*', *d*' and *g*') which eventually quicken into a more melodically expressive final blessing. This section is marked at its beginning by a downward shift in vocal register and in general by its wide range. The last phrase brings the music back to the pitch region of the prayer's opening and concludes on high *b-flat*' (*doh*').

The greater melodic expressiveness nearing the end of the prayer results in a musical division of the last two lines into four phrases, thus giving a ten-phrase musical structure. The overall tonal layout, viewed through a developing series of phrase-end notes, is mapped as follows:

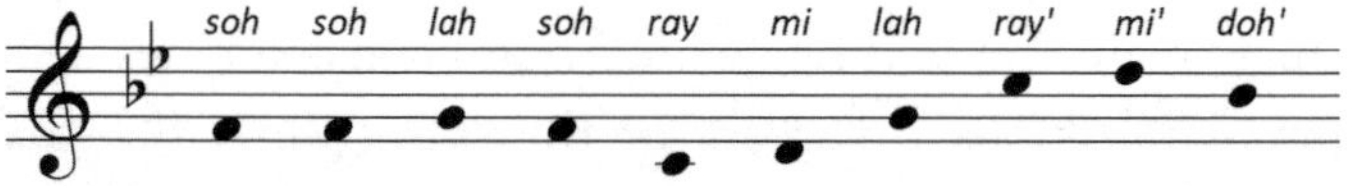

3.2 Seán Ó Riada, *Ceol an aifrinn, Iontróid*: phrase-endings

The declamatory nature of the prayer may account for Ó Riada's decision to begin and end on a high tessitura, features which would be less typical of the Munster tradition of 'big' songs (amhráin mhóra). This approach is repeated in two other declamatory mass ordinary texts containing strong elements of praise: *An ghlóir* (beginning and ending, leaving out the concluding 'Amen') and the *Sanctus* (ending only).[5]

In the second half of the piece, apart from the apparent plan of the composer to set out a wide tonal canvas and to reflect the developing litany by means of a very obvious rising movement, there is no detectable attempt at word-painting in terms of attaching particular significance to the personages mentioned. The cumulative build-up of the litany structure provides the impetus for a musical movement which culminates in the final 'Is beannaithe Thú' breaking out of recitative and into song, thus concluding the prayer with melodic savour.

KYRIE ELEISON

A Thiarna, déan trócaire	*Lord, have mercy.*
A Chríost, déan trócaire.	*Christ, have mercy.*
A Thiarna, déan trócaire.	*Lord, have mercy.*

3.3 Seán Ó Riada: *Ceol an aifrinn, Kyrie eleison* (bars 13–15)

Ó Riada chooses a basic AABBAA call/response format for this simple syllabic setting which 'recites' at mid-range on *f'* (*soh'*) and combines with downward and upward inflections to *d'*, g' and, in the case of phrase B, *b-flat'* (*doh'*). The rhythm (set in a triplet-based 9/8 structure) is very much that of the spoken invocation, and it combines with the recitational melodic style to produce an effect which is very much in harmony with the Kyrie's litanic origins,[6] as expressed in the following opening invocations from the Gregorian Litany of the Saints:

3.4 Gregorian Litany of the Saints

The tonally stable, litanic effect which characterises Ó Riada's first setting of this text renders it eminently repeatable in liturgical situations, and throughout Ireland to this day, even in English-language celebrations, it remains the setting most frequently, and most willingly, intoned by liturgical presiders. The chant's intrinsic tonal stability is further enhanced by a tonic pedal which supports the repeated progression I–IV^6_4–I.

AN GHLÓIR

Gloria in excelsis Deo.
Et in terra pax hominibus bonae voluntatis.
Laudamus te. Benedicimus te. Adoramus te. Glorificamus te.
Gratias agimus tibi propter magnam gloriam tuam. Domine Deus, Rex caelestis, Deus Pater omnipotens. Domine fili unigenite Iesu Christe.
Domine Deus, Agnus Dei, Filius Patris. Qui tollis peccata mundi, miserere nobis.
Qui tollis peccata mundi, suscipe deprecationem nostram.
Qui sedes ad dexteram Patris, miserere nobis.
Quoniam tu solus sanctus.
Tu solus Dominus.
Tu solus altissimus, Iesu Christe. Cum Sancto Spiritu, in gloria Dei Patris. Amen.

Glóir do Dhia sna harda. *Glory to God in the highest.*
Agus ar thalamh síocháin do lucht a pháirte.
And on earth peace to people of goodwill.
Molaimid Thú. Móraimid Thú. Adhraimid Thú.
We praise You. We bless You. We adore You.

Tugaimid glóir duit.	*We glorify You.*
Gabhaimid buíochas leat as ucht do mhórghlóire.	*We give You thanks for Your great glory.*
A Thiarna Dia, a Rí na bhFlaitheas,	*Lord God, King of Heaven,*
a Dhia, a Athair uilechumhachtaigh.	*God, the Father almighty.*
A Thiarna aonmhic, Íosa Chríost.	*Lord, only son, Jesus Christ,*
A Thiarna Dia, a Uain Dé, Mac an Athar.	*Lord God, Lamb of God, Son of the Father.*
Tusa a thógas peacaí an domhain,	*You, who take away the sins of the world,*
déan trócaire 'rainn.	*have mercy on us.*
Tusa a thógas peacaí an domhain,	*You, who take away the sins of the world,*
glac lenár nguí.	*accept our prayer.*
Tusa atá i do shuí ar dheis an Athar,	*You, who sit at the right hand of the Father,*
déan trócaire 'rainn.	*have mercy on us.*
Óir is Tú amháin is naofa.	*For You alone are holy.*
Is Tú amháin is Tiarna.	*You alone are the Lord.*
Is Tú amháin is ró-ard, a Íosa Críost,	*You alone are the most high, Jesus Christ,*
mar aon leis an Spiorad Naomh	*one with the Holy Spirit*
i nglóir Dé an tAthair.	*in the glory of God the Father.*
Amen.[7]	*Amen.*

24
glóir duit. Gabhai-mid buío-chas leat as ucht do mhór-ghlóir-e. A
28
Thiar-na Dia, a Rí na bhFlai-theas, a Dhia, a Ath-air ui-le-chumhach-taigh. A
30
Thiar-na aon-mhic, Ío-sa Chríost. A Thiar-na Dia, a Uain Dé, Mac an
33
A-thar. Tu-sa a thó-gas pea-caí an domhain, déan tró-cai-re 'rainn.
36
Tu-sa a thó-gas pea-caí an domhain, glac le-nár nguí.

3.5 Sean Ó Riada: *Ceol an aifrinn, An ghlóir* (bars 16–48)

Ó Riada's through-composition of this extended, broadly tripartite (praise-petition-praise) prose text follows directly on from the Gregorian tradition, providing as it does discrete, self-contained musical responses to the various types and lengths of phrases, and weaving them into a musically coherent whole. From a textual point of view, it is evident that each phrase has its own purpose, which cannot be fulfilled until the final syllable is uttered. To the same degree at least, if not more powerfully, may the final note or destination of a musical phrase be said to exercise power over the preceding elements:

> Though any chant is made up of all the notes and intervals, the note that ends it holds the chief place, for it sounds both longer and more lasting … The beginning of a chant and the ends of all its phrases … need to cling close to the note that ends the chant. It is no wonder that music bases its rules on the last note, since in the elements of language, too, we almost everywhere see the real force of the meaning in the final letters or syllables …[8]

An analysis of the final notes of Ó Riada's setting produces the following overall plan:

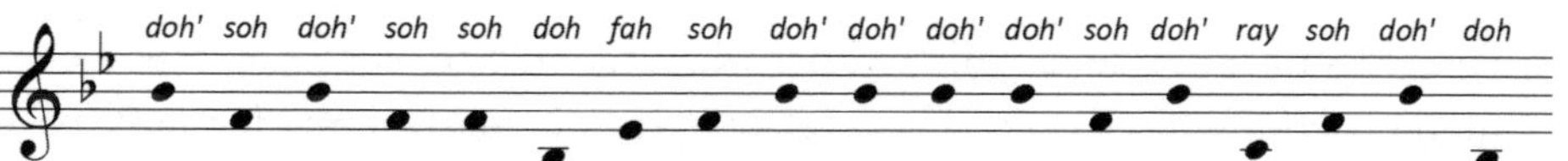

3.6 Sean Ó Riada: *Ceol an aifrinn, An ghlóir: phrase endings*

The consistent structural importance of *doh*' (eight cadences) throughout the delivery of this extended text is the main feature of the above diagram. In terms of importance, it is followed by *soh*. This hierarchical dominance is maintained in the context of the single biggest governing influence on the composition of the movement: that of recitative.

Recitative

Of the 167 syllables in the text, less than one-third are non-recitational in character. High *b-flat*' (*doh*') carries the majority of recitational passages. This is the pitch at which, significantly, the piece is in*tone*d, and in addition to the very deliberate recitations at the triple praise litany ('Molaimid Thú. Móraimid Thú. Adhraimid Thú'), the triple petition litany ('Tusa ..., déan trócaire orainn. Tusa ..., glac lenár nguí. Tusa ..., déan trócaire orainn'), and minor recitations in bars 26 and 41–42, it is the pitch which ends each significant section of the text (bars 33, 39 and 46 – immediately prior to the 'Amen'). In terms of recitational passages *f'* (*soh*) comes next in quantity, with examples in bars 30–31 and 40–41, but perhaps of more significance is its structural use as a 'bridging' pitch between the higher and lower registers of the wide tonal spectrum chosen by the composer (see bars 23–28 and again 29–33). Low *b-flat* (*doh*), *e-flat'* (*fah*) and *c'* (*ray*) have one recitational passage each in bars 28, 29 and 44 respectively.

Litanic Elements

Of particular compositional interest are the very deliberate rising gestures which begin the internal repetitions of both triple litanies already mentioned. Even more important to the overall development of the piece, however, is the four-fold rising litany of praise which brings the text from the low *doh* of bar 28 through to the high *doh'* register of bar 33. This approach has already been used in the opening *Iontróid* (bars 5–8) and will return later as the main compositional device in the *Agnus Dei*.

In his survey of Gregorian compositional approaches to the Gloria, Willi Apel identifies certain commonalities with regard to the melodic setting of litanic sections of the text.[9] These relate to the obviously limited number of musico-rhetorical 'spins' a composer can put on, for instance, a short, three-fold litany. In formal terms, these may span the distance from a static AAA form to a more rhetorically dynamic ABC concept.

Of the Gloria's four litanies, the first of them, the four-fold 'Laudamus te/ Benedicimus te/ Adoramus te/ Glorificamus te', is effectively reduced to a three-fold form in the Irish version (see line 3 of *An ghlóir* text), whereas the second, three-fold litany, 'Domine ... omnipotens/ Domine ... Iesu Christe/ Domine. ... Filius Patris' assumes a four-fold format in the Irish translation (see lines 6–9 of Irish text). The last two litanies correspond formally in their textual structures, thereby providing a secure point of departure for direct comparisons. Focusing on the first of these, the 'Qui tollis'/ 'Tusa a thógann' series, Ó Riada's ABC format (bars 34–39) concurs in broad formal terms with the corresponding passages in Gloria I, VII and VIII.[10]

In rhetorical terms, however, only Gloria I provides a close match for Ó Riada's rising, developmental approach:

3.7 *Liber usualis,* Gloria I

Looking at the final 'Quoniam tu solus'/'Óir is Tú amháin' litany, Ó Riada's AA1B approach (bars /40–44), while matched in formal terms only by Gloria I 'ad libitum',[11] appears to present, in terms of the dramatic shift in both direction and register of its third phrase, something quite different rhetorically from anything that may be found within the standard Gregorian corpus of Gloria settings. The variety of musical approaches to these fixed texts observed above simultaneously encapsulates for us Guido's principle of 'double-melody' and McGee's description of music employing, in combination with the text, its own parallel yet referentially independent systems of rhetoric.[12] These litanies provide a useful point of departure for further consideration of the question of text/music aesthetics.

The 'Non-relationship' of Words and Music

The Gregorian Gloria's final litany 'Quoniam tu solus sanctus, tu solus Dominus, tu solus altissimus', with its strongly suggestive final phrase ('You alone are the Most High'), provides a useful departure point for consideration of possible correlations of a 'referential' or 'emotional' nature between text and melody. In the Gregorian tradition a wide variety of approaches is in evidence. These range from the static AAA form of Gloria VI, and the ternary ABA approach of Gloria IV to the more musically developmental ABC forms of Gloria II and Gloria X:[13]

3.8 *Liber usualis*, Gloria VI, IV, II and X

This obvious freedom of approach suggests an artistic aesthetic which is not driven by referential considerations or trapped by visual stimuli. Placing each of the above litanies back in their overall melodic context reveals to what extent their forms are governed by considerations of (a) musical rhetoric, and (b) the larger melodic picture.

In Ó Riada's setting of the litany, we search in vain for an example of 'word-painting' at the textually significant 'is Tú amháin is ró-ard, a Íosa Críost' ('you alone are the most high, Jesus Christ'). Ó Riada's choice at this point (bars /42–44) is determined by what will best serve the musical unfolding of the Irish text. From a compositional perspective, by this stage in the piece the upper melodic regions have been extensively mined – something new is needed to sustain the musical journey. From the musico-rhetorical point of view, this phrase represents the final litanic phrase of the main body of the text. In contrast to, or as a relief from, all the previous rising litanic elements, Ó Riada redirects the musical movement towards low *ray* and in doing so prepares the ear, and the entire musical composition, for the conclusion on the lower tonic which will come in four bars' time.

We have already seen in the *Iontróid* the pre-eminence of text structure (and, by implication, 'number') in generating the musical response. A potent example of how this approach overrides any music/text relationships of a 'referential' or 'emotional' nature may be seen by comparing the two triple litanies already referred to (bars 21–25; 34–39). Even though the emotional content is as differentiated as it can be in the context of the Gloria, i.e. praise vs. petition, we find, however, that it is the similarity in textual *form* (i.e. triple litany) which prompts the composer to return to the music of the first example in crafting a musical solution for the second:

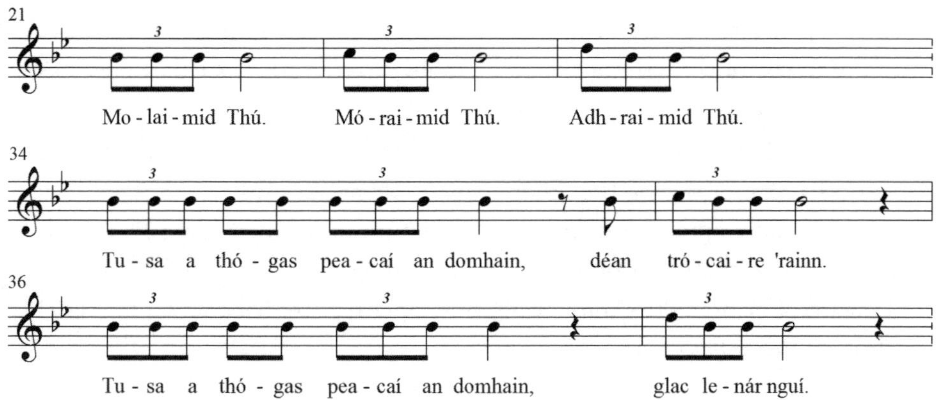

3.9 Seán Ó Riada: *Ceol an aifrinn, An ghlóir* (bars 21–23 and 34–37)

Melismas

Ó Riada's Gloria setting is syllabic in style with a small number of mild but highly effective melismatic features. The phenomenon in the Gregorian repertoire of melismas on 'unimportant' syllables is already well documented in chant studies.[14] John Stevens refers to their use in early medieval song on certain words such as 'O' and 'Tu' and contemplates the possibility of a rhetorical impulse for this phenomenon. He concludes that a proper explanation for 'this striking and un-numerical effect may be simpler – and deeper – as a natural feature of human song in all ages'.[15]

In Ó Riada's first setting of *An ghlóir*, the sonic properties of the key word 'glóir' certainly appear to have drawn forth from the composer some sort of onomatopoeic response, which results in all three appearances of the word (excluding the opening intonation of the priest) being treated in a melismatic fashion. Falling on a strong rather than on a weak textual accent, these melismas occur in bars 24 (seven notes), 27 (three notes) and

45 (four notes), with the first of them being closest in spirit to the gratuitous nature of chant-associated melismas.

Ó Riada breaks out of the syllabic pattern on two remaining occasions. In the first of these, a short three-note figure given to the final syllable of 'is Tú amháin' (bar 42) is quite significant in rhetorical terms. This occurs in the third statement of a litany where the previous two had placed the stress on 'Tú'. Here, the increase of musical weight on the final (accented) syllable brought about by the melisma adds a deliberate intensity to the final repetition. It also demonstrates the composer's willingness to break out of the by now rhythmically predictable patterns established by previous litanic elements.

The fifth and remaining melisma, which, significantly, occurs on the sonically open 'A-' of the final 'Amen' (bars /47–48) is not merely a proportionally appropriate concluding gesture to the preceding text, such as we find in the traditional Gregorian settings. Here, it also functions as a means of bringing the music from the upper register back down to a final close on low *b-flat* (*doh*).

AN PHREAFÁID

S. Go raibh an Tiarna libh. — *The Lord be with you.*
P. Agus leat féin. — *And also with you.*
S. Tógaigí bhúr gcroíthe in airde. — *Lift up your hearts on high.*
P. Tá siad tógtha 'nairde chun an Tiarna 'gainn.
We have lifted them up to the Lord.
S. Gabhaimis buíochas leis an Tiarna ár nDia.
Let us give thanks to the Lord our God.
P. Is ceart agus is cóir sin. — *That is right and fitting.*

3.10 Seán Ó Riada: *Ceol an aifrinn, An phreafáid* (bars 49–54)

The preface dialogue between presider and congregation is structurally centred around the reciting note *f'* (*soh*). The three congregational responses all begin and end on this note. Only the presider's second and final invocations conclude on a more declamatory *b-flat'* (*doh'*), the dialogue's other significant tonal pole. The phrase-end structure works out as follows:

soh/soh: doh'/soh: doh'/soh

Ó Riada's setting follows the principle inherent in the traditional Gregorian version, by which the presider/pastor goes ahead of his flock, to prepare, as it were, the melodic ground for it. The Gregorian version, seen here below, adopts a less musically dramatic approach, alternating the phrase-ending pitches of *doh* and *ray* in the following manner, *ray/ray: doh/doh: ray/doh*:

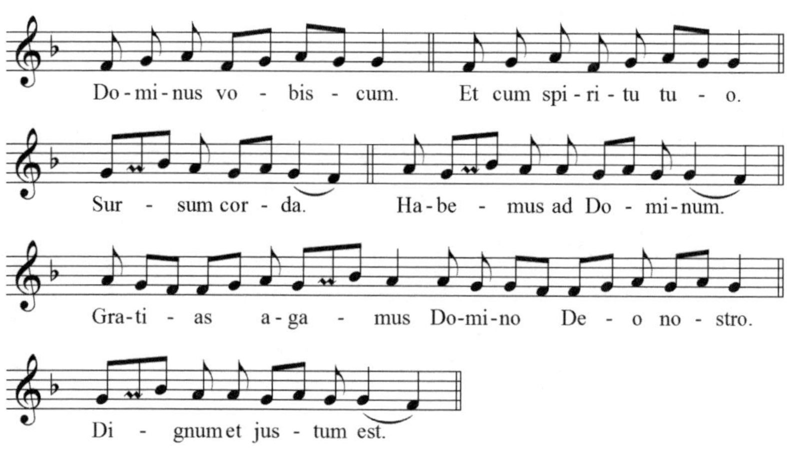

3.11 Gregorian Preface dialogue

The Roman principle of unaccompanied presidential chanting is adhered to in spirit as Ó Riada limits himself to single-note cues for the presider, while providing full chordal accompaniment for the people's responses. These follow the form ABB, with the melodic structures of A and B forming harmonically compatible mirror images of each other:

3.12 Seán Ó Riada: *Ceol an aifrinn, An phreafáid* / response structures

For the preface itself, Ó Riada suggests that the presider might recite it on *f* (*soh*) or on a psalm-tone if he so wishes. The composer does not suggest a tone but presumably envisages an adaptable two-line formula along the lines of the traditional Gregorian tone which would provide a suitable tonal link between the opening dialogue and the ensuing *Sanctus*. Although the possibilities for the employment of native 'reciting' tones of this type exist,[16] the issue of identifying a standard tone for Irish-language preface texts was not addressed in *An leabhar aifrinn*,[17] the first Irish translation of the *Roman Missal*.[18]

SANCTUS

Is Naofa, Naofa, Naofa Thú,	*Holy, Holy, Holy are You,*
a Thiarna, Dia na Slua.	*Lord, God of Hosts.*
Tá neamh agus talamh lán de do ghlóir.	*Heaven and earth are full of Your glory.*
Hósanna sna harda.	*Hosanna in the highest.*
Is beannaithe'n té 'tá ag teacht	*Blessed is he who is coming*
in ainm an Tiarna.	*in the name of the Lord.*
Hósanna sna harda.	*Hosanna in the highest.*

3.13 Seán Ó Riada: *Ceol an aifrinn, Sanctus* (bars 55–64)

The opening *soh/doh'* melodic oscillations of this acclamation distil and re-emphasise the elemental nature of the particular traditional melodic terrain which Ó Riada is mining. The Irish translation of this text divides into six phrases of varying length,[19] presenting, as it does in both Latin and English, certain challenges for the composer. The phrases are presented below in terms of number of textual accents, notes of destination and musical content:

4 (*b-flat'*) A
3 (*c''*) B
4 (*f'*) C
2 (*b-flat'*) A1 *
5 (*f'*) C1 **
2 (*b-flat'*) A1
(*Telescoped version of A; **Developed version of C)

The tightness and unity of the thematic weave ABCA1C1A1 is the result of Ó Riada's decision to use the same melodic gesture for the 'Is Naofa' and 'Hósanna' phrases.[20] The four-accent (as opposed to three- in the Latin and English) make-up of the opening line, which enables the motif to be stated twice, is the result of a peculiarity in the Irish translation in which the first line may be rendered in English as follows:

> 'Holy, Holy, Holy *are you*,
> Lord God ...'

Thus the question of pre-existent *number* (i.e. quantity of syllables or accents in lines) may be seen to have a potential bearing on the resulting form of the piece.[21]

The melodic composition of the *Sanctus* alternates declamatory material (principally phrase A) with more lyrical content, and the full extent of the range (an octave and a fourth) is covered in the opening two phrases. Ending on high *doh'* (*b-flat'*), the movement shares this characteristic with two other short, declamatory texts in the collection – *Iontróid* and *Iomann iargomaoineach*. Ó Riada's detailed attention to the rhythmic declamation of the words continues to feature in this succinct and exclusively syllabic setting. The Hosannas draw forth no melismas; instead the melodic momentum is directed upwards towards the final word, 'harda'.

AN PHAIDIR

Ár nAthair atá ar neamh,
go naofar tAinm,
go dtaga do ríocht,
go ndeántar do thoil ar an dtalamh
mar a níthear ar neamh.
Ár n-arán laethiúil tabhair dúinn inniu
agus maith dúinn ár bhfiacha
mar mhaithimid d'ár bhféichiúna féin.
A's ná lig sinn i gcathú,
ach saor sinn ó olc.

Our Father who art in heaven,
hallowed be your Name,
your kingdom come,
your will be done on earth
as it is in heaven.
Give us this day our daily bread
and forgive us our debts
as we forgive our own debtors.
And lead us not into temptation,
but deliver us from evil.

3.14
Seán Ó Riada: *Ceol an aifrinn, An phaidir* (bars /65–77)

The general textual layout of the Our Father prayer, with its patchwork of asymmetrical phrases, presents the composer with a significant challenge in terms of providing a comprehensive and unified response. The traditional Gregorian setting limits itself to a very restricted tonal range (a perfect fourth, for the most part), working with the greatest of textual and musical sensitivity around a *mi* reciting pitch:

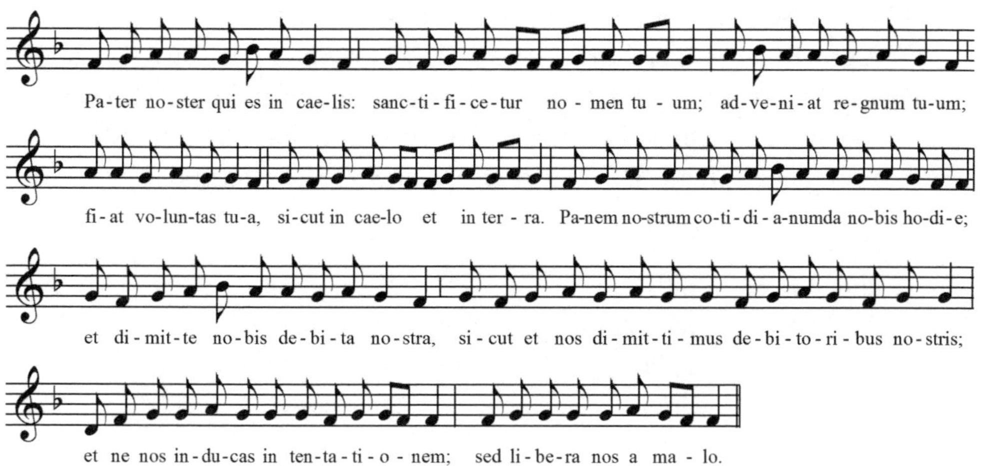

3.15 Gregorian 'Pater noster'

Ó Riada, by contrast, uses the full potential of the Munster song range (in this case an octave and a diminished fifth) to carry the text in a more demonstrative and melodically expressive way; apart from the repeated litanic figures mentioned below, the setting contains no recitational elements. The overriding constraint, as in all liturgical composition, is provided by the rhythmic or numerical qualities of the text – in this case an Irish composition – which ultimately dictate the musical unfolding of the prayer.

The Irish translation of this traditional prayer follows for the most part the structure and proportions of the Latin model. Only in the opening section does a comparatively shorter second line and the distinctive Irish expression of the subjunctive set up a different textual dynamic,[22] giving a terse, rhythmically unified trio of invocations which have the character of a litany:

Go naofar tAinm	(sanctificetur nomen tuum)
Go dtaga do ríocht	(adveniat regnum tuum)
Go ndéantar do thoil	(fiat voluntas tua)

Here, as in other such places throughout the mass (notably *Iontróid*, *An ghlóir* and *Agnus Dei*), Ó Riada responds in kind, in this case with the repeated melodic figure *soh-lah-fah-soh* adapted to *soh-lah-fah-mi* on the third statement (see bars 66–69) to facilitate a textual 'run-on'.

A general analysis of the text reveals all ten lines beginning on a textual upbeat. In response to this, Ó Riada chooses as his main driving element a filled-in third motif and the use of this, both ascending and descending, in six of the ten phrases gives the piece much of its character and identity:

Phrase	**Solfa**
Phrase 1:	mf/s
Phrase 5:	d'r'/m'
Phrase 6:	r'd'/t
Phrase 7:	dr/m
Phrase 9:	sl/t
Phrase 10:	dr/m

3.16 Seán Ó Riada: *Ceol an aifrinn, An phaidir*: solfa phrase openings

In terms of length, this setting matches the offertory hymn *Ag Críost an síol* which it resembles in its opening melodic gesture and its overall range. However, it is closer in textual character, and almost identical in size (fifty-two versus fifty-three words) to the prose-based *Iontróid* and, like the aforementioned, demonstrates a logical tonal plan with respect to phrase-end notes:

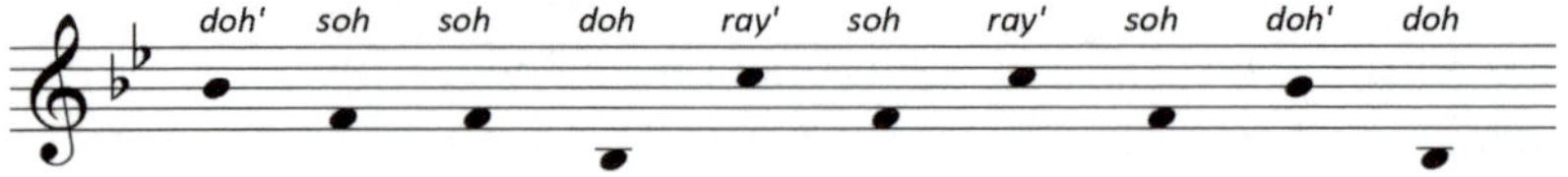

3.17 Seán Ó Riada: *Ceol an aifrinn, An phaidir*: phrase endings

We have already seen how in such a broad tonal canvas the fifth degree *soh* (*f*') functions as a kind of internal melodic 'hinge', providing access to both the upper and lower melodic strata. In *An phaidir* we find it consistently held in position on either side by its auxiliaries *lah* and *fah*.

AGNUS DEI

A Uain Dé, a thógas peacaí an domhain, déan trócaire ’rainn.
A Uain Dé, a thógas peacaí an domhain, déan trócaire ’rainn.
A Uain Dé, a thógas peacaí an domhain, tabhair dúinn síocháin.

Lamb of God, who takes away the sins of the world, have mercy on us.
Lamb of God, who takes away the sins of the world, have mercy on us.
Lamb of God, who takes away the sins of the world, grant us peace.

3.18 Seán Ó Riada: *Ceol an aifrinn, Agnus Dei* (bars /78–86)

The Gregorian settings of this AAB tripartite litanic text present themselves in a variety of musical forms:[23]

AAA	Agnus Dei I, III, V, VI, XVII, XVIII, 'Ad libitum' I and II
ABA	X, XII, XV, XVI
AAB	VII
ABA	II, IV, VII, VIII, IX, XIII, XIV (common petitions)
ABC	XI (common petitions)

Interestingly, only one setting, Agnus Dei VII, aligns itself completely with the form suggested by the text. Focusing on the earliest known syllabic setting (and therefore the one most likely to have been sung by congregations) of Mass XVIII,[24] we note the monothematic musical approach suggesting the earlier history of the Agnus Dei as part of a litanic text.[25] Another feature of the text retained by the Church suggesting this connection is the fact that the petitions 'miserere nobis' and 'dona nobis pacem' share the same number of syllables and basic accentual pattern. From a compositional perspective, this accounts for the fact that in the vast majority of chant settings, these texts receive identical melodic treatment. It would seem that, in this particular aspect of the Agnus Dei, syllabic quantity (or 'number'), as opposed to sound (rhyme) or textual content, shapes the form.

Questions of quantity and form obviously have a bearing on Ó Riada's first Irish-language setting of the Agnus Dei. The respective petitions 'déan trócaire orainn' and 'tabhair dúinn síocháin' do not match either in terms of accent or syllable count and so a different melodic solution is required for each. In relation to form, Ó Riada's petitions follow the pattern suggested by the text, thus producing an AAB structure, with B clearly distinguished from its predecessors by the introduction of the flattened seventh. For the three invocatory portions, however, he opts for a rising ABC-type structure, reciting respectively on the ascending pitches of *soh*, *doh'* and *mi'*.[26]

Ó Riada's setting establishes itself from the outset on the fifth degree, *soh*, and each of the three lines concludes at that pitch. As in the other litanic (*Kyrie*) and dialogical (*An phreafáid*) elements in the mass, Ó Riada selects an open-ended tonality that seems appropriate to the nature of the text, one indeed which resonated convincingly with the modal character of the earliest-known Roman rite setting, the aforementioned Agnus Dei XVIII:

3.19 Agnus Dei XVIII

Hymn Settings

This section considers five metrical, strophic hymns, three from within the body of *Ceol an aifrinn*, associated with the offertory, communion and post-communion/recessional, and two others which Ó Riada includes in an Appendix (Aguisín). Though their regular, conventional forms render them secondary to the irregular, asymmetrical prose forms on which this study has chosen to concentrate, they nevertheless contain material that is of certain cultural, historical, textual and compositional interest.

OFRÁIL: AG CRÍOST AN SÍOL

Ag Críost an síol, ag Críost an fómhar,
With Christ is the seed, with Christ, the harvest,
i n-iothalainn Dé go dtugtar sinn
into God's barn may we be gathered.
Ag Críost an mhuir, ag Críost an t-iasc
With Christ is the sea, with Christ, the fish,
i líontaibh Dé go gcastar sinn.
in the nets of God may we be caught.
Ó fhás go haois, is ó aois go bás,
From growth to age and from age to death,
do dhá láimh, a Chríost, anall tharainn
your two hands, O Christ, be round about us.
Ó bhás go críoch, ní críoch ach athfhás,
From death to the end, no end but a rebirth,
i bParrthas na nGrást go rabhaimid.
in the Paradise of Graces may we be found.

3.20 Seán Ó Riada: *Ceol an aifrinn, Ag Críost an síol* (bars /87–102)

The text of this native prayer presents Christ as an ever-present saving figure throughout the journey of life and beyond its end, bringing those who hope in him to resurrection and to 'the Paradise of the Graces'[27]. Its construction bears all the hallmarks of a grand litany cast within the regularised confines of accentual poetry. The eight-line structure divides into four couplets which follow the classic Christian prayer movement of praise/acknowledgement followed by petition. The litanic dynamic is enhanced by end-of-couplet agreement (sinn/sinn/-ainn/-mid) and the repetition structures built into each couplet (XXY throughout).

With respect to phrase *beginnings* the overall textual form might be described as AABB. However, the dynamics of Ó Riada's chosen melodic form follow the pattern AABA1, a modified version of one of the most common traditional melodic forms. Each couplet contains eight accents and Ó Riada's four-bar articulation reflects the driving two-accent pulse inherent in the text. Each of these pulses is given a discrete melodic gesture and each large-scale melodic phrase comprises four of these gestures linked together to form a coherent melodic unit. A detailed breakdown reveals the following form (the sign / representing line divisions):

A	A	B	A1
ab/cd	*ab/cd*	*ef/bb*	*ab*^{1}*/gh*

Of particular interest is the re-framing of motif *b* in the B phrase as the opening gesture of a line instead of its by-then-established role as a type of 'answering phrase'. This thrifty and telling re-use of motifs is a compositional technique which may be observed in the following 'classic' melodies from the native tradition: 'Slán le Máigh' (*ab ab cd d*^{1}*b*), 'Táimse im chodladh' (*ab ab cd db*),[28] 'The Bonny Bunch of Roses O!' (*ab ac de bc*).[29]

Motif *b* predominates throughout Ó Riada's melody and, with its distinctive flattened seventh, provides an essential element of the composition's tonal character. The overall melodic range extends to the full compass (octave and a fifth) of the big major-mode Munster songs. The melody displays many modal characteristics already noted in the mass, e.g. *soh* as a melodic hinge in wide-range melodies; structural oscillation between *soh* and *doh'*; *lah* and *fah* as important auxiliaries of *soh*. Similarities in scale and melodic range with *An phaidir* have already been noted:[30] their distinctive opening and closing melodic gestures are almost identical and, of the ten pieces in the mass they share with only two other items (*An ghlóir* and *Iomann comaoineach*) an ending at the lower tonic pitch (standard for the bigger traditional songs).

IOMANN COMAOINEACH: GILE MO CHROÍ

Gile mo chroí do chroíse, 'Shlánaitheoir
Light of my heart, thy heart, dear Lord divine,
agus ciste mo chroí do chroíse d'fháil im chomhair;
my treasure bright thy heart to keep in mine;
ós follas gur líon do chroí dom ghrása, a stóir,
since thy heart filled, dear Lord, with love for me,
i gcochall mo chroí do chroíse fág i gcomhad.
let mine be cloak to fold and comfort thee.[31]

3.21 Seán Ó Riada: *Ceol an aifrinn, Gile mo chroí* (bars 103–122)

Ó Riada's communion hymn is a setting of a poem entitled 'Duan chroí Íosa', by the eighteenth-century Munster poet Tadhg Gaelach Ó Súilleabháin. The five-stanza composition expresses the poet's recognition of his Saviour's abiding love, his acknowledgement of Christ's suffering and death, and his own desire for conversion. It is set in the traditional four-line, five-accent poetic metre known as 'amhránaíocht' ('singing') and contains the internal assonances and uniform rhyming scheme typical of the genre. A definitive melodic version of the poem, to the tune of the Munster air 'Sa mhainistir lá', is contained in the collection *Londubh an chairn*[32] with accompanying notes stating that this was the air the poet had in mind for the words which he composed:

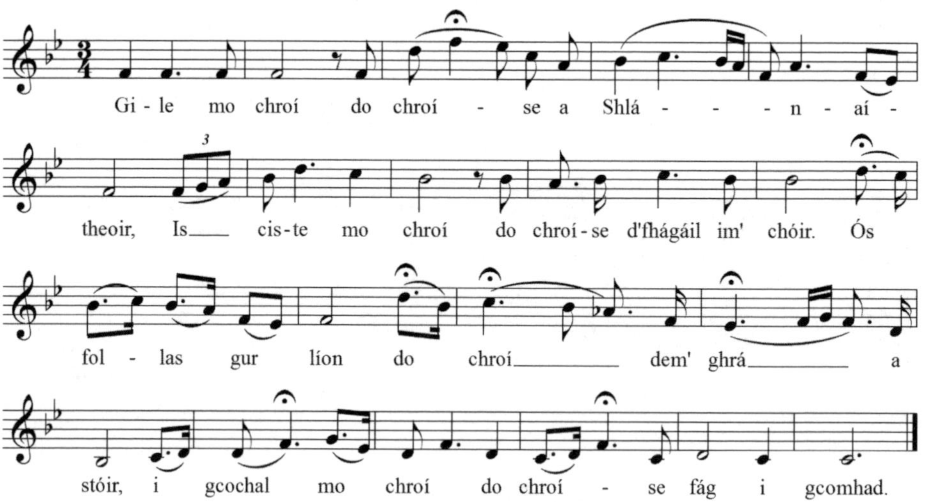

3.22 'Sa mhainistir lá' (from *Londubh an chairn*)

This earlier version of the tune is marked by a distinctive modality (focusing on *soh* and ending on *ray*) and by a developing melodic form ABCD.

While Ó Riada's melodic response to Ó Súilleabháin's text has tonal elements in common with the traditional version (similar range, strong emphasis on *soh*), it is marked out by a different, indeed distinctive, formal structure, being cast in the binary melodic form ABAB (strictly speaking ABA1B1, the second couplet introducing standard traditional melodic variants). An examination of the text, however, reveals that the succession of thoughts that comprise the composition is expressed in the form of couplets, giving the whole structure a dynamic akin to that of Hebrew psalmody:

> Brightness of my heart, your own heart, O Saviour
> And my heart's satisfaction to have your heart with me.
> (Literal translation of opening couplet)

The rhetoric of Ó Riada's musical response to this couplet-based structure involves a 'setting-out' A phrase, based around the tonic arpeggio, starting on *soh* and cadencing on high *doh'* (bar 107). The 'answering' B phrase distinguishes its identity by means of a dominant triad-based passage followed by a balancing cadence on low *doh* (bar 112). Continuing the four-line round, the second couplet introduces *fah* as a climactic variant in the upper (A) range (bar 115), a gesture which is re-echoed in the lower (B) register (bar 120).

In terms of its rhythmic complexity and ornamental detail, the notation of *Gile mo chroí* bears the greatest witness amongst the contents of *Ceol an aifrinn* to the influence of the solo sean-nós singing style. We find here the full ornamental repertoire of 'cuts' (bars 109, 117, 119), mordents (bars 103, 108, etc.) and 'rolls' (bar 105) written into the melody. Confirming the direct and conscious link with the tradition and the specific tune is Tomás Ó Canainn's account of how *Gile mo chroí* was set to music by Ó Riada for the funeral mass of Mort Ó Sé, as a tribute to the singer whose version of 'Sa mhainistir lá' he had very much admired.[33]

IOMANN IARGOMAOINEACH: RÉIR DÉ GO NDEINEAM

Réir Dé go ndeineam,	*May we do the will of God*
agus beatha na naomh go dtuilleam.	*and may we earn the life of the saints.*
Solas na bhFlaitheas go bhfeiceam,	*May we behold the vision of Heaven*
agus glóire na n-aingeal go gcloiseam.	*and hear the glory of the angels.*

3.23 Seán Ó Riada: *Ceol an aifrinn, Réir Dé go ndeineam* (bars 123–126)

The composer's direction regarding this short four-line text is that it may be sung after communion or as a recessional hymn. The traditional prayer text,[34] apparently suggested to Ó Riada by one of the singers, Tadhg Ó Mulláin,[35] is an apt choice for the end of the Sunday celebration of mass.

The litanic influence which so permeated both Roman and, more especially, native elements throughout this mass setting, exerts its influence once more in this final quartet of hope-filled resolutions. Ó Riada's melody focuses in declamatory fashion on high *doh'* for three of the four short phrases, dropping down the octave to low *doh* only in the third phrase. This general structure mirrors to a significant degree the melodic shape and dynamic of the mass's opening movement, the *Iontróid*. Ó Riada's setting is upbeat, with the syncopated speech rhythms of the melody vigorously replicated in the four-part keyboard arrangement of the opening two phrases, the only such example in the entire mass.

Aguisín (Appendix)

Beyond the boundaries of the mass setting, but included in the overall collection in *Ceol an aifrinn*, are two ancillary hymn settings which have no fixed liturgical designation. The first of these, *Bí, a Íosa, im chroíse*,[36] a four-stanza devotional text, is constructed of four-line verses with each four-accent line comprising twelve syllables:

Bí, a Íosa, im chroíse i gcuimhne gach uair
Be in my heart, O Jesus, and in my memory every hour.
Bí, a Íosa, im chroíse le haithrí go luath
Be in my heart, O Jesus, for early repentance.
Bí, a Íosa, im chroíse le cumann go buan
Be in my heart, O Jesus, for love without end.
Ó, a Íosa, ' Dhé dhílis, ná scar Thusa uaim
O Jesus, faithful God, *do not separate Yourself from me.*

3.24 Seán Ó Riada: *Ceol an aifrinn, Bí, a Íosa, im chroíse* (bars /127–142)

Each verse has a unified rhyming scheme with respect to line-endings, hence, in verse one: *uair/luath/buan/uaim*. The textual form, once again litanic in style, might be described as AAAB with respect to line-openings. Ó Riada's melody, set in a minor (*ray*) mode, follows a more developmental route, mapping out an AA1BC structure, with the openings of the first three phrases nevertheless maintaining a rhythmic and motivic unity in keeping with the litanic drive of the text.

A RÍ AN DOMHNAIGH

A Rí an Domhnaigh, tar le cabhair chugam is fóir in am ón bpian mé.
A Rí an Luain ghil, bíse buan liom is ná lig uaitse féin mé.
A Rí na Márta, a chroí na páirte, déan díonadh Lá an tSléibh dhom.
A Rí Céadaoine, saor ó ghéibhinn mé, cé fad' óm chaoimhghein féin mé.

O King of Sunday, come to my aid, and save me in time from punishment.
O King of the bright Monday*, be with me always and never let me from you.*
O King of Tuesday, heart of paradise, be my advocate on the Day of Judgement.
O King of Wednesday, free me from confinement, even if I am far from my gentle birth.

3.25 Seán Ó Riada: *Ceol an aifrinn, A Rí an Domhnaigh* (bars /143–159)

The text of the final hymn, *A Rí an Domhnaigh*, written by the nineteenth-century Uíbh Ráthach poet Tomás Rua Ó Súilleabháin (1785–1848), is one of the more recent examples of the tradition in Irish native poetry of 'dánta aithreachais' (poems of repentance) whereby the poet, weighed down by thoughts of his mortality and by guilt for the misdeeds of his life, makes an eloquent plea to God to show him mercy. Each verse contains four couplets comprised of a four-accent line followed by one of three accents. This rhythmic template is a traditional one, and the text could have lent itself to any one of a number of traditional melodies such as that of the famous Connemara lament, 'Anach Cuain'.[37] Nóirín Ní Riain, however, provides us with the following definitive information concerning Ó Riada's choice of melody:

> In a publication of the poetry of Tomás Ruadh Ó Súilleabháin edited by James Fenton, the tune reference to this poem is 'Na bearta crua'. Seán Ó Riada set this poem to a version of 'Na bearta crua' which was printed in 'Veritas' [*The Veritas Hymnal*] as his own composition.[38]

The following transcription by Nóirin Ní Riain of the Uíbh Ráthach (Iveragh/South Kerry) version of the hymn, collected in the earlier part of the twentieth century from Cáit Ní Ailíosa of Glenmore, Waterville, confirms 'Na bearta crua' as the pre-eminent version, and the starting point for Ó Riada's melodic setting:[39]

3.26 'Na bearta crua'

Instead of opting for the more common traditional 'Anach Cuain'-type approach in which the natural textual accents would tend to be given longer time values, he chooses instead as his template the more tersely constructed 'Na bearta crua' model. By so doing, he limits himself to an almost exclusively syllabic approach, maintaining consistent quaver movement until the end of the couplets. (Only in the third climactic couplet of this AABA form is there a relaxation or 'broadening-out' of the rhythmic delivery.) This approach brings the syllabic composition and numerical basis of the poetic lines into sharper focus, with a resulting musical emphasis on melodic economy. In the absence of longer accented notes, the bar-line assumes a greater prominence in relation to the rhythmic articulation of the text and serves its delivery with the greatest of flexibility.

The plagal melodic disposition and narrower range (readily associated with Gregorian mode 6) of this melody sets it apart from the other major-mode pieces in the collection, and Ó Riada chooses the key of F as a suitable pitch area for its delivery. Ó Riada, it would seem, took a particular interest in this melody, considering its basic structure to be something of a traditional archetype spanning various textual genres, as may be deduced from his Suite for harpsichord,[40] where he includes it as a type of 'middle way' between the light-hearted 6/8 'Túirne Mháire' and the more substantial 'An Brianach óg'.[41]

Ceol an aifrinn: A Tonal Summary

The compositions of the main body of *Ceol an aifrinn* explore in various ways the characteristically wide melodic range (typically an octave and a fourth/fifth) of larger-scale major-mode songs from the Munster sean-nós tradition.[42] A key signature of B flat presumably prescribes the pitch area which in Ó Riada's opinion would be the most suitable for choral or congregational singing. Taking the final note as a modal determinant, Ó Riada sets his pieces in either the *doh*- or nearly-related *soh*-mode. Of the ten pieces, three (nos 1, 6 and 10) end on high *b-flat'* (*doh'*), four (nos 3, 4, 7 and 9) end on low *b-flat* and three (nos 2, 5 and 8) end at mid-range on *f'* (*soh*). It is worth noting again that, of these, the first, 'high' group (*Iontróid*, *Sanctus*, *Iomann iargomaoineach*) are united by the declamatory nature of their texts and a relatively short performance duration. The second, 'low' group (*An ghlóir*, *Ofráil*, *An phaidir* and *Iomann comaoineach*) feature longer texts, two of which are in regular verse form. The last, *soh*-mode group is characterised either by a litanic (*Kyrie*, *Agnus Dei*) or dialogic (*An phreafáid*) structure.[43]

Taking the collection as a whole, the prominence of *f'* (*soh*) may frequently be observed as the 'recitational' carrier and musical destination of many textual phrases. Conclusive evidence of its structural importance in the overall modal context, and in the mind of the composer, may be seen in Ó Riada's direction that the preface may be chanted by the priest on this single pitch. By means of this 'reciting-note', the opening dialogue (*An phreafáid*) is structurally connected with the resulting *Sanctus* acclamation. The other important pitch for recitational delivery is that of high *b-flat'* (*doh'* – see especially *An ghlóir* and *Agnus Dei*), and the tension between these two tonal centres generates much of the musical energy which Ó Riada uses to drive his compositions forward.

Ceol an aifrinn: Keyboard Accompaniments

If the melodic settings of *Ceol an aifrinn* can be said to have emerged from the cultural reality of the Múscraí Gaeltacht, then it may equally be suggested that the keyboard accompaniments provided by the composer reflect an accurate translation of a musician at work within an ongoing liturgical reality, not simply at the level of setting the melodies off to good artistic effect, which he manages to do, but at the more basic level of sustaining, encouraging and, where necessary, controlling the singing of his male choir. An interesting decision taken by the composer from the outset is to separate musically the accompaniment from the melody and to frame the upper voice at the alto rather than the soprano range.[44] While this undoubtedly represents the composer's confidence in the primacy of the sung unison line and in his singers' ability to sustain it, there may also have been governing acoustical/textural factors which necessitated this type of approach.[45]

Ó Riada's use of texture exemplifies the long-established principle describing the primary role of musical instruments in liturgy as that of 'supporting the singing'.[46] Best typified by the opening *Iontróid*, at the core of the accompaniment is a standard four-part configuration which holds sway until the melodic climax of the piece, when it broadens out to five and ultimately six parts. Four-part writing is the exception rather than the norm in a highly declamatory setting such as *An ghlóir*, in which a seven-part underlay frequently features (see bars 21–27, 34–39). This movement also features the only time in the mass setting where the accompaniment independently intervenes as a means of generating momentum for the singing (bars 34 and 36). At the other end of the textural spectrum is Ó Riada's treatment of the two 'Hosanna' phrases from the *Sanctus*. The first of these well-defined melodic gestures (bar 60) generates its own momentum and for the opening of the second (bar 63), Ó Riada dispenses entirely with the keyboard part.[47] Both spare and richly textured approaches are employed in a musically developmental way in the *Iomann comaoineach*, the first couplet being delivered over a tonic drone and the second opening out to a more fully developed, quite expressive chordal accompaniment.

The harmonic palette drawn on by the composer leans heavily on the primary major-key colours of I, IV and V, with the last of these featuring regularly in dominant seventh form (see for instance the *Iontróid*, *Ofráil*, *An phaidir*, *Iomann comaoineach*). More distinctive is his use of the secondary chords of II^7 and III^7 in the course of the *Sanctus* and in the litanic sections of the *Iontróid* and *Agnus Dei*.[48] The harmonic movement largely adheres to a classical dynamic, with chord changes being sensitively used to help drive the melody forward and the customary quickening of harmonic movement evident towards cadence points. Of special interest, however, is Ó Riada's use of the bass part, whose movement he controls in various ways to enhance the musical and liturgical context. In the vigorous settings of *Iomann iargomaoineach* and *A Rí an Domhnaigh*, for instance, the solid consistency of the accompaniment is largely achieved by a limited and low tessitura for the bass-line. More significant is his extremely effective use of tonic-based (e.g. entire *Kyrie eleison*, bars 21–23, 33–39 of *An ghlóir*) and dominant pedal-points (see *An phaidir*, bar 74) which add a notable stability and breadth to the melodic delivery. The nature of the accompanimental layout with the alto line resting above draws attention to the harmonic effects of movement in sixths and thirds, sometimes present simply due to the nature of the changing chords, at other times used by the composer to more deliberately expressive effect.[49]

Ceol an aifrinn: Integrating Tradition

> I would like to hear a man coming out of Mass whistling the Our Father, or hear a man making hay whistling the Our Father.'[50]

This statement is evidence of how closely woven into the local cultural/musical fabric Ó Riada envisaged his music as being. More than that, one senses that with this statement, the composer, convinced as he is of its healthy integration within that culture, is rejecting the notion of any artificial or false dichotomy between the sacred and the secular (and, by extension, their modes of musical expression). Liturgy and its music, in Ó Riada's view it would seem, are to draw their energy and inspiration from the lives they are meant to nourish.

We have already seen in our examination of the strophic hymn settings, the obvious influence on the composer of native melodic forms (*Ag Críost an síol*, *Bí, a Íosa*), down to the re-use (*A Rí an Domhnaigh*) and re-casting

(*Gile mo chroí*) of specific melodies. In the latter we saw how, for the funeral of a local sean-nós singer, Ó Riada was anxious to weave musically into the religious text something of the living spirit of the deceased. These hymn settings, while revealing much in terms of Ó Riada's cultural and artistic inspiration, do not represent anything particularly significant on a compositional level. They remain simply adoption or, at best, minor adaptation, albeit of a high quality, of pre-existing traditional musical forms.[51]

The asymmetrical prose texts of the Roman mass ordinary, however, present an entirely different challenge, and in this respect it is instructive to return to Ó Riada's opening quote which, amongst the various texts he could have chosen, singles out the *An phaidir* setting as the piece he would like to hear on the lips of the local people. In forging an acceptable native musical solution for this seminal Christian liturgical prayer text, with its textually irregular agglomeration of praise and petitionary elements, Ó Riada, it would seem, sensed that he had achieved something significant and worthwhile.[52] Furthermore, one may deduce from Ó Riada that the ultimate validation of the enterprise for him was to see the *An phaidir* melody flowing back out of the liturgical arena into the living culture whence it came.

The seven prose texts in the collection constitute the bulk of *Ceol an aifrinn* (leaving out the Appendix, they account for 85 of 130 bars) and of these seven, the opening three pieces *Iontróid*, *Kyrie* and *An ghlóir* account for over half the material. Through-composed in the classic Gregorian manner, these pieces may be said to sum up – in terms of modality, melodic range and style, and music/text relationships – the defining characteristics of the mass setting (the succeeding mass movements produce little that is new on any of these fronts). These characteristics include the following: major-mode, large-range melodic canvas; the prominence of *doh'* and *soh* as important structural notes within this tonal canvas; and the regular use of these two pitches as centres of recitation. Of these characteristics, the first two could readily be identified in any one of a number of songs within the Munster tradition. The recitational element, however, which we have noted to be a prominent and crucial ingredient in Ó Riada's accommodation of these irregular (and, in the case of *An ghlóir*, extremely long) prose texts, is more elusive and less readily identifiable within the context of a song tradition more commonly associated with symmetrical texts and phrasal melodic structures.

Sung or 'chanted' prose recitations do, of course, exist within the Gaelic tradition,[53] as indeed they do in other European folk traditions.[54] Within the Irish context, this type of musical delivery may be found in the *caoine* (lament) genre, of which a relatively small number of examples exist.[55] The following tonally relevant excerpt is from one of the most famous of them, *Caoine Airt Uí Laoghaire*, which is intimately associated with Múscraí, the region surrounding Cúil Aodha:[56]

3.27 *Caoine Airt Uí Laoghaire*

The basic musical formula, a psalmodic-type structure typical of the genre, in this case couched in a clearly major modality, is stated twice in the above excerpt. Evident in the first statement is the structural and recitational prominence of *doh'* and *soh* as principal carriers of the prose text.

That Ó Riada had an active interest in these chanted recitations is evidenced by the composer's visit to the South Kerry district of Uíbh Ráthach during the 1960s in search of local *caoine* singers.[57] In terms of its significance as a possible musical template for the prose settings of Ó Riada's *Ceol an aifrinn*, however, the basically static, repetitive melodic structure of the *caoine* model falls well short of the mark. To realistically fill any such role, a larger-scale, more developmental musical structure would be required which successfully combines recitational style with characteristic melodic elements, and spans the full ambit of traditional major-mode Munster song. While Ó Riada is unlikely to have consciously drawn inspiration from any specific model, many of the characteristics of *Ceol an aifrinn* outlined above do come together in a particular way in the following song, which as much as any other may be said to encapsulate an essential ingredient of the spirit of Cúil Aodha:[58]

3.28 'An poc ar buile'

The light-hearted subject matter of the narrative song 'An poc ar buile' ('The angry puck-goat'), composed by Cúil Aodha native Dónal Ó Mulláin, is cast in a musically substantial form which combines recitative-style verses with a vigorous refrain. Apart from the similarities in mode (major) and range (octave and a fourth), we note the structural prominence of *doh'* and *soh*, confirmed by the existence of recitational passages at both these pitches, recalling similar recitations encountered in *Kyrie eleison*, *A Uain Dé* and *An phreafáid* and, notably, in the opening phrases of *Ceol an aifrinn* itself:

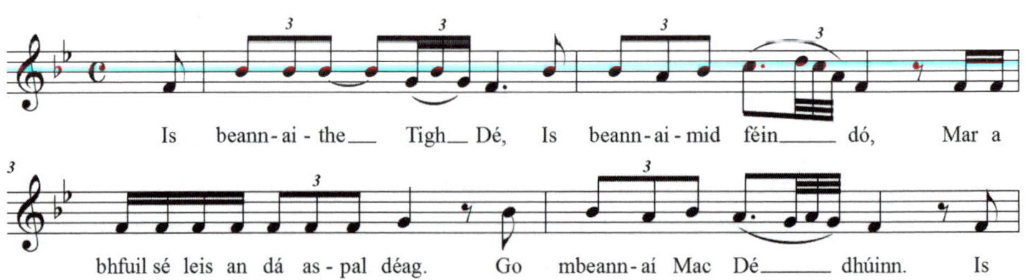

3.29 Seán Ó Riada: *Ceol an aifrinn, Iontróid* (bars /1–4)

The melodically incremental sequence of motifs A, B and C (Example 3.28), which helps to set the song on its way, finds an interesting parallel in Ó Riada's setting of the following litanies from *An ghlóir*:

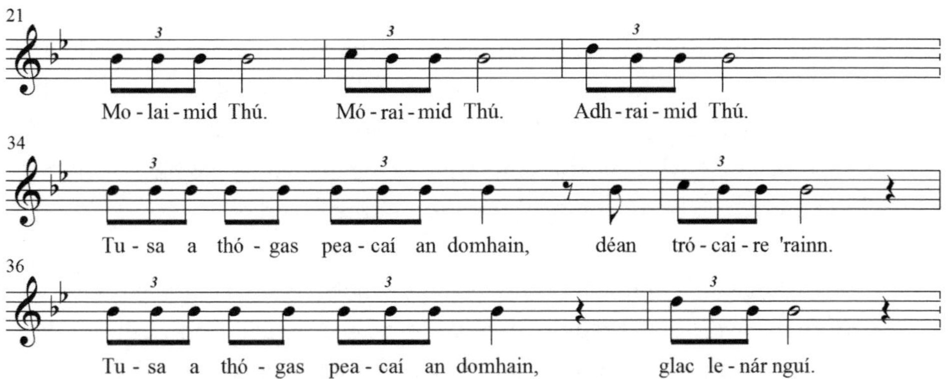

3.30 Seán Ó Riada: *Ceol an aifrinn, An ghlóir* (bars 21–23; 34–37)

The striking musical gesture (D), which concludes and tonally summarises the song, finds a close conceptual and actual melodic parallel in *An ghlóir*'s concluding 'Amen':

3.31 Seán Ó Riada: *Ceol an aifrinn, An ghlóir* (Amen) and conclusion of 'An poc ar buile'

Such comparisons, while not intended to be conclusive, are nevertheless worth noting. While both compositions may be said to be generally expressive of a particular tonal and aesthetic tradition associated strongly with Munster song, they do nevertheless correspond in some distinctive ways. Of the two, Ó Mulláin's is the earlier composition, but only by a decade or so, having been first heard, interestingly, at the 1956 gathering of Dámhscoil Mhúscraí, the annual forum for the public presentation and critical appraisal of new compositions, recited in speech and in song. Whether or not 'An poc ar buile' may have constituted a conscious or unconscious model for *Ceol an aifrinn* is open to debate. What is certain, however, and ultimately more significant, is the fact that Seán Ó Riada, in seeking to integrate his first mass setting into the cultural context of Cúil Aodha, consciously drew on the 'characteristic expressions' of a rich local musical practice, while at the same time being guided, as we have seen, by a keen awareness of the 'musical tradition of the Church':

> Adapting sacred music for those regions which possess a musical tradition of their own ... will require a very specialized preparation ... It will be a question in fact of how to harmonise the sense of the sacred with the spirit, traditions and *characteristic expressions* [my italics] proper to each of these peoples. Those who work in this field should have a *sufficient knowledge both of the liturgy and musical tradition of the Church*, [my italics] and of the language, popular songs and other characteristic expressions of the people for whose benefit they are working.[59]

4

Aifreann 2: Seán Ó Riada

Introduction

In this analysis of Seán Ó Riada's *Aifreann 2*, focus is maintained on the aesthetic connections between music and words, and mounting evidence attests to a relationship largely free of any referential or emotional ties, but inescapably grounded in the numerical constitution of the text.

The use of a Gregorian frame of reference for the mass ordinary is continued, one which will prove useful as we ponder the artistic impulse behind some of the settings in a mass commissioned by the Glenstal Benedictines, a community devoted to the practice of Gregorian chant. To the Gregorian framework we may now add as a parallel track the compositional model of the composer's first mass, *Ceol an aifrinn*. In the ordinary settings of *Aifreann 2*, the natural patterns of Irish text-declamation draw from the composer certain rhythmic responses, some of which are new, and others which may be seen to owe much to those established in the earlier mass. As with *Ceol an aifrinn*, the prose settings of this second mass constitute the primary focus of the analysis, and consideration of these will be followed by a separate section dealing with the hymns.

The main question to emerge from the analysis of *Aifreann 2*, however, relates to modality, and Ó Riada's selection and inventive working, within an unaccompanied, purely monophonic context (his original score includes no keyboard part) of a structurally interesting tonal terrain. This question will be interpreted through classic and new understandings of mode, as viewed from the standpoints of plainchant and ethnomusicology. Finally, Seán Ó Riada's second mass setting introduces a number of liturgical elements not dealt with in *Ceol an aifrinn*. These will be seen to occur in the context of what may be described as a more fully developed conception on the composer's part of the musico-liturgical roles of the congregation and priest.

Contents

1. *Iontróid (Críost liom)*
2. *Kyrie*
3. *Gloria*
4. *Alleluia/ Roimh an soiscéal/ Ag deireadh an tsoiscéil*
5. *Ofráil* (hymn: *A Íosa bháin*)
6. *An phreafáid*

7. *Sanctus*
8. *Tar éis an choisreachadh*
9. *Deireadh an phaidir eochairistigh*
10. *Ár nAthair*
11. *Agnus Dei*
12. *Iomann comaoineach* (hymn: *Gurab tú mo bhoile*)
13. *Iomann ceiliúrtha* (hymn: *Beannaigh sinn, a Athair*)

This mass was commissioned by Dom Paul McDonnell of Glenstal Abbey and was first performed there in 1970 as part of an annual summer congress of religious. The original manuscript contains words and melody only,[1] but Ó Riada accompanied the mass on the organ at its first performance and the original score together with a tape recording of the event formed the basis of the only published version of the mass. This edition, published by Tomás Ó Canainn in 1979,[2] including a keyboard transcription by Eilís Cranitch is, however, incomplete, omitting as it does the *Alleluia/ Roimh an soiscéal/ Ag deireadh an tsoiscéil* and *An phreafáid*. It also contains a psalm setting which is not by Ó Riada but by Ó Canainn himself (included albeit at the request of Dom Paul McDonnell) and a re-publishing of the hymn *Bí a Íosa* from the Aguisín (Appendix) of the first mass. For the purposes of this study, therefore, attention will be focused on the original Ó Riada vocal score, referring in a general way, where helpful, to the published version.

New Liturgical Elements

The Second Vatican Council's 1967 Instruction on Music in the Liturgy, *Musicam sacram*, highlighted the pre-eminence in the Roman liturgical tradition of chanted liturgical prayers and dialogues involving priest and congregation.[3] As already noted in chapter one, Ó Riada had attended a conference on this document in Glenstal around the time of its promulgation[4] and, even as he worked on *Aifreann 2*, plans were advancing in the broader English vernacular context towards the publication of a new 'Roman Missal'.[5] Glenstal's respected position in terms of its daily interaction with the musical traditions of the Roman rite and its active interest in the demands of the 'new' liturgy were bound to have some influence on the new commission.

Ceol an aifrinn had, in fact, contained directions for the singing of the liturgically important Preface together with its dialogue (*An phreafáid*). *Aifreann 2* contains a new setting of the dialogue (there are no directions regarding the delivery of the preface itself), and includes settings for three other important ritual exchanges involving priest and people: the mystery of faith (*Tar éis an choisreachadh*), doxology/Amen (*Deireadh an phaidir eochairistigh*) and the acclamations at the gospel (*Roimh an soiscéal/ Ag deireadh an tsoiscéil*), these last associated with a further liturgical innovation of Ó Riada's second mass, a congregational *Alleluia* setting with its verse.[6] The new elements reflect no doubt the input of Glenstal itself into this commission, hence Dom Paul's subsequent description of the mass as liturgically 'more complete' than its predecessor.[7]

Supplementary Texts

The sung items at the entrance (1), offertory (5), communion (12) and recessional (13) belong to the realm of indexical rather than fixed liturgical texts, and here, as in the first collection, Ó Riada avails of the freedom afforded him to draw on a rich store of native religious texts for his raw material. His selection on this occasion, however, appears to be a more considered one, given the incentive for the collection (a proper commission) and the liturgical milieu in which it would be performed (an annual congress of religious at Glenstal Abbey). Hence we find at communion a setting of the eighth-century Irish vernacular Christian hymn *Gurab tú mo bhoile* ('Be thou my vision') and, for the celebration's entrance procession, a combination of two short excerpts from the more well known *Lúireach Phádraig* (St Patrick's Breastplate). Both of these texts, together with that of *Beannaigh sinn a Athair* ('Bless us, Father'), may be found in the Irish hymn collection *Dánta Dé*,[8] suggesting this as an important reference source for Ó Riada. The devotional setting *A Íosa bháin* completes the quartet of indexical sung items. Of these four texts, three are metrical, strophic compositions, and the remaining one is a non-strophic, prose-based *Iontróid*, thus repeating exactly the pattern previously established in *Ceol an aifrinn*.

Tonality

During Ó Riada's frequent visits to Glenstal, Dom McDonnell recalls that 'many hours were spent while the monks plied him with questions on Irish modal music, plain-chant, and the possible assimilation of one into the other'.[9] An examination of the tonality of *Aifreann 2* reveals a departure from the direct *doh/soh* major modality found in *Ceol an aifrinn* into a tonal world that is more nuanced, elusive and, in Peadar Ó Riada's opinion, 'interesting'.[10]

The predominant modal context might be described as mixolydian (major, with flattened seventh) on *d*'. We note with interest, however, the following variety of pitch- endings in the prose-based settings of the mass:[11]

Iontróid	(*d*')
Kyrie	(*d*')
Gloria	(*g*')
Alleluia	(*a*')
An phreafáid	(*d*')
Sanctus	(*d*'')
Tar éis an choisreacadh	(*a*')
Deireadh an phaidir eochairistigh	(*a*')
Ár nAthair	(*d*')
Agnus Dei	(*g*')

The above table, with its predominant emphasis on *d* (lower and upper) and structural leanings towards *a*' and *g*', presents in macrocosm the essential properties of the Gregorian mode 7, a tonality latent with structural ambiguity.

Mode 7

In discussing the Gregorian repertoire of introits, chant scholars tend to comment on the structural ambiguity which characterises those antiphons associated with mode 7 of the *oktoechos* system.[12] The essence of this ambiguity, defined by Hiley as hinging on the relative structural importance in any piece of the fourth or the fifth degree above the final note, may be seen in a distilled form in the melodic configuration of the mode 7 psalm-tone, a standard melodic formula designed to accompany and sustain all antiphons in that mode:

4.1 Mode 7 psalm-tone

We note first of all the predominant reciting note, *a'*, which carries the main portion of the text. We observe also, however, the structural importance of the note *g'* towards the beginning and end of the musical formula, in other words those points where the psalm engages with the antiphon. The *d'* which opens and closes the formula represents the final of the mode, the note to which *g'* and *a'* relate by means of intervals of a fourth and a fifth above. Finally, we acknowledge the characterising influence of *c"* as the highest note of the psalm-tone a minor seventh above (or, in transposed form, a major second below) the final.

The nature of mode 7 and its internal tonal relationships may be seen then as a useful conceptual template against which to frame ensuing discussions concerning the tonality of the various movements, beginning with the *Iontróid* of Ó Riada's *Aifreann 2*.

IONTRÓID: CRÍOST LIOM

Críost liom,	*Christ be with me,*
Críost romham,	*Christ before me,*
Críost im dhiaidh,	*Christ behind me,*
Críost os mo chionnsa,	*Christ over me,*
agus Críost fúm,	*and Christ beneath me,*
Críost ina chónaí i mo chroíse,	*Christ living in my heart,*
Críost fós ó dheas díom,	*Christ even to the south of me,*
Críost ó thuaidh.	*Christ to the north.*
Ón Tiarna tig slánú,	*From the Lord comes salvation,*
ón Tiarna tig slánú.	*from the Lord comes salvation.*
Go raibh do shlánú, a Thiarna	*May your salvation be, O Lord,*
inár measc go saol na saol.	*in our midst forever and ever.*

4.2 Seán Ó Riada: *Aifreann 2, Iontróid* (bars 1–18)

The structural ambiguity referred to above is distilled and encapsulated in the opening phrases of the *Iontróid*, the mass-setting opening, as it were, with a statement of the main musical argument: *a*', the fifth, contending with *g*', the fourth, over a foundational *d*'. The text, though laid out in verses in *Dánta Dé*,[13] is essentially irregular, comprising a series of litanic invocations imploring the protection of Christ, leading to a repeated affirmation that 'salvation comes from the Lord' and closing with a petition that this salvation will ever abide amongst His people. The pattern of the text, together with the musical form articulated by Ó Riada's responses to it, might be laid out in the following terms:

Críost liom	(A)
Críost romham	(A)
Críost im dhiaidh	(B)
Críost os mo chionnsa	(C)
agus Críost fúm	(A)
Críost ina chónaí i mo chroíse	(B+C)
Críost fós ó dheas díom	(D)
Críost ó thuaidh	(A1)
Ón Tiarna tig slánú	(E)

ón Tiarna tig slánú (E)
Go raibh do shlánú, a Thiarna (B1)
inár measc go saol na saol (F)

The figure of Christ dominates the opening eight-fold litany, and an overriding musically unifying factor in this opening section is the consistent repetition of the word 'Críost' on *a*', a pitch which, in the manner of a plainchant tenor, retains its ruling character throughout the remaining four phrases. Working in both directions from this fixed tonal point, the composer fashions a tapestry of responses that explore a classic mode 7 ambitus, cadencing variously on *g*' (x4), *d*'' (x2), *a*' (x2), *c*'' (x1), and *d*' (x1), to produce an overall melodic structure with a satisfying sense of balance and proportion.

While the component responses are at times dictated by considerations of textual *structure* (such as, for instance the repeated assertions of lines 9 and 10) or *rhetoric* (a climactic *e*'' on the emphatic word 'fós'), the question of *number* (in other words, the *number* of syllables carrying the meaning of the various lines), as we shall see, exercises a huge degree of influence on the fashioning of the individual phrases, and, as a result, on the overall form.[14] This influence is most obvious in the A (two syllables) – B (three) – C (five) formal pattern of lines 2, 3 and 4, but it is also present in a different way in the opening two lines. In *textual* terms, the opening five lines form a unit comprising an opening statement followed by two paired contrasts, thus giving a possible structural reading of ABB1CC1. While the second and third lines, for example, clearly form a pair in terms of *sense* (Christ before/behind me), lines 1 and 2 form a pair in terms of *number* (two syllables each), rhythmic delivery and even sound ('Críost liom/Críost romham'), and so Ó Riada sets them to the same *a*'-*g*' motif A (a motif that returns quite naturally for the delivery of the similarly structured 'Críost fúm' in the fifth line). Ó Riada's musical form for the opening five lines, AABCA (generated, as we have seen, by number rather than sense), counterpoints rather than aligns itself with the form of the text, and the effectiveness of the overall result reminds us once more of Guido d'Arezzo's concept of a 'double-melody', i.e. the 'melody' of the text and that of the music running concurrently.[15]

The return of A in line 5 ('agus Críost fúm') is at once a completion and a new beginning. It is as if the repetitions of A provide stability while all the time the inherent tonal properties of the motif (*a'-g'*) are delivering energy and musical impetus. A developed repetition of A (A1) in line 8 concludes the principal litany of the prayer. Focusing on the other elements within this opening section, we notice the incremental syllabic and melodic development (*c''-d''*) of B and C (noting their skilful combination in the carrying of line 6, the longest in the prayer), through to the climactic D phrase (line 7), which takes in the piece's highest note *e''*.

The concluding four lines, with their opening declamatory repetitions ('Ón Tiarna tig slánú' x 2), are fashioned so as to form a melodically integrated and musically logical continuation of the piece, and the larger-scale melodic structure of the final two lines spans the more leisurely unfolding of what might be termed the only fully fledged couplet in the whole text. The petitionary tone of this last phrase is further enhanced by the prominence of *b'*, largely insignificant up to this point in the movement.

The melodic range outlined in this piece (essentially an octave, plus its upper and lower auxiliary notes) sets the limits for the subsequent movements of the mass. A syllabic style predominates, balanced occasionally by mildly melismatic elements.

KYRIE

S.	A Thiarna, déan trócaire.	*Lord, have mercy.*
P.	A Thiarna, déan trócaire.	*Lord, have mercy.*
S.	A Chríost, déan trócaire.	*Christ, have mercy.*
P.	A Chríost, déan trócaire.	*Christ, have mercy.*
S.	A Thiarna, déan trócaire.	*Lord, have mercy.*
P.	A Thiarna, déan trócaire.	*Lord, have mercy.*

In the Gregorian tradition, the six-fold Kyrie/Christe/Kyrie form has received a variety of treatments, from the monothematic approach of its litanic origins,[16] through to the more developed forms of eleventh-century mass settings.[17] In his first mass setting, Ó Riada set the *Kyrie* in the simple AABBAA form suggested by the text. The *Aifreann 2 Kyrie* adopts a more sophisticated approach, with each new pair of invocations receiving a different melodic opening (the ending word 'trócaire' has the same melodic motif for all invocations, being transposed down a fifth for the last) and the final pair crucially cast in the dynamic of call/response or question/answer,

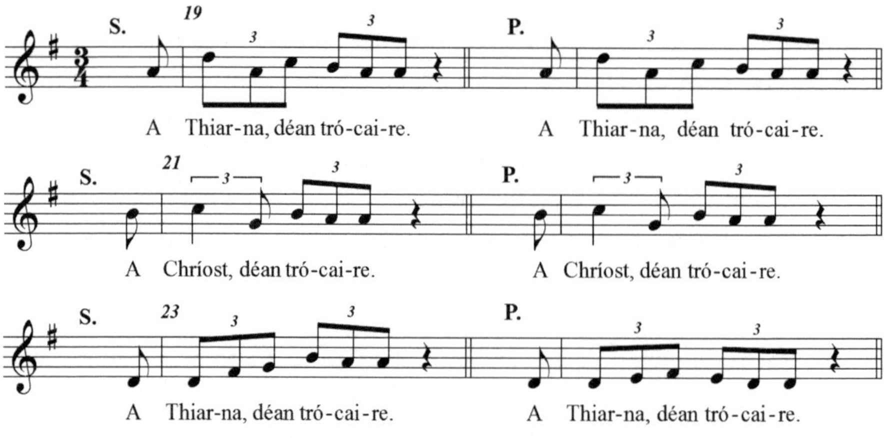

4.3 Seán Ó Riada: *Aifreann 2, Kyrie* (bars /19–24)

producing a formal layout of AABBCC1. This last innovation breaks the cycle of slavish repetition (typical of many post-Vatican II vernacular settings) and does so in a musically convincing manner, conferring in the process a greater dignity on the congregation.[18]

In the *Kyrie* the second pair of tonal protagonists are introduced, *d''* for the first 'Kyrie' petition, and *c''* for 'Christe'.[19] The relationship between these companion pitches (in higher *and* lower registers) will generate much of *Aifreann 2*'s tonal energy and identity, as indeed a similar relationship may be seen to do in the following mode 7 excerpt from the Gregorian tradition:[20]

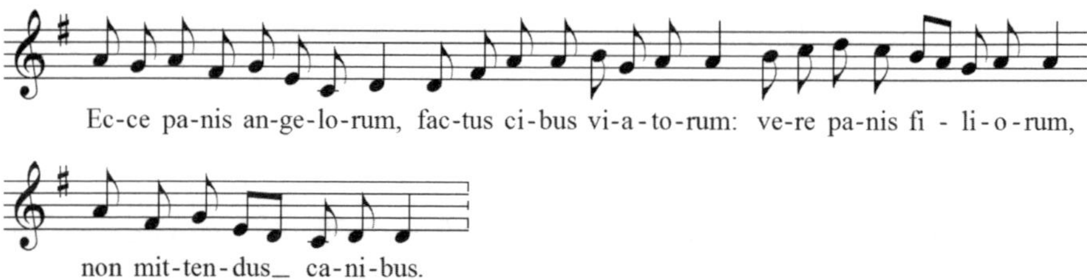

4.4 'Ecce panis angelorum' verse from sequence *Lauda Sion*

The two pitches of *d''* and *c''*, which help characterise his setting of the *Kyrie*, will play an important structural role later on in Ó Riada's mass-setting, particularly in the *Gloria*, *Sanctus* and *Agnus Dei*. Of the remaining pitches the fifth degree, *a'*, the destination of five of the six invocations, is structurally prominent throughout, and the piece concludes, like the opening *Iontróid*, on the conventional mixolydian 'tonic'.

GLORIA

Glóir do Dhia sna hardaibh. *Glory to God in the highest.*
Agus ar thalamh síocháin do lucht a pháirte.
And on earth peace to people of goodwill.
Molaimid Thú. Móraimid Thú. Adhraimid Thú.
We praise You. We bless You. We adore You.
Tugaimid glóir duit. *We glorify You.*
Gabhaimid buíochas leat as ucht do mhórghlóire.
We give You thanks for Your great glory.
A Thiarna Dia, a Rí na bhFlaitheas,
Lord God, King of Heaven,
a Dhia, a Athair uilechumhachtaigh.
God, the Father almighty.
A Thiarna aonmhic, a Íosa Críost.
Lord, only son, Jesus Christ,
A Thiarna Dia, a Uain Dé, Mac an Athar.
Lord God, Lamb of God, Son of the Father.
Tusa a thógas peacaí an domhain,
You, who take away the sins of the world,
déan trócaire orainn. *have mercy on us.*
Tusa a thógas peacaí an domhain,
You, who take away the sins of the world,
glac lenár nguí. *accept our prayer.*
Tusa atá i do shuí ar dheis an Athar,
You, who sit at the right hand of the Father,
déan trócaire orainn. *have mercy on us.*
Óir is Tú amháin is naofa. *For You alone are holy.*
Is Tú amháin is Tiarna. *You alone are the Lord.*
Is Tú amháin is ró-ard, a Íosa Críost,
You alone are the most high, Jesus Christ,
mar aon leis an Spiorad Naomh
one with the Holy Spirit
i nglóir Dé an tAthair. *in the glory of God the Father.*
Amen. *Amen.*

4.5 Seán Ó Riada: *Aifreann 2, Gloria* (bars 25–63)

Tonality

Within the body of Gregorian mode 7 introits, some notable examples – such as the Christmas day 'Puer natus' or 'Viri Galilei' from the feast of the Ascension – demonstrate a strong structural leaning towards the fourth degree above the final.[21] In the opening *Iontróid* of Ó Riada's *Aifreann 2*, as we have seen, the fourth (*g'*) competed over a foundational *d'* with the fifth degree (*a'*), with *a'* proving more influential by the end of the piece. With the *Gloria*, however, *g'* literally comes into its own at key points of beginning, middle and, most notably, the end (bars 26–27; 37–41; 60–63), to such an extent that it is possible to speak of a shift in tonal foundations within the mass. To describe this shift as a key-change is at best a rather crude way of identifying what is essentially a change of emphasis within the existing modal structure – as can be seen, the majority of the text is couched within the *d'*-based mixolydian modal parameters already established in the *Iontróid* and the *Kyrie*. However, Ó Riada does choose to begin and end clearly in a mode 6-type major tonality, with *g'* as the new tonic (*doh*), and it is from this starting point that an analysis is most usefully pursued. In spite of this bi-polar tonal alternation (corresponding to Gregorian modes 6 and 7), however, the principal tonal protagonists from the mass's opening two movements, *g'*, *a'*, *c''* and *d''* (now *doh*, *ray*, *fah* and *soh* respectively), continue to exert their major structural influence and remain very much in control of the musical journey.

Melodic Style

The *Aifreann 2* setting of the Gloria is characterised by far fewer repeated notes and a more consistently flowing melodic style than its predecessor in *Ceol an aifrinn*. However, while the setting is much less reliant on recitational-type passages, it is more reliant on the device of motivic repetition. (A comparison between the settings of three of the text's four significant triple litanies bears this out.) In *Ceol an aifrinn*, the recitational principle is consistently present, but always within the context of a dynamic tonal plan, whereas in the second mass, only one of the litanies – the largest of them – employs recitative, and here the litanic phrases are simply repeated with no significant melodic development:

4.6 Seán Ó Riada: *Aifreann 2, Gloria* (bars 46–51)

It is interesting also to compare the overall tonal plans of both settings in respect of their phrase-endings:

Ceol an aifreann

Aifreann 2

4.7 Seán Ó Riada: Gloria settings: phrase endings

In *Aifreann 2*, the presence of *soh* (lower and higher *d*) and nearly-related *ray* (*a*') in all but two of the piece's cadences give the impression of the internal melodic activity taking place against the structural backdrop of a dominant open-fifth mode 7 type drone. This effect, together with the melodic repetitions referred to above, contribute to an overall tonal character that is more static and tonally grounded, in contrast with the more structurally mobile setting of *Ceol an aifrinn*. Apart from the tonic-based opening intonation and closing cadence (both of which, interestingly, feature the word 'Glóir'), the only internal structural shift in the direction of the 'home' *g*'-based tonality happens with the litany 'A Thiarna Dia, a Rí na bhFlaitheas ... a Íosa Críost' (bars 36–42).[22]

Ó Riada's second setting of the Gloria text is, as has already been mentioned, further stabilised by a more tightly woven thematic design in which various motifs return again and again, developing where necessary to meet the subtle demands of changing text patterns. The two principal motifs, A and B, together with their adaptations, draw their energy from the inherent properties of the tonality (the *c'/d'* and *g'/a'* relationships respectively):

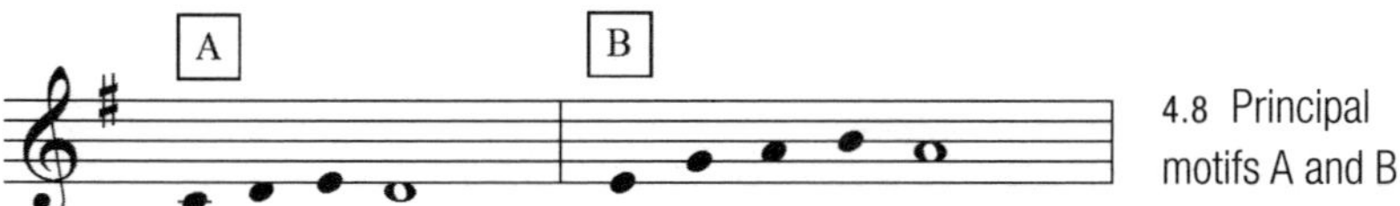

4.8 Principal motifs A and B

Together they inhabit twenty-two of the piece's thirty-nine bars, appearing towards the beginning and middle, and dominating the final section of the piece. An example of the composer's flexible treatment of one motif, B, may be seen by tracking its appearances as the text progresses:

4.9 Seán Ó Riada: *Aifreann 2, Gloria* (bars 33–34; 43–45; 58–59)

The 'hidden' recurrence of motifs has already been discussed in relation to traditional melodic composition and Ó Riada's *Ceol an aifrinn.*[23] By this conscious or subconscious compositional device, a motif is concealed by placing it in an uncharacteristic position, for instance as a phrase 'answer' following a pattern of 'opening' type statements, or vice versa. The latter is the case with the descending fourth motif (bars 28–29) which closes the opening couplet and reappears (as a form of tonal echo up a fourth) later (bars 36–37) as the opening of a new section:

4.10 Seán Ó Riada: *Aifreann 2, Gloria* (bars 28–29; 36–37)

Returning once more to phenomena associated with the tonal structure, it is interesting to note the behaviour of the lower *d'* pitch. Because of its association with motif A, it is linked indissolubly with the succeeding structural pitch, *a'* of motif B. The higher *d''* pitch, when it does appear, seems, on the other hand, to be naturally attracted downwards to the tonic, *g'*. The continuation of the musical flow over such a large body of text would seem to depend on this 'open' structural relationship, one which is not definitively closed until the very definite *d'*-*g'* melodic gesture of the final bar.

Rhetoric, Word-Painting

The static, grounded tonality of this setting of the Gloria has already been referred to, and contrasted with the more mobile tonal dynamic of Ó Riada's *Ceol an aifrinn*. This quality was also noted in relation to the absence, compared to the earlier setting, of melodic development in the course of litanic passages. In rhetorical terms the contrasting nature of the two approaches may be seen by comparing the tessiturae of the crucial opening triple-litany of praise 'Molaimid Thú, Móraimid Thú, Adhraimid Thú':

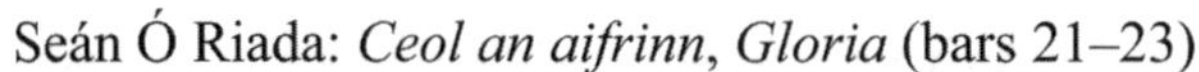
Seán Ó Riada: *Ceol an aifrinn*, *Gloria* (bars 21–23)

Seán Ó Riada: *Aifreann 2*, *Gloria* (bars 30–32)

As can be seen, *Ceol an aifrinn* adopts a very obvious declamatory position, using upper *doh* as its basis. *Aifreann 2* on the other hand, treats the same text in a completely different manner, using the lowest notes of the tonal scheme to deliver it. The aesthetic questions raised by this may be partially answered by a return to Peadar Ó Riada's statement concerning the setting of certain standard text-elements:"For 'heaven" and "earth", you might use a high note and a low note, or a bright note and a dark note, *or you might go the opposite way* ... [my italics]'.[24] However, matters of even greater bearing on the tonal positioning of any given passage in a long text such as the Gloria might include questions of (a) the overall melodic plan, and in a piece characterised (as this is) by a more gradual melodic development, (b) the melodic material immediately preceding it. Ó Riada's declamatory opening phrase leads naturally and gradually down to the lower register and to the beginning of the litany referred to above.

Considerations of overall structure and strategic melodic planning may also account for the passages of *g'*-based melody, all of which are nevertheless associated with textual elements of praise and 'glory' to God.[25] However, since we have no information regarding Ó Riada's compositional method in this discipline, we must be careful not to attribute too much weight to the notion of a very deliberate, pre-determined tonal plan.[26]

Melismas

There is only one melisma in this setting, and it happens, unsurprisingly, on the richly onomatopoeic word 'nglóir' (bar 60).[27] The musical context is culminatory in nature and takes place four bars from the end, with the six-note melisma beginning on the melodic apex of the piece's tonal structure (*d''* and its upper auxiliary, *e''*, which has not been heard since the piece's opening section), triumphantly heralding the return of the tonic 'home' tonality, and echoing the tonic 'Glóir' with which the piece began.

ALLELUIA/ ROIMH AN SOISCÉAL/ AG DEIREADH AN TSOISCÉIL

Alleluia, Alleluia	*Alleluia, Alleluia*
Alleluia, Alleluia	*Alleluia, Alleluia*
Nach álainn ar na sléibhte	*How lovely on the mountains*
tá cosa an dea-scéalaí!	*are the feet of the one who brings good news!*
Tuar na síochána é,	*Tower of peace is he,*
ola an tsuaimhnis é,	*Oil of gladness is he,*
fógróir na slánaithe é.	*Announcer of salvation is he.*
Alleluia, Alleluia	*Alleluia, Alleluia*
Alleluia, Alleluia	*Alleluia, Alleluia*
S. Go raibh an Tiarna libh.	*The Lord be with you.*
P. Agus leat féin.	*And also with you.*
S. Sliocht as an soiscéal naofa	*A reading from the holy gospel*
do réir Matha/Marc/Lúcáis/Eoin.	*according to Matthew/Mark/Luke/John.*
P. Glóir duit, a Thiarna.	*Glory to you, O Lord.*
S. Sin é briathar Dé.	*This is the word of God.*
P. Moladh duit, a Chríost.	*Praise to you, O Christ.*

Roimh an Soiscéal:

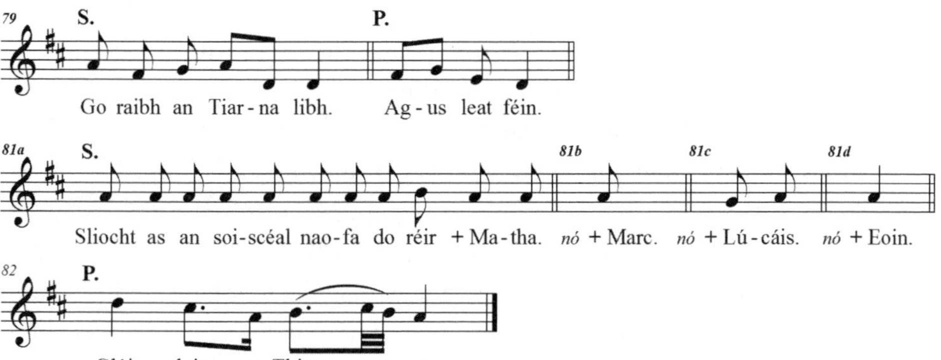

Ag deireadh an tSoiscéal:

4.12 Seán Ó Riada: *Aifreann 2, Alleluia/ Roimh an soiscéal/ Ag deireadh an tsoiscéil* (bars 64–84)

The Gregorian tradition of the Alleluia involves an elaborate choir-oriented acclamation and an equally elaborate verse. The nature of the Glenstal commission would appear to have demanded a more assembly-friendly setting, in keeping with the Vatican II aim of restoring various liturgical elements to the people.

Ó Riada here conceives of the Alleluia and the dialogues surrounding the gospel as forming a distinctive and unbroken musical unit. Both elements begin and end on *a'*.[28] Alone among the mass-parts these elements carry a key signature of two sharps, *f#* and *c#*, thus signalling a clear departure from the single sharp tonality of the other movements. The question naturally arises as to why Ó Riada, who had selected a mixolydian tonality, pregnant as we have seen with so many possibilities, chose not to have fashioned a suitable Alleluia from the same material. The version that he has produced struggles to justify such a radical tonal shift and ranks as probably the least convincing of all the musico-liturgical elements in the mass. Are there other forces at work here? In an extended version of the earlier-quoted passage from *The Achievement of Seán Ó Riada*, Dom Paul McDonnell gives us a revealing insight into the composer's instincts regarding chant and orality, as shared with the Glenstal monks during the 1960s:

> Many hours were spent while the monks plied him with questions on Irish modal music, plain-chant and the possible assimilation of one into the other … One did not always agree with him, especially when he took some plain-chant *troparia* and sang it in *sean-nós* fashion.[29]

Was Ó Riada possibly trying to prove his point with this *Alleluia*? Certainly the model seems to have been a double-alleluia motif taken from an Eastertide mode 2 antiphon for the office of None, presented here at the relevant pitch:[30]

4.13 Alleluia from *Antiphonale monasticum*

Here is Ó Riada's vernacularised version with the opening and closing tonal modifications:

4.14 Seán Ó Riada: *Aifreann 2, Alleluia* (bars 64–65)

The result, identifiable with an open-ended Irish *soh*-mode structure, places the music firmly in the tonal region of Gregorian mode 8. While Ó Riada's modification of the tonality of a stock Gregorian melody may have appeared to the Glenstal monks a merely cavalier gesture, contemporaneous work in chant scholarship around the revolutionary concept of 'archaic modality' proposed by the Benedictine Dom Jean-Claire at Solesmes reveals a solid tradition amongst the earliest chant sources for this type of phenomenon.[31] Dom Daniel Saulnier, successor to Dom Jean-Claire at the monastery's palaeography department, proposes the two antiphons as an example of the repertoire's apparent flexibility in relation to final notes:[32]

4.15 from *Les modes grégoriens*

An apparent flexibility with regard to final notes in another orally based melodic tradition is referenced in the work of ethnomusicologist James Cowdery. As previously discussed in chapter two, Cowdery, in attempting to define inherent processes governing tune relationships, development and transmission within the Irish melodic tradition, attests to the primacy of melodic *contour* over other musical considerations, elevating it to the status of a principle, which he terms the 'outlining principle'. Following this principle, he states that in an orally derived repertoire such as Irish music: 'contour will out, cadence and final notwithstanding'.[33]

In apparently playing fast and loose with the canonical melodies of the *Antiphonale monasticum*, Ó Riada's musical instincts were, after all, it would appear, not far off the mark, either from the standpoint of the generative processes of Irish traditional music, or the evidence of melodic comparisons from the chant repertoire itself.[34]

Alleluia verse

The text of the verse consists of a straightforward scriptural passage,[35] followed by a more stylised continuation in litany form:

How lovely on the mountains
are the feet of the one who brings good news!
Tower of peace is he,
Oil of gladness is he,
Announcer of salvation is he.

The opening passage occupies, like the *Alleluia* itself, the traditional terrain of a mode 8 psalm-tone (covering the area between the final and the fourth above), even if the melodic style here is more lyrically mobile than the recitative approach of a psalm-tone. This lyrical mobility of the verse and its stylistic kinship with the *Alleluia* is very much in keeping with the Gregorian Alleluia tradition and provides a positive example of Ó Riada's concurrence with the underlying *principles* (as opposed to the surface pitches) of a chant genre. The three litanic invocations are united tonally by their endings, while the composer varies the beginnings in accordance with the structural potentialities of a mode 8-type tonality. The opening two invocations of the triple litany focus on the lower tetrachord of the mode, with the final one taking in the outer limits of the mode in a manner strongly reminiscent of mode 8 tracts:[36]

4.16 *Liber usualis*, 517

The ritual dialogues before and after the Gospel (*Roimh an soiscéal* and Ag *deireadh an tsoiscéil*) maintain the mode 8 character (upper tetrachord only), with the opening ritual exchange (linked possibly with the immediately succeeding *An phreafáid*) in a different but closely related tonality. One interesting detail which reflects Ó Riada's abiding concern with natural word accentuation is the melodic modification provided for the introduction of gospel passages by the evangelist 'Lúcáis'.[36]

AN PHREAFÁID

S. Go raibh an Tiarna libh — *The Lord be with you.*
P. Agus leat féin. — *And also with you.*
S. Tógaigí bhúr gcroíthe in airde
Lift up your hearts on high.
P. Tá said tógtha 'n airde chun an Tiarna 'gainn.
We have lifted them up to the Lord.
S. Gabhaimis buíochas leis an Tiarna ár nDia.
Let us give thanks to the Lord our God.
P. Is ceart agus is cóir sin. — *That is right and fitting.*

4.17 Seán Ó Riada: *Aifreann 2, An phreafáid* (bars 85–91)

Comparisons were made in the case of the Preface dialogue from *Ceol an aifrinn* with the traditional Gregorian version vis-à-vis the 'leading' musical as well as textual role of the priest. In *Aifreann 2* the priest still leads the way, but the musical dynamic set up by Ó Riada is born of a broader conceptual framework which allows the congregation its own identity, one which is characterised by a greater sense of freedom and independence. The seeds of this vision were already present in the final 'non-repetition' of the *Kyrie*, and while it may well have more to do with Ó Riada's knowledge and expectations of the soon-to-be-assembled Glenstal gathering than any theological or musical vision regarding congregations in general, it reveals more effectively than any liturgical instruction could, and to a greater extent than any other piece in the mass, the full dignity of the congregation 'at play' in a liturgical celebration. The six-fold interplay is cast within the forward-moving dynamic of a developing melody, and the phrase-end notes produce the following logical pattern:

d' – d': a' – a': a' – d'

The most noteworthy exchange, in both rhetorical and melodic terms, is the second one. Here the priest's command 'Lift up your hearts on high' is emphatically owned by the congregation and taken further in the response, translated more literally as 'They are lifted on high to the Lord by us'. The idea of the congregation going further than the priest, yet remaining united to him, is perfectly expressed in the musical setting which moves the melodic plot on by introducing *c''* as an upper decoration of *a'*, in classic mode 7 manner.[38] The priest's subsequent completion of the upward musical journey builds on what has been independently achieved by the congregation, and the last ten notes of this exchange represent an interesting link with an earlier movement:

Seán Ó Riada: *Aifreann 2, An phreafáid* (bars 90–91)

Seán Ó Riada: *Aifreann 2, Kyrie* (bars /23–24)

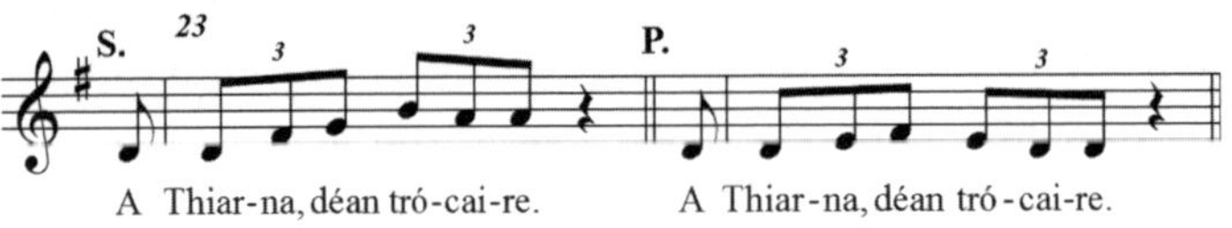

4.18

Given the similarities between the opening exchange of the mass and the above-quoted passage, the *Kyrie*, it could be suggested, has provided both the conceptual framework and melodic starting point for *An phreafáid*.[39]

SANCTUS

Is Naofa, Naofa, Naofa Thú,
A Thiarna, Dia na Slua.
Tá neamh agus talamh lán de do ghlóir.

Hósanna 'sna harda.
Is beannaithe 'n té 'tá ag teacht
in ainm an Tiarna.
Hósanna 'sna harda.

Holy, Holy, Holy are You,
Lord, God of Hosts.
Heaven and earth are full of
Your glory.

Hosanna in the highest.
Blessed is he who is coming
in the name of the Lord.
Hosanna in the highest.

4.19 Seán Ó Riada: *Aifreann 2, Sanctus* (bars /92–103)

Ó Riada's second setting of the Sanctus text reveals, amongst all the mass-movement settings of *Aifreann 2*, the most radical departure from the rhythmico-textual 'template' established in *Ceol an aifrinn*. In the earlier setting we saw how Ó Riada took full advantage of the Irish translation of the opening triple 'Sanctus', one which provides the composer with an exceptionally musically friendly four-accent text. In *Aifreann 2*, however, Ó Riada chooses a more leisurely (dare one say 'static') approach which, though lacking the natural forward drive of the original conception, is nevertheless full of interesting resonances. In the first place, the three unchanging *g'-a'-a'* repetitions of 'Naofa' ('Holy') may be said to mirror the opening repeated melodic gestures of the *Iontróid*, with which the mass began, and they mine once more the dynamic tonal ambiguities of the authentic mixolydian mode. An even more interesting resonance emerges when we recall once more the origins and destination of this Glenstal-commissioned work, Ó Riada's 'frequent visits' to the Abbey and his musical engagement with the monks and furthermore, the heightened sense of history and tradition (already noted in his selection of ancillary hymn texts) which informed his approach to this task. Could it be that, in this melodic opening of his second Sanctus setting, Ó Riada is acknowledging, consciously or otherwise, the oldest and most familiar of all Gregorian settings, Sanctus XVIII?[40] Here are the two openings:

4.20 Sanctus XVIII; Seán Ó Riada: *Aifreann 2, Sanctus* (openings)

Certainly if Ó Riada wanted to reproduce the motivic dynamic of the earlier setting into the Irish language, he would have no option in accentual terms but to transfer the gestural weight found above (but, notably, in no later Gregorian setting of the text) at the end of the Latin word to the beginning of the Irish one. The upward directional movement also seems to particularly suit the Irish word (in any case one cannot imagine Ó Riada, conscious as he was of the melodic resourcefulness of his native heritage, resorting to a direct mimicking of the Gregorian melody). The idea of a mirror image is completed on the structural melodic level with Ó Riada's *g'-a'-b'* movement symmetrically matching the tonal drive of the *b'-a'-g'* structure of the chant. Structural comparisons aside, however, where Ó Riada's setting seems to flounder momentarily is with the third identical 'Naofa' motivic repetition. The Gregorian version develops at this point and the earlier-mentioned *Iontróid* also moves off after two motivic repetitions.[41]

Modality

The *d'* which launches the pattern discussed above forms with its near neighbour *g'* an immediate tonal summary of this piece. The question is, are we to treat it as a *d'*-based mode 7 melody (it begins and ends on that pitch) with a characteristic flattened seventh and a strong internal emphasis on the fourth degree *g*'? Or instead, as a more straightforward concert *g*-based mode 6 melody which begins and ends on *d*', the fifth degree? To a certain extent, we are in new tonal territory here: the *Sanctus* is the only mass movement that ends on a high *d*''. It is a testament (the strongest yet) to the flexible character of the tonality that one could in fact proceed with confidence on either path. A revisiting of the broader liturgical context surrounding the Sanctus, and articulated by the composer in his earlier *Ceol an aifrinn* setting, may help us here. The earlier setting demonstrates his clear understanding of the liturgical link between Preface dialogue, Preface and Sanctus and his musically integrated response underlines that understanding. It could hardly be otherwise in the case of the later *Aifreann 2*; and the clearly mixolydian character of *An phreafáid* (it shares the same range as the *Sanctus*) suggests mode 7 as the more likely path to follow.

Form and Musical Style

The tightly woven and unified form of the earlier *Ceol an aifrinn* setting (ABCA1C1A1) has already been noted. It contrasts with the more disparate thematic character of the *Aifreann 2* setting, summarised below, together with respective phrase-end notes:

A (*b*')
B (*f#*')
C (*f#*')
D (*d*'')
E (*d*')
D (*d*'')

As already mentioned, the final note of the piece (*d*'') signals a new melodic departure in the mass.[42] New also are the tonal effects produced by the use, for the first time in the mass setting, of *b*' and *f#*' as phrase-end notes. The increased prominence of these notes results also in new intervallic leaps (major sixth, bars 97–98 and 101) and relationships (diminished fifth, bars 96–97 and 99–100). The melodic style, as in the other movements, retains, however, an overall stepwise character.

In formal terms, apart from the melodic repetitions of the two 'Hósanna' phrases, the piece does employ other, perhaps less obvious, unifying devices.

Phrases C and E, for instance, follow something of the Gregorian tradition of musically unified 'Pleni sunt' and 'Benedictus' elements,[43] in their sharing of the same distinctive *g'*-based tonality and major sixth leaps. Even more noteworthy is the fact that the repeated *g'*- *a'*-*a'* motif, which characterised the opening phrase A, is re-echoed in a different but structurally related tonal area (*c''*-*d''*-*d''*) at the end of the D phrase (bar 100). In this way our four principal tonal characters exert their influence over the beginning, middle and end of the movement, fashioning unity out of apparent diversity.

TAR ÉIS AN CHOISREACADH

S. Fógraimís rúndiamhair an chreidimh.
Let us proclaim the mystery of faith.

P. A Íosa, fuair Tú bás ar ár son;	Jesus, You died on our behalf;
d'éirigh Tú ó na mair[i]bh;	You rose from the dead;
tiocfaidh Tú 'rís.	You will come again.

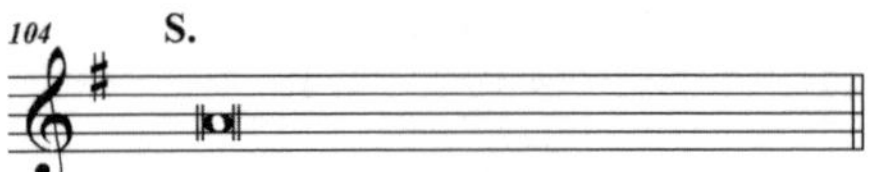

4.21 Seán Ó Riada: *Aifreann 2, Tar éis an choisreacadh* (bars 104–105)

The memorial acclamation' (Ó Riada entitles it 'After the Consecration') is the first of the new post-Vatican II liturgical elements that Ó Riada introduces in his *Aifreann 2* setting.[44] This dialogue between the priest and the people consists of a solo invitation followed by a communal proclamation.

The acclamations at the gospel saw *a'* being used in recitational fashion, though in the context of a mode 8 tonal configuration. Here we see the pitch coming into its own for the first time within a genuinely mixolydian melodic framework, where its distinctive energy is used to introduce, sustain and conclude a brief but textually potent acclamation. Following the chanted monotone invitation on *a'*, Ó Riada carves the text three discrete and distinctive melodic phrases out of the mixolydian modal structure. The concluding melodic pattern of the first of these (*a'b'g'd'*) is completely fresh in terms of the mass setting so far, and its tonal energy adds a new twist to the modal dynamic.

The upward sweep of the middle phrase ('you rose from the dead') concludes with an *a'-d''* (perfect fourth) movement ('tú ó na mairbh') that is matched by the opening *g'-c'* gesture of the final phrase. The modally incomplete ending of the proclamation on *a'* seems particularly suited to the nature of the text,[45] a dynamic that finds a ready parallel in the official chant version found in the *Missale romanum*:

4.22 *Missale romanum*, 'Mysterium fidei'

DEIREADH AN PHAIDIR EOCHAIRISTIGH

S. Is tríd, agus leis, agus ann,	*Through him, and with him and in him,*
a thugtar gach onóir agus glóir duitse,	*all honour and glory are given to You,*
a Dhia, an tAthair uilechumhachtach,	*God, the almighty Father,*
mar aon leis an Spiorad Naomh,	*one with the Holy Spirit,*
trí shaol na saol.	*forever and ever.*
P. Amen.	*Amen.*

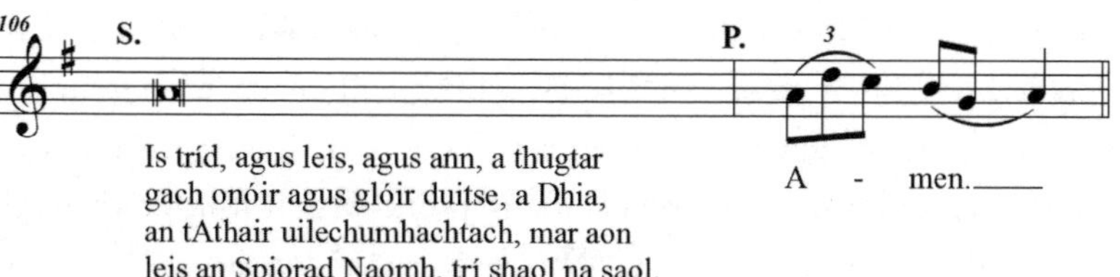

4.23 Seán Ó Riada: *Aifreann 2, Deireadh an phaidir eochairistigh* (bars 106–107)

The public recitation of the doxology together with its 'Amen' as a conclusion to the Eucharistic Prayer was another new Vatican II liturgical development with implications for music. As expressed some years later in the *General Instruction of the Roman Missal*, 'the praise of God is expressed in the doxology, which is concluded and affirmed by the assent of the people'.[46] It is unclear to what extent Ó Riada might have had access to experimental English-language versions (the *Roman Missal* was not yet published), but he may have been familiar through Glenstal with the official Latin musical version from the newly released *Missale romanum* (published in March 1970).[47] In this version, with its text skilfully adapted to the traditional Gregorian preface-tone, the musical burden of praise lay with the celebrating priest, the people's assent coming in the form of a simple concluding 'Amen':

4.24 Doxology from *Missale romanum*

It is interesting, then, to note Ó Riada's reversal of this dynamic in his first and only essay in the genre. The *Aifreann 2* setting has the priest delivering the main body of the text on a single reciting note *a'* (the normal mixolydian reciting pitch) and the congregation responding with a relatively florid, though *a'*-centred 'Amen'. Regarding the priest, Ó Riada's musical choice seems to be freely made and not determined by any limiting circumstances on the celebrant's part (the priest's role in the preface dialogue, for instance, is quite challenging and musically developed).

It seems wise, then, to view this on a broader scale, taking into account also the preceding *Tar éis an choisreachadh*, a liturgical entity with which it shares almost identical characteristics: priest/people dialogue; initiated by a recited passage, and a tonally open starting point which follows through to the end of the people's response. This pattern is continued with the introduction and delivery of the immediately ensuing *An phaidir*.

AN PHAIDIR

S. Aitheanta an tslánaitheora …
de mhisneach againn a rá:
P. Ár nAthair atá ar neamh,
go naofar tAinm,
go dtaga do ríocht,
go ndeántar do thoil ar an dtalamh
mar a dhéantar ar neamh.
Ár n-arán laethiúil tabhair dúinn inniu,
agus maith dúinn ár bhfiacha
mar a mhaithimidne d'ár
bhféichiúna féin.
Agus ná lig sinn i gcathú,
ach saor sinn ó olc.

P. *The example of the Saviour …*
we have the confidence to say:
C. *Our Father who art in heaven,*
hallowed be Your Name,
Your kingdom come,
Your will be done on earth
as it is in heaven.
give us this day our daily bread
and forgive us our debts
as we forgive our own debtors.
And lead us not into temptation,
but deliver us from evil.

4.25 Seán Ó Riada: *Aifreann 2, An phaidir* (bars 108–128)

In the earlier discussion of Ó Riada's first setting of this text, the Irish and Latin translations of the prayer were compared, as was Ó Riada's compositional approach with that of the traditional 'Pater noster'. In *Aifreann 2* the same Irish translation provides the starting point for the composer, and while the setting itself is not in any way radically different from its predecessor in terms of the accentual rhythmic declamation of the text,[48] certain areas such as form, melodic expression and modality merit some attention.

Ó Riada adopts a classic mode 7 tonality which stretches to one degree on either side of the *d'-d''* octave, and relies almost exclusively on the fifth degree *a'* as an internal structural note. The major-mode tonality and reliance on the fifth bring it very close to the tonal world of its predecessor in *Ceol an aifrinn*, and produces certain structural and gestural similarities, such as the following mirror-image settings of the opening phrase:

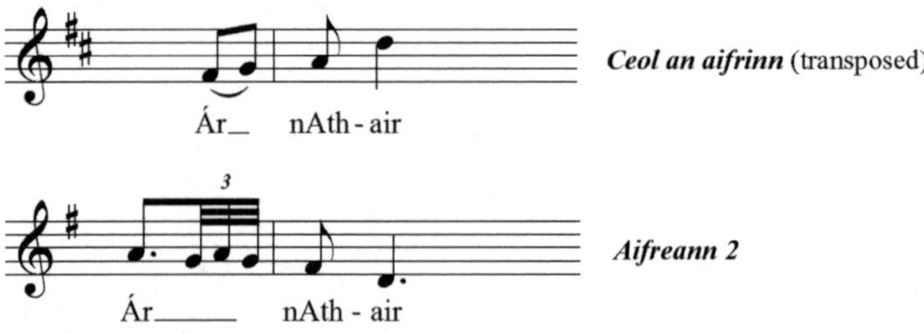

4.26 Seán Ó Riada: *Ceol an aifrinn (bar /65); Aifreann 2* (bar /110)

However, once under way, the characteristic patterns and relationships of authentic mixolydian tonality soon begin to hold sway. Briefly summarised, the tonal argument can be reduced to an ABA interplay of melodic patterns constructed on the arpeggio patterns of the tonic *d'* and the flattened seventh, *c'*.[49] The tonal structure outlined above mirrors, more closely than Ó Riada's first essay in the genre, the broadly tripartite nature of the prayer, particularly as it is articulated in both the Latin language and in the standard Gregorian melodic setting:

4.27 'Pater noster'

The XXY musical form of the above may be defined in terms of (X) the melodic repetitions beginning the 'Pater noster' and 'Panem nostrum' sections (occasioned possibly by the almost identical sonic properties of their two opening phrases) and (Y) the change of tessitura which marks the final petition couplet. In the Irish text, while the corresponding phrases 'Ár nAthair' and 'Ár n-arán' are quite similar in terms of sound and number of syllables, they are radically different in accentual terms, thus making the possibility of a musical gestural repetition very unlikely. The ABA form found in Ó Riada's *Aifreann 2* setting, and referred to above in purely tonal terms, extends also into the thematic realm, with the composer's ternary-type repetition of A reflecting potentialities latent in the structural make-up of the Irish translation:[50]

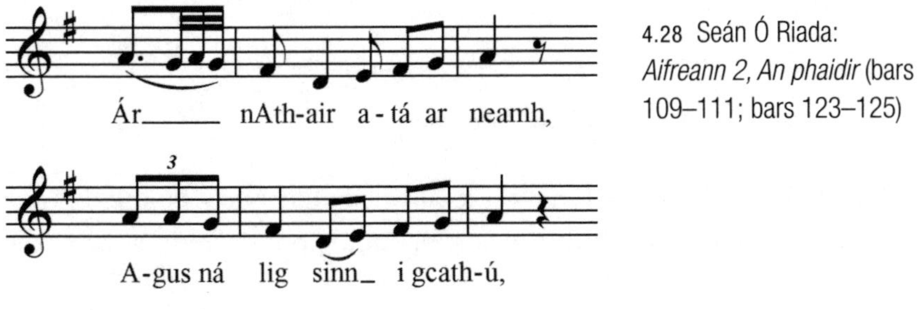

4.28 Seán Ó Riada: *Aifreann 2, An phaidir* (bars 109–111; bars 123–125)

In terms of overall structure, the open-ended *a'* cadence at the end of the first A section (bar 116) is balanced in the end of prayer reprise of A by a closed cadence on *d'* (bar 128), with the final couplet presenting a type of condensed recapitulation of all the available tonal elements (including - and this within the umbrella of traditional Irish modality – a sharpened seventh, *c#"*).[51]

In thematic terms the middle *c'*-based B section begins with a rising filled-in minor third, mirroring the corresponding falling gesture of A. Indeed it is interesting to note all the phrases in the prayer which begin with a filled-in third motif, and to further compare in tonic solfa terms their beginnings with the corresponding phrases of the *Ceol an aifrinn* setting:

Aifreann 2		***Ceol an aifrinn***	
Phrase 1:	*sf/m*	Phrase 1:	*mf/s*
Phrase 5:	*rm/f*	Phrase 5:	*d'r'/m'*
Phrase 6:	*sl/ta*	Phrase 6:	*r'd'/t*
Phrase 7:	*rd/ta*	Phrase 7:	*dr/m*
Phrase 8:	*sf/m*	Phrase 9:	*sl/t*

4.29 Seán Ó Riada: *An phaidir*, comparative phrase openings

The similarity of musical approach in handling the pervasive textual upbeats of the prayer is noteworthy, with the *Aifreann 2* setting being characterised by a greater mix of directional changes than its predecessor. Turning to phrase-endings, as already mentioned, *a'* (in this context *soh*) retains a dominant structural role throughout, as evidenced by the following table:

(* preferred over the following *fah*, which I take to be a passing note.)

4.30 Seán Ó Riada: *Aifreann 2, An phaidir*, tonal layout

The static character of the tonal plan outlined above may be highlighted by means of a comparison with the corresponding phrase endings from the *Ceol an aifrinn* setting:

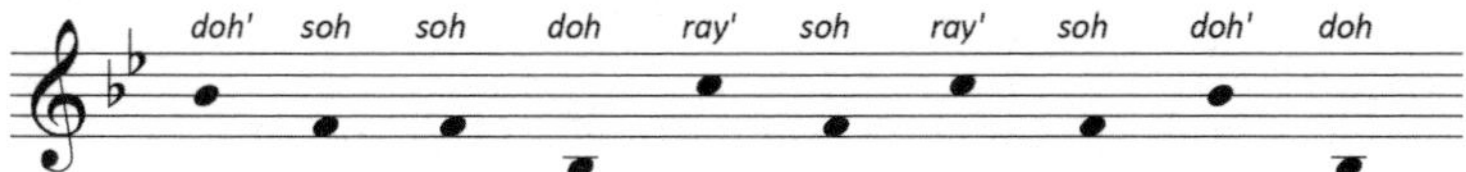

4.31 Seán Ó Riada: *Ceol an aifrinn, An phaidir*, tonal layout

The melodic movement in the *Aifreann 2* setting, as elsewhere in the mass, is more deliberate in its journey, with a type of tension-release principle which sees melodic ascents generally gained by step, being balanced by descents regularly featuring leaps of a third. The one exception to this comes at the end of the prayer's opening triple litany, 'go naofar tAinm/ go dtaga do ríocht/ go ndéantar do thoil ar an dtalamh', where after two stepwise approaches to *c*', *d*'' is gained by means of an upward leap of a fourth:

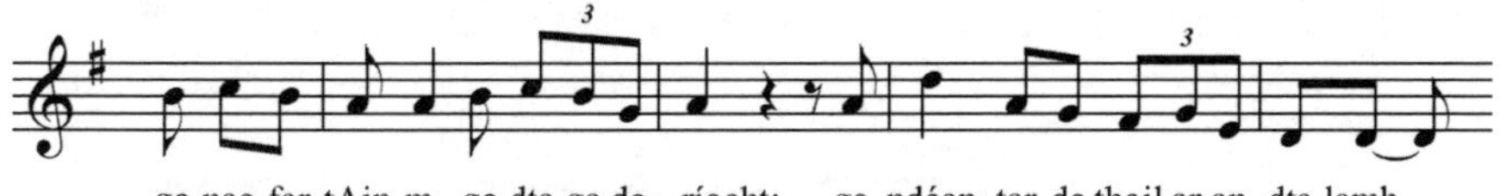

4.32 Seán Ó Riada: *Aifreann 2, An phaidir* (bars 111–115)

This example of progressive melodic 'questing', such a regular feature of the triple litanies of *Ceol an aifrinn*, is rare in the context of *Aifreann 2*, where the vast majority of such passages are delivered in a musically static manner. The closest related example from amongst the other movements of this mass may be found in the opening lines of the *Iontróid*:

4.33 Seán Ó Riada: *Aifreann 2, Iontróid* (bars 3–4)

AGNUS DEI

A Uain Dé, a thógas peacaí an domhain, déan trócaire orainn.
A Uain Dé, a thógas peacaí an domhain, déan trócaire orainn.
A Uain Dé, a thógas peacaí an domhain, tabhair dúinn síocháin.

Lamb of God, who takes away the sins of the world, have mercy on us.
Lamb of God, who takes away the sins of the world, have mercy on us.
Lamb of God, who takes away the sins of the world, grant us peace.

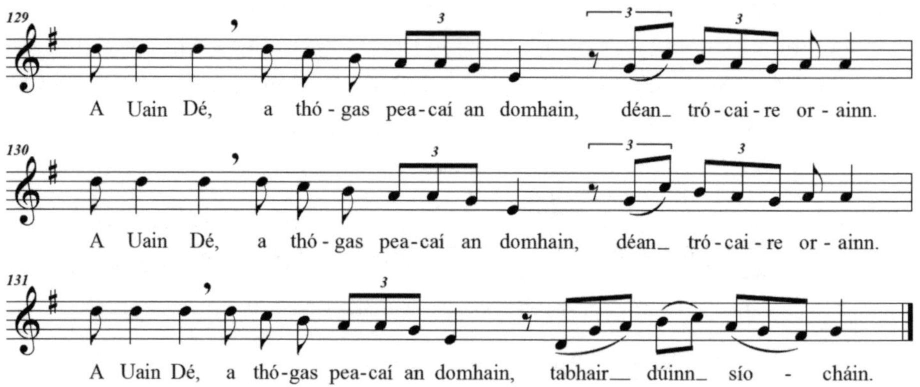

4.34 Seán Ó Riada: *Aifreann 2, Agnus Dei* (bars 129–131)

Ó Riada's *Ceol an aifrinn* setting of this text (invocation + petition) was cast in the following form:

A+X
B+X
C+Y

The three repetitions of the invocation followed a developmental musical path while the petitions followed the form suggested by their texts. The *Aifreann 2* setting works out as follows:

A+X
A+X
A+Y

Here we see a musical form completely aligned to that of the text, stressing the repetitive and inherently litanic nature of this liturgical element. In this sense it recalls the equally repetitive setting from the Gregorian Requiem Mass XVIII, a melody which would have been well known to Ó Riada not just from his visits to Glenstal, but from pre-Vatican II liturgies in general.

Staying with the question of formal comparisons, it is instructive to look at the broader musico-textual canvas of *Aifreann 2* itself and compare Ó Riada's setting of this triple litany with the very similarly structured petitionary section from the *Gloria*:

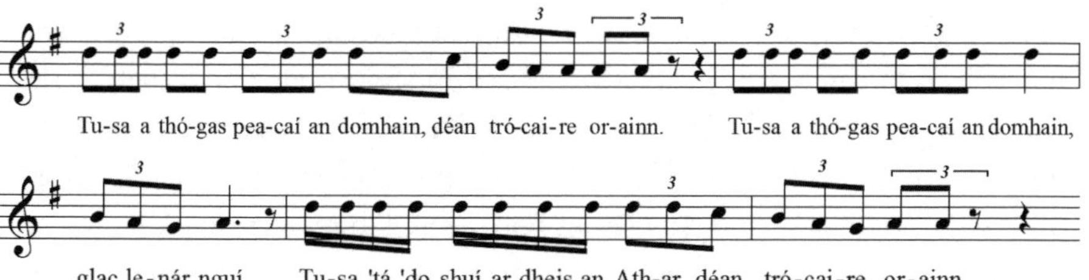

4.35 Seán Ó Riada: *Aifreann 2, Gloria* (bars 46–51)

Both litanies share the musically defining elements of an opening *d''* recitation and the same concluding cadence on *a'*. The main difference lies in the treatment of the invocations. In the case of the *Gloria*, these are delivered in a purely functional manner. Being cast within a long and constantly varying structure (both textually and melodically) such as the *Gloria* is, Ó Riada's recitational treatment marks their textual distinctiveness and provides the necessary musical relief within the whole melodic plan. In the *Agnus Dei*, where the piece consists simply of the three invocations with their petitions, there is more room for consideration to be given to melodically expressing the content of the invocations. It may be noted at this point, as we discuss the last of the congregation-oriented mass parts, that Ó Riada tries to imbue each communal ritual gesture, however small or large, with a degree of musical savour sufficient to make it worth the singing. In his avoidance of a purely functional approach he is at once mindful of the inherent power of music, true to a richly melodic native folk heritage, and aware of what is needed to galvanise and sustain the singing of a liturgical assembly.

Tonality

In the opening *Iontróid* of the mass, *g*' and *a*' contended for structural supremacy within a broad *c*'-*e*'' tonal horizon. The tonal argument based on the relationship between these pitches lay at the heart of the melodic activity throughout the subsequent mass parts and was resolved in various ways. The *Gloria* and *Sanctus*, as we have seen, leaned heavily towards *g*', the former being the only movement so far to end on that pitch, having also set out in the same tonality. The *Agnus Dei* presents us with yet another twist in the tonal tale. The *d*''-*a*' relationship which frames the first two repetitions of the text has already featured in shorter elements such as the *Tar éis an choisreachadh* and the 'Amen' (*Deireadh an phaidir eocharistigh*), both of which ended on *a*'. This relationship is also present to a significant degree in the *Iontróid* and *An phaidir*, both of which resolve on *d*'. However, the most fruitful line of comparison, both in terms of text structure and content, is with the *Kyrie*, which would seem to have provided the musical template for the *Agnus Dei*:

Seán Ó Riada: *Aifreann 2, Kyrie* (bars /19–20)

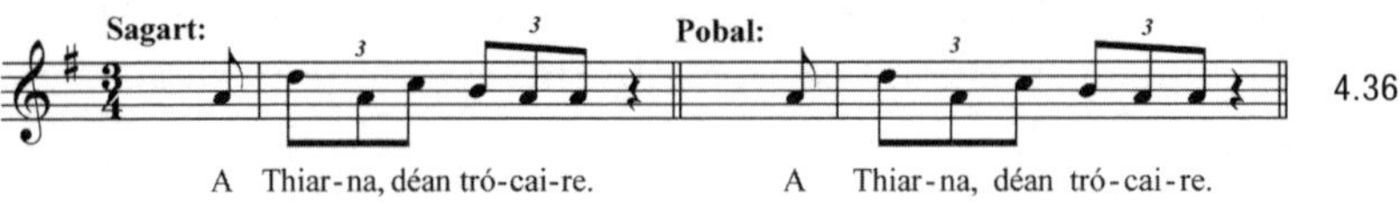

Seán Ó Riada: *Aifreann 2, Agnus Dei* (bar 129)

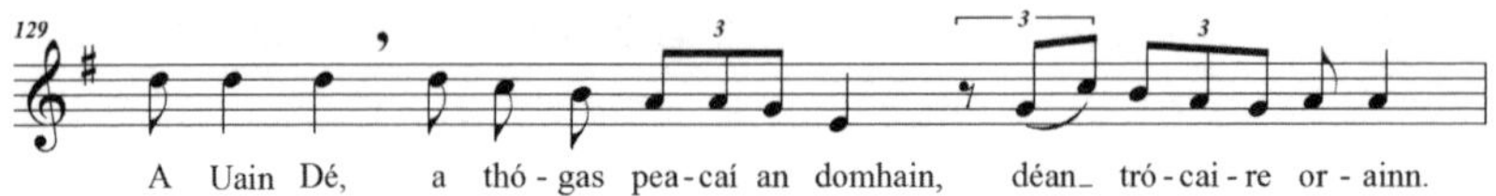

The *Kyrie*, while admittedly taking a more interesting formal, melodic and, ultimately, liturgical path in its final invocation, nevertheless replicates the modal drive of the *Iontróid* and *An phaidir* in its tonal resolution on *d*'. Ó Riada could easily have repeated this classic tonal scheme in his *Agnus Dei* by providing any one of a number of suitable closing melodic gestures, e.g.:

4.37 Seán Ó Riada: *Aifreann 2, Agnus Dei*, alternative melodic closing

However, he prefers to capitalise one final time on the possibilities inherent in his chosen mixolydian terrain. His tonal shift in the direction of *g'* gives modal force to the textually modified final invocation, while at the same time adding a distinctive new musical 'event' to the mass setting. It is worth clarifying in what manner this distinctiveness surpasses that of the *Gloria*, the only other movement which ends on *g'*. In the case of the *Gloria*, a more comprehensive tonal shift was intimated with the *g*-based intonation, conclusion and intermediary section. In the *Agnus Dei*, however, the situation is somewhat different. Since the framing structural pitches of its first two lines situate it firmly in a *d''*-based mixolydian tonality, the unexpected shift in the final petition towards the fourth degree emphasises, in the most forceful manner yet, the varied musical options which the composer feels this tonal scheme affords him.

Hymn Settings

In addition to the prose-style *Iontróid*, Ó Riada supplied three ancillary strophic compositions, one for the offertory (*Ofráil*), one for communion (*Iomann comaoineach*) and a final one, entitled *Iomann ceiliúrtha* (celebratory hymn), the words of which clearly suggest it as a recessional-type text. These three pieces are marked out as tonally separate from the main elements of the mass, two of them being cast in a minor mode 1 type tonality, and the third operating within the context of a major tonality featuring alternating sevenths.

OFRÁIL – A ÍOSA BHÁIN

A Íosa bháin, id' láthair gheobhad	*Purest ['white'] Jesus, I come into your presence*
Ag caoi do bháis 'san Árdchrois mhóir,	*lamenting your death on the great High Cross,*
Ó aois go bás ag tál na ndeor	*from age to death shedding tears*
'S ag maoidheamh mo ghrádh do'n Slánaitheoir	*and declaring my love for the Saviour*
Ó, a Shlánaitheoir.	*O, (my) Saviour.*

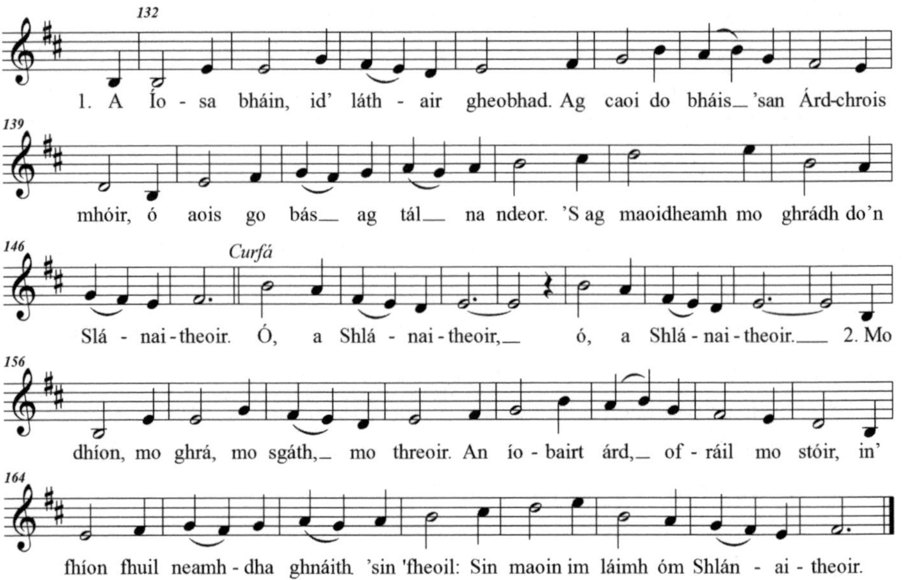

4.38 Seán Ó Riada: *Aifreann 2, A losa bháin* (bars /132–171)

This text follows the syllabic pattern 8.8.8.8.5.[52] The five-line form of the composition, though very much rarer than the standard four-line template, has a number of textual and musical equivalents in the native tradition.[53]

To carry the words of the text, Ó Riada supplies a continually evolving mode 1 type melody, whose consistently-sharpened sixth degree places it within the category of traditional minor-mode melodies, defined by Breathnach as the 'ray mode'.[54] The phrase-end notes *e'*, *d'*, *b'*, *f#'*, *e'* help to articulate a form which might be described as ABCDD[1], with the fifth line being ingeniously derived from the fourth:

4.39 Seán Ó Riada: *Aifreann 2, A Íosa bháin* (bars /144–151)

This type of motivic displacement from a weak structural position (in this case, the second bar of a phrase) to a strong one (phrase beginning) adds both unity and interest to the melody and is a further example of the 'thrift' which frequently characterises the compositional aesthetic of orally grounded musical cultures.[55]

IOMANN COMAOINEACH: *GURAB TÚ MO BHOILE*

Gurab Tú mo bhoile, a Choimhdhe chroí
Be Thou my vision, O Lord of my heart
ní níneach eile acht Rí seacht nimhe.
be nothing else but the King of the seven heavens.
Gurab Tú mo mhachtnamh de ló agus d'oíche,
Be Thou my only thought by day and night,
gurab Tú mo radharc i mo chodladh choíche.
in sleep, my abiding vision.

Gurab Tú mo labhradh, gurab Tú mo thuigse,
Be Thou my speech, be thou my understanding,
go madh Tusa domsa, go madh mise Dhuitse.
be Thou my portion, and I Thine.
Gurab Tusa m'athair, gurab mé do leanabh,
Be Thou my Father, and I Thy child,
gurab Tusa liomsa, agus mise leatsa.
be Thou with me, and I with Thee.

4.40 Seán Ó Riada: *Aifreann 2, Gurab Tú mo bhoile* (bars /172–187)

Ó Riada selects an ABAC melodic form for this early strophic text,[56] the characteristic rhythms of which he adapts within an overall triple metre. The repeated A phrase in the melody reflects the consistent appearance in lines 1 and 3 of each of the four verses of the same textual motif 'Gurab Tú'. The key signature (two sharps) and broad mode 1 tonality recall the *Ofráil* melody, but it is distinguished from the latter by a more energetically rhythmic textual pattern, in which each line is characterised by opening upbeat semiquavers and a closing quaver/crotchet syncopation.

IOMANN CEILIÚRTHA: BEANNAIGH SINN, A ATHAIR

Beannaigh sinn, a Athair,	*Bless us, O Father,*
agus beannaigh sinn, a Chríost.	*and bless us, O Christ.*
Go gcumhdaigh sibh ár n-anama	*May you both bless our souls*
go dtigimid arís.	*until we return again.*
Beannacht leat, a Thigh Dé,	*Blessings on you, House of God,*
agus beannacht Dé 'nár dtimcheall.	*and the blessings of God around us.*
Nár sgaradh uainne grásta Dé	*May the grace of God not leave us*
go bhfillimid chun a Theampaill.	*until we return to his Church.*

4.41 Seán Ó Riada: *Aifreann 2, Beannaigh sinn, a Athair* (bars 188–195)

Ó Riada's first mass, *Ceol an aifrinn*, concluded with a setting of one of a number of short native prayers associated with the end of the liturgy. In *Aifreann 2* another such prayer, *Beannaigh sinn, a Athair*, is selected by the composer, and though the text is slightly longer (two short verses instead of one), the musical approach is similar. Both settings are strongly rhythmic with a clearly major-key tonal character (the *Aifreann 2* setting includes one instance of a flattened seventh). Both begin on the upper end of the tonal range and in the course of the melody clearly outline the interval of an octave. The composer's brief, vigorous and joyful musical treatment of these texts, together with the title of the *Aifreann 2* example – translated 'celebratory hymn' – gives us an insight into his understanding of the sung musical requirements, such as they exist, of this part of the rite.[57]

From 'Mode' to 'Tune-Family': Recontextualising the Tonal Content of *Aifreann 2*

> It was so difficult to write the second one. How do you rethink the same text? How do you approach the same text in the same idiom and produce something entirely different? ... When you are writing a single melodic line with the most basic harmony, usually just a drone, it is the most hellish job to try and think of another melodic line for the same text and still be full of conviction and sincerity. (Seán Ó Riada)[58]

The above quote reminds us of the extremely tight aesthetic limits Seán Ó Riada chose to work within for his *Aifreann 2*, limits which essentially reduced the composer's means of expression to unison composition on the diatonic scale. We have seen, nevertheless, how, in his setting of the prose-based items of the mass, Seán Ó Riada moved with freedom and assurance within the sophisticated tonal relationships of this 'given' musical structure.

The relationships played out by the principal tonal protagonists *a'*, *g'*, *d'* and *c'* parallel those observable in a mode 7 configuration of the diatonic scale, which undergirds both melodic traditions. The main difference in Ó Riada's tonal structuring of the texts of *Aifreann 2* is his freedom in using *a'* and g' not just as internal structural notes, but also as *finals* in their own right. The modal potentialities relating to the positioning or re-positioning of the final, already noted in the composer's tonal modification of the chant-based gospel *Alleluia*, are framed within an Irish context in the following statement from Richard Henebry, whose *Handbook of Traditional Irish Music* contained one of the earliest attempts to deal comprehensively with the question of traditional tonality:

> The most remarkable feature of human music in its form is that presented by the wandering of the tonic ending. For there are no less than four places in the octave on which tunes *may be made to close* [my italics], with a full and satisfying sense of completeness. Those places shall here be called modal tonics ... [59]

Ó Riada's instinctive approach, however, combined with the particular challenges provided by the variety of textual shapes and sizes, takes him beyond the commonplace structures of standard Irish tonalities into a less obvious tonal world, leading his son Peadar to describe the mass as 'more interesting' and drawing the following response from Tomás Ó Canainn:

> Níl sé fréamhaithe sa sean-nós mar a bhí an chéad Aifreann, ach, ag éisteacht leis, ní bhéadh amhras ar bith ort ná gur ceol Éireannach é ...' [*It isn't rooted in the 'sean-nós' the way the first* Mass *was, but, listening to it, you would be in no doubt that it was Irish music ...*][60]

If we are to identify aspects of this mass setting which are out of the ordinary or 'more interesting', attention is naturally drawn to the *Gloria*, which because of its textual irregularity and sheer length appears to have stretched the composer the furthest in tonal terms. In the *Gloria* setting, with its *d'*/*g'* tonal fluctuation, Ó Riada seems to have instinctively drawn on a less common *bi-polar* modal template to help him sustain an uncommonly long textual journey.[61] The composer, as we have already seen, returned to this template in the *Sanctus* and, even more tellingly, in the *Agnus Dei* which, like the *Gloria*, cadences on g'.

Melodies with competing leanings towards the fourth and fifth degree above the final, though certainly less common in the Irish tradition, are nevertheless marked out by their distinctiveness, a fact which renders them more readily susceptible to scholarly interest. James Cowdery, whose book *The Melodic Tradition of Ireland* makes a significant contribution to literature concerned with compositional aspects of Irish music, brings together a sub-group of such airs within the context of a study of a larger 'tune-family' framework, a concept promulgated through the work of ethnomusicologists such as Samuel Bayard and Bertrand Bronson.[62] While Cowdery's principal focus has more to do with 'migrating phrases' than with modal concurrences, the relevant airs do nevertheless exhibit strong tonal similarities. The airs in question include those associated with 'Sail óg rua', 'Plúirín na mban donn óg', 'Lord Gregory' and the following one, 'Iníon an Fhaoit ón ngleann':[63]

4.42 'Iníon an Fhaoit ón ngleann'

At the head of the family, however, on account of its compositional richness, Cowdery proposes 'The Blackbird', an air belonging to the category of 'long dance', an instrumental genre characterised, interestingly enough, by extended and asymmetrical structures. Like the example above, it ends on *d'*, having set out in the tonal region of *g'* which contends along the way with the strong tonal pull of *a'*. Of particular interest, at the end of Cowdery's detailed analysis of the various tunes within the family, is the following 'weighted' tonal model which he distils from his comparisons, and which amounts to little short of a modal template in itself:[64]

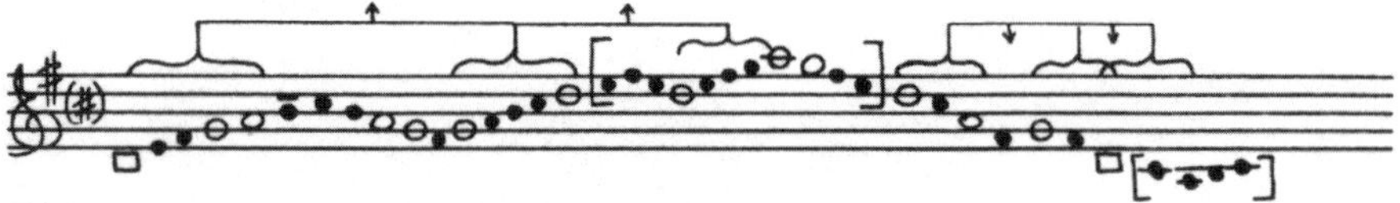

4.43 'The Blackbird': 'weighted' tonal model[65]

Ó Riada's prose settings of *Aifreann 2* seem to a degree to resonate very convincingly with such a tonal template. However, with his adoption of a bi-polar structure for the *Gloria*, and the various degrees (*d*', *d*'', *a*' and, in particular, *g*') in which his tunes are 'made to close',[66] Ó Riada appears to have stretched conventional boundaries. In his *Aifreann 2*, the composer's heightened awareness of modal potentialities allied to a perceptive interaction with the individual nature, length and liturgical purpose of each text have combined effectively to fashion melodic responses which help to rede-'fine' the notion of traditional Irish modality, placed at the service of liturgical word and rite.

5

Aifreann Eoin na Croise: Peadar Ó Riada

Introduction

This third mass setting of the Ó Riada cycle, an oral composition by Peadar Ó Riada,[1] represents both elements of continuity and, as we shall see, significant development along the musical continuum. While the compositional traditions of Gregorian chant remain as general reference points for the common liturgical elements of the mass, specific settings from *Ceol an aifrinn* and more particularly *Aifreann 2* emerge as more potent and influential models for *Aifreann Eoin na Croise* which, notably, lacks a Kyrie and Gloria. The composer's use of the ancient Muscraí prayer 'An marnabh' as the backdrop for the opening chant signals from the outset a very particular cultural context, the characteristic musical expressions of which will be shown to sustain the musical composition.

Different in scale is the prose content of the mass, which almost equals that of the combined settings of *Ceol an aifrinn* and *Aifreann 2*, the dimensions of the text and Ó Riada's compositional approach to it prompting useful initial and ultimately illuminating comparisons with the tradition of oral epic. The melodic setting of the extended *Opening Chant*, itself a significant conceptual development, raises questions relating to the compositional craft of large-scale melodic construction, and here also we encounter the first examples of the highly controlled, organically derived keyboard accompaniments provided by the composer throughout the mass. The *Opening Chant*'s textual canvas is characterised by a series of litanic passages, and the oral influence of parallelism dominates the textual structure of the extended *Salm* setting, the first to appear in the combined Ó Riada corpus. Other liturgical developments in *Aifreann Eoin na Croise* centre on the ritual elements involving priest and people, thus building on the liturgical advances of Seán Ó Riada's second mass.

The *Aifreann 2* concepts of bi-modality and structural oscillations between the tonic, fourth and fifth scalar degrees find strong echoes in the tonal landscape selected by Peadar Ó Riada to sustain this large-scale composition, whose extremely wide range of two octaves seems to be naturally divided by the composer into a series of tetrachords. Tetrachordal divisions also provide the tonal context for the issue of motivic construction which emerges, as the analysis progresses, as the central compositional question of *Aifreann Eoin na Croise*. Such is the significance of motivic construction for the mass itself and for broader issues surrounding the generation of vernacular liturgical music, that a full chapter (chapter six) is devoted exclusively to it.

Contents

> This Mass originated out of a desire to draw people into a more meditative form of worship. The music, prayers and chants of the liturgy prepare us to become attentive and receptive to the word of God. The opening chant chosen here is 'An marnabh', the oldest prayer in Muscraighe Uí Fhloinn. The five short prayers sung simultaneously with the opening chant are meant to awaken in us that which we have inherited from our people – the linking of past and future – the present. Time is transformed in the House of God. Thus we hope to find the 'Cosán Draíochacht' (The Secret Ladder) to the presence of God. (Peadar Ó Riada)[2]

So reads the introduction to Peadar Ó Riada's *Aifreann Eoin na Croise* (Mass of John of the Cross), commissioned in 1990 by the Carmelite Community of St Teresa's, Clarendon Street, Dublin, for a mass marking the quatercentenary of the death of St John of the Cross. Having composed the mass and taught it to his choir, the composer, whose normal medium is oral transmission,[3] was eventually persuaded to produce a hand-written score which was then integrated into the mass booklet for the occasion.[4] The mass setting, conceived as a unified entirety,[5] contains musical settings for the following elements:

1. *Opening Chant* (combining 'An marnabh' and five native prayers):
   1a. *Go mbeannaíthear duit*
   1b. *Umhlaím duit*
   1c. *Im' chroí 'tá 'n t-olc*
   1d. *Bronnaim m'anam ort*
   1e. *Admhaím do Dhia mhóir*

2. *Salm 139*
3. *Aililiúia*
4. *Guí an phobail*[6]
5. *Is Naofa*
6. *Rúndiamhair an chreidimh*[7]
7. *Is tríd/ Amen mór*
8. *Ár nAthair–Síocháin*
9. *A Uain Dé*
10. *An cosán draíochta*

New liturgical developments within the combined Ó Riada corpus include the *Salm*, *Guí an Phobail* (Prayer of the Faithful), the Communion Rite sequence *Ar nAthair–Síocháin* and, of course, the lengthy and formally distinctive *Opening Chant*.

The borrowed item, *Rúndiamhair an chreidimh* (Memorial acclamation), provides a helpful key to placing this mass setting in some sort of context. Arriving some twenty-one years after *Aifreann 2*, *Aifreann Eoin na Croise* represents the third in the series of Cúil Aodha-associated mass settings. Seán Ó Riada's *Ceol an aifrinn*, the original of the triptych, was 'home-grown', arising to fill a local need; *Aifreann 2*, though an outside commission, subsequently won its place in the regular Sunday worship of Cúil Aodha, significantly replacing *Ceol an aifrinn* as the preferred setting. This third mass, in including the borrowed item identified above, implicitly identifies itself as part of an unbroken continuum, happy to take at least one of its starting points from its immediate predecessor.

Musical Score of the Mass

Fr Christopher Clarke, one of those primarily responsible for commissioning the mass, recounts how, in order to obtain a written version of the music, he had to coax the composer up to Dublin and work with him through the night to produce, six hours later, a partial draft of the score.[8] In the weeks leading up to the first performance, a completed version of this draft was prepared by Ronan McDonagh, the organist at

Clarendon Street, by means of a series of faxed communications between Cúil Aodha and Dublin, a process acknowledged by both Ó Riada and McDonagh as 'approximate' and 'unsatisfactory'. For the purposes of this study, therefore, I have produced an entirely new score, based partly on the completed written draft, but transcribed principally from a recording of the first performance.[9] In this transcription the rhythmic delivery of the text freely alternates triplet with duple rhythms, with the former being more characteristic throughout.[10] Following the principle proposed by Lord and Treitler, and confirmed by Peadar Ó Riada's original score layout and observed manner of composition,[11] that the oral composer 'works in phrases', I have adopted the principle of inserting bar lines at the end of the textual phrases,[12] instead of trying to impose any potentially artificial metrical overlay on the phrasal pattern. Such an approach ensures the primacy of the verbal text, and by this means also the reader/singer can more clearly see, to paraphrase John Stevens, that 'the form of the text is the form of the music'.[13]

OPENING CHANT

A key starting point for Peadar Ó Riada in undertaking the challenge of *Aifreann Eoin na Croise* was obviously the nature of the commission and the contemplative spirituality of St John of the Cross:

> The tone of the Mass itself is meant to be contemplative – very much in the dark so as to see the light if you know what I mean. It is ideally a communal prayer occasion where the spiritual world is the focus and not the daily life and its venal and petty or light thoughts. I find that this stream of spiritual communication fits the Irish humour around here at least. It brings a stillness or peace. This then is the basis of my frame of mind and from whence I come as I apply those long pedal notes and cast phrases and thoughts adrift on their surface.[14]

The *Opening Chant* tries to express something of this spirituality through the use of five native prayers sung at various stages over a continuous monotone chanting of 'An marnabh', a substantially long text associated in the Múscraí area with prayers for the dead. The chanting of 'An marnabh' (the composer suggests that this might be done by the congregation) is sustained throughout on a bass A, providing a musical context out of which the various, more melody-driven prayers emerge, these to be delivered by soloist or choir. The bass A provides the foundational pitch for an authentic (wide-range) major tonality which will build upwards as the chant progresses to a range of an octave and a fifth, and in the prayer's final phrase will extend down a fourth to *E*, thus giving an overall range of two octaves.

1a: *Go mbeannaíthear duit*

Go mbeannaíthear duit, a theampaill Dé,
All hail to you, temple of God
an áit a gcónaíonn mo Shlánaitheoir, Íosa Críost,
where dwells my Saviour, Jesus Christ,
Muire agus an dá aspal déag — *Mary and the twelve apostles*
ag guí or[a]m féin inniu. — *praying for me today.*[15]

5.1 Peadar Ó Riada: *Aifreann Eoin na Croise, Go mbeannaíthear duit* (bars 1–5)

The melodic style of *Go mbeannaíthear duit*, which begins at the lower end of the vocal register, is controlled and fairly tightly woven with no dramatic gestures, befitting the introductory nature of the prayer, the composer's intent to prepare people 'to become more attentive and receptive to the word of God',[16] and, of course, the epic proportions of the *Opening Chant* itself.[17] Allied to this are the triple text/music repetitions of bars 4 and 5, which also harmonise with the composer's stated aim, i.e. to 'draw people into a more meditative worship',[18] and which also correspond very closely with the universal processes of folk narrative, as may be seen from the following extended passage from Olrik:

> Another important principle of *Sage* composition is the *Law of Repetition* (*das Gesetzder Wiederholung*). In literature, there are many means of producing emphasis, means other than repetition. For example, the dimensions and significance of something can be depicted by the degree and detail of the description of that particular object or event. In contrast, folk narrative lacks this full-bodied detail, for the most part, and its spare descriptions are all too brief to serve as an effective means of emphasis. For our tradition of oral narrative, there is but one alternative: repetition. A youth goes into the giant's field three days in succession and each day he kills a giant. A hero tries three times to ride up the glass mountain. Three would-be lovers are magically rendered immobile in one night by a maiden. Every time that a striking scene occurs in a narrative, and continuity permits, the scene is repeated. This is necessary not only to build up tension, but to fill out the body of the narrative. There is intensifying repetition and simple repetition, but the important point is that without repetition, the *Sage* cannot attain its fullest form. The repetition is almost always tied to the number three.[19]

Ó Riada's threefold 'intensifying repetitions' of the key phrase 'ag guí orm' (bars 4 to 5) signal, at the very beginning of this mass setting, a particular approach to words which will involve strategic repetitions and elisions of received text elements.

The short four-line text is one of a number of native prayers associated with entry into a church. The lines are of unequal length, working out accentually as follows: 4, 6, 4, 3. The text structure suggests two couplets, a reading which is reflected in the tonally related mirror-image cadences of the first couplet,[20] and (leaving aside for a moment the repeated elements of bar 4) the thematically related concluding one. The musical form might be read as ABCC1, and the overall melodic journey, with its steady build-up to a climactic third phrase, follows a pattern readily associated with strophic Irish melodies.

The range extends to just over an octave and, taking the opening A as tonic, the four phrases end respectively on the third, octave, sixth and fifth above.[21] The conclusion of the prayer's final phrase at the *soh*-based *e* pitch signals a more open-ended tonal dynamic. Meanwhile, attention is momentarily re-directed to the continually chanted words of 'An marnabh'.

1b: *Umhlaím duit*

Umhlaím duit, a Íosa Críost, *I bow before you, Jesus Christ,*
umhlaím duit, a Mhaighdean ghlórmhar,
I bow before you, O glorious Virgin,
umhlaím duit a chrann deas *I bow before you lovely tree [Christ]*
agus a chrann atá len' ais. *And the tree that is beside you. [Our Lady]*
Screadaim ar Rí na bhfeart, *I cry aloud to the all-powerful King*
peacaí a thugas liom isteach *that the sins I have taken into His presence*
gan iad a ligeann liom amach. *He may not allow to depart with me.*

5.2 Peadar Ó Riada: *Aifreann Eoin na Croise, Umhlaím duit* (bars 6–14)

This seven-line text begins with a genuflection-type litany ('I bow before you, Jesus Christ/ I bow before you, Glorious Virgin ...') which follows naturally on from the preceding entry-type prayer, and which is followed in turn by a desperate plea for forgiveness of sins. The four-line opening section, which has Jesus and Mary as its focus, is cast in litany form for the first three lines. For the fourth, however, it emphatically dispenses with the device of text repetition in favour of a more rhetorically compelling structure. This textual movement suggests a build-up of tension in the prayer, one which is dramatically released in the climactic beginning to the second section, 'I cry aloud to the all-powerful King'.

Ó Riada mirrors the stable and developing elements of the text movement by retaining the distinctive falling-seventh melodic motif for the three deliveries of the litanic 'Umhlaím duit' (bars 6, 7 and 8) and, in a manner recalling the litanies of Seán Ó Riada's *Ceol an aifrinn*, by steadily and very consciously building up the melodic tension note-by-note (beginning on *a*) and bar-by-bar until a climactic *e'* is reached at the beginning of the fifth line of text (bar 10). The drama of this line is further enhanced by the presence of a falling fifth and by the first appearance of the flattened seventh, *g*. This pitch continues as the tonally dominant element of the following line, giving a distinctive mixolydian character to the second half of the prayer.[22] With only one line remaining and a lot of musical tension to be dispelled, Ó Riada brings the litanic device once more into play as he thrice repeats the final line 'that He may not allow my sins to depart with me' at a low tessitura, set to another melodic gesture outlining a falling fifth.[23]

A large range (octave and a fourth) and wide intervallic leaps (fifths, sixths and sevenths) characterise this, the most musically dramatic of all the opening chant's constitutive elements. The keyboard accompaniment continues in a similar fashion to the previous setting with, however, thirds and sixths harmonies giving way to starker unison colouring during the closing triple litany. The melodic span of the text's final three lines covers the full range of the piece which concludes on low *B*, a major second above the drone (an even more open-ended pitch than the *e* which concluded the first prayer), suggesting a stronger conceptual link with the next melody-driven text. The interim period is meanwhile bridged by the re-emerging into the musical foreground of the 'An marnabh' recitation.

1c: *Im' chroí 'tá'n t-olc*

Im' chroí 'tá'n t-olc,
im' bhéal agus im' chois;
triúr a chuirim á chosc,
an tAthair, an Mac 'san Spiorad Naomh.

Whatever sin is in my heart,
in my mouth or in my feet;
to guard against them I invoke
Father, Son and Holy Spirit.

5.3 Peadar Ó Riada: *Aifreann Eoin na Croise, Im' chroí 'tá'n t-olc* (bars 15–18)

The melodic span of the previous piece's final three lines covered the full range of the piece, with little or no relief by way of the compensatory directional changes which are associated with traditional melody. In other words, in aesthetic terms, the concluding section of that prayer appears to have left a yawning gap in the melodic outline. The text of *Im' chroí 'tá'n t-olc* is placed into this chasm. Its heavily penitential content suggests this prayer as a natural continuation of the preceding one and the musical treatment also suggests continuity and compensation. By starting on *e*, it resolves and completes the descending *a/g/f#* structural melodic journey of the previous piece, and with its melodic outlining, by means of rising stepwise movement, the interval of a seventh (albeit in a very deliberate, and in traditional melodic terms uncharacteristically relentless manner), it effectively balances the extremely steep descent of the previous piece.[24]

Yet at its end, *Im' chroí 'tá'n t-olc* itself, like its predecessor, feels detectably incomplete. This short text's four-line structure, it would seem, serves a broader compositional necessity – that of a type of rising 'link passage' – even though it could be argued that the rhetoric of the litany-type build-up of the opening textual couplet suggests some sort of melodic ascent. In view of the apparent functionality of this piece, above all others in the cycle, in serving a larger-scale melodic plan then, we note with interest the chosen pitch of destination for the piece, *b*, a ninth above the tonic A, accompanied by a type of dominant seventh harmony, maintained over the persistent tonic drone.

1d: *Bronnaim m'anam ort*

Bronnaim m'anam ort, a Íosa Críost,	*I offer to you O Jesus Christ, my soul,*
ní iarrfad ort é choíche ná go brách.	*I shall not ask it back for ever more.*
Cuirim m'achainí chugatsa, a Mhuire,	*I beseech you, O Mary,*
m'anam a bheith ar do dheasláimh	*to take my soul in your right hand*
ar urlár do thí féin.	*on the floor of your own house.*

5.4 Peadar Ó Riada: *Aifreann Eoin na Croise, Bronnaim m'anam ort* (bars 19–23)

In this fourth prayer the believer's soul is offered to Christ and to the protection of Mary. Thus is completed a passage, begun in the first prayer, from praise, to penitence, to trust. In musical terms also there is a very clear sense of the completion of a melodic journey which began with *Go mbeannaíthear duit*. This sense of completion is evident not only in tonal terms, as we shall see, but also in the way the composer, for the first time, appears to look back musically and to draw on earlier thematic material.

The five-line text consists of an opening couplet (addressed to Christ) followed by a three-line portion (addressed to Mary). Beginning on *a* (thereby resolving the unfinished business of the previous prayer), it opens with a recapitulation of the melodic motif which was repeated three times at the end of the opening prayer (bars 4–5). The *a-e* movement of the opening line is balanced by the more rhetorically emphatic *a-b* of the second. The melodic gesture at the end of this phrase (bar 20) recalls the conclusion of the previous prayer (bar 18) and re-emphasises the compensatory nature of this pitch area as a further response to the earlier dramatic descent of *Umhlaím duit*. The composer's emergent sense of balance and counterbalance, from couplet composition to larger-scale melodic formations, which undoubtedly has its roots in the Irish song tradition, finds a close parallel in the following passage from Guido d'Arezzo regarding melodic composition in medieval monophonic song: 'If you then fill in the gaps, space out the constricted places, draw together the overextended, and broaden the over-condensed, you will make a unified, polished work.'[25] A lower tessitura, based around *e*, is chosen to sustain the 'Marian' lines three and four, leading to a cadential melodic homecoming, for the first time in the music, on A, to the accompanying textual image 'on the floor of your own house'.

While separated textually and, as we have seen, rhetorically, Christ and Mary are bound together by a melodic cross-weave which sees the concluding motif of the opening 'Christ' couplet (bar 20) repeated immediately down a fourth to open the 'Mary' section (bar 21).[26] The strong sense of internal thematic unity in this fourth prayer is further enhanced by the close melodic ties of line four with the opening line of the prayer, suggesting, then, an overall musical form of ABB1A1C.

Parallel thirds and sixths still form the basis of the accompanimental approach, but in this 'concluding' prayer where we have already noted a sense of musical recapitulation, a concomitant relaxation of the strict discipline of a melody-driven approach can also be detected in the occasional rhythmic and melodic independence of the alto part. This sense of ease and relief accords well with the sentiments of the text which describes the handing over forever of the believer's soul to Christ, in hopeful expectation also of the company of Mary.

1e: *Admhaím do Dhia mhóir*

Admhaím do Dhia mhóir na n-uile chumhacht
I confess to Almighty God
ó lá mo bhaisteadh go lá mo thórraimh,
from the day of my baptism to the day of my wake,
trí smaointe mo chroí,
through the thoughts of my heart,
trí radharc mo shúl,
through the sight of my eyes,
trí chlos mo chluas,
through the hearing of my ears,
trí ráite mo bhéil,
through the speech of my mouth,
trí chúrsa mo rian,
through the course of my path,
trína ndúirt nach raibh fíor,
what I have said that was not true,
trínar gheallas is nár chomhlíonas,
what I have promised and not fulfilled,
trínar réabas de do dhlíthe is ded' aitheanta naofa.
through thy laws, holy commandments, which have broken.
Iarraim an aspalóid ort anois féin,
I ask absolution from you now,
in ainm Íosa Chríost,
through the name of Jesus Christ,
ar eagla nár iarras riamh í mar ba chóir,
in case I have not asked it already as I ought,
agus nach mairfinn len í a n-iarraidh arís:
and in case I may not live to ask it again:
in ainm an Athar, an Mhic
in the name of the Father, the Son
agus an Spioraid Naoimh.
and of the Holy Spirit.
Amen.
Amen.

5.5 Peadar Ó Riada: *Aifreann Eoin na Croise, Admhaím do Dhia mhóir* (bars 24–36)

32
trí - nar gheall - as is nár chomh - líon - as,
33
trí - nar réa - bas de do dhlí - the is ded' aith - ean - ta nao - fa.
34
Iarraim an aspalóid ort anois féin in ainm Ío - sa Chríost,
35
ar eagla nár iarras riamh í mar ba chóir, is nach mairfinn len í a n-iarraidh a - rís:

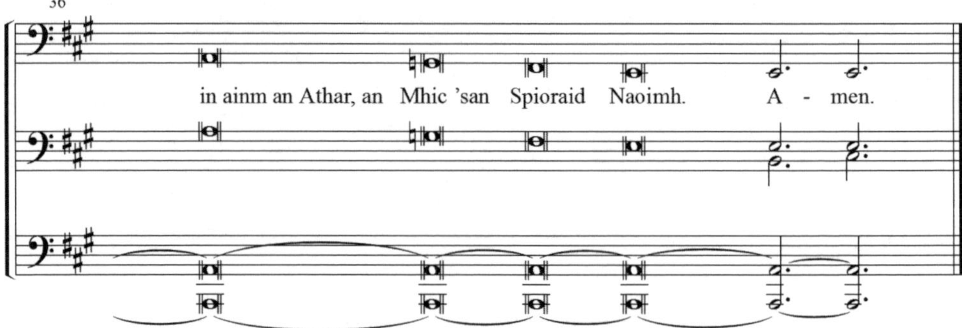

The last of the five prayers, a native version of the Act of Contrition, is proportional in size to the sum of the preceding four. Because of its textual link with the introductory rites of the mass, it forms a type of bridge, or ladder, from the native spirituality of the other prayers into the universal/official forms of the Roman rite. From here the mass continues with a spoken Kyrie, the composer having dispensed with the standard opening ritual exchanges of the mass.

By virtue of its sheer size and liturgical nature, *Admhaím do Dhia mhóir* is marked out as separate from the first four prayers. In musical terms its separateness has already been signalled by the tonal 'full stop' at the end of the previous prayer. However, since the first four prayers themselves constitute a type of cumulative Act of Contrition, and this text re-presents their concerns in a more intense and formally unified way, we should not be surprised that Ó Riada consciously or unconsciously draws on musical links to what has gone before and binds the final prayer to its four predecessors by means of a type of musical bringing together of various thematic elements.

It is with one of these thematic recollections that Ó Riada begins the prayer. He sets the first line to the thematic motif already identified as connecting the first and final prayers of the opening quartet (see bars 5 and 19). This motif, a typically traditional melodic shape characterised by a general *ag#ef#e* movement, was on both these occasions presented in an A-major context, ending on the fifth above the A drone. Now, however, it is presented beginning on the fourth degree *d*, giving us a *dc#ABA* movement. Because of the prominence of A in the motif, it is difficult to be certain at this point if in fact a significant tonal shift has taken place. Ó Riada's setting of the second line, outlining a *d*-based triad (bar 25), confirms, however, that it has. This dimensional shift at the very beginning of the final prayer to a different step on the tonal ladder very effectively confirms, as suggested above, that this prayer is of a different order from its predecessors. The tonal change from A towards *D* on the twenty-fifth line of text is quite striking after such a long period of stability, and its refreshing tenor signals a type of quickening towards action, in this case, it could be suggested, the liturgical action of the mass. The *D*-based tonality is maintained, through the presence of a *g* (natural), into the first part of the prayer's central section, an extended eight-part penitential litany. The first six intonations of this litany consist of a series of dramatically widening intervals extending upwards by step from a foundational *e*.[27] The continuous structural influence of the fifth degree *e*, at the melodic basis of the litany (with the drone A beneath that again) gradually steers the tonality back towards an A-centred tonic one, so that by the litany's final invocation, *g#* comfortably re-emerges as part of a triple re-instatement (recalling the close of the first prayer, bars 4–5) of the opening thematic motif, at its original pitch.[28]

The final section of the prayer and, by extension, of the opening chant of this mass, now begins. In it, the believer asks for absolution 'in the name of Jesus Christ'. This is done in the context of another musical recollection, this time from the opening lines of the very first prayer *Go mbeannaíthear duit* (see bar 2). The expressive motif *c#df#e*, almost hidden from view because it is so close to the beginning of that prayer and which has not been heard since then, re-emerges here in stronger relief, being used twice in succession to deliver in recitative fashion the two remaining petitionary couplets (bars 34, 35). The ensuing blessing (bar 36) which draws this prayer to a close, and with it the various activities of the *Opening Chant*, seems at first sight to present something entirely new on the musical plane. New, certainly, is the extremely low tessitura which frames its stepwise descent down a perfect fourth (*doh-ta-la-soh*), from A, through the flattened seventh G, down to lower *E*, towards the furthest extremity of the bass range.[29] Thematically however, it could be regarded as a motivic distillation of an identical, though more structurally drawn-out movement already noted in our discussion of the central prayer, *Umhlaím duit – agf#e* (bars 10–15).[30] This motif's sheer contour, its open-ended tonality, its position and, above all, its elemental melodic make-up (underlined by unison accompanimental writing) hint at a musical significance which may go beyond the confines of the *Opening Chant*.

SALM 139

Freagra (*Response*)

Má deirim go bhfolóidh an dor[a]chacht mé
If I ask darkness to cover me
agus go mbeidh solas an lae ina oíche liom,
and light to become night around me,
ní dor[a]cha leatsa an dor[a]chacht:
that darkness is not dark to you:
is comhsholas duit lá agus oíche. *night is as bright as day.*

Bhéarsa (*Verse*)

Scrúdaíonn tú mé, a Thiarna, agus is eol duit mé;
O Lord, you examine me and know me;
más luí dom, más suí dom, is eol duit é;
you know if I am lying or sitting down;
is eol duit mo rún is mé i bhfad uait. *you read my thoughts from far away.*
Más siúl dom, más suan dom, feiceann tú mé.
Whether I walk or lie down, you are watching.
Is eol duit mo shlíte go léir; *You know all my ways;*
sula gcluintear focal ar mo theanga,
before a word is heard on my mouth,
a Thiarna, is eol duit ar fad é. *O Lord, you know it through and through.*
Im dhruideann tú ar chúl is ar bhéal mé;
You fence me around, behind and in front;
agus leagann do lámh orm de shíor.
and you continually keep your hand on me.
Is ró-iontach, ró-uasal liom an t-eolas seo
Such knowledge is beyond my understanding,
agus téann sé thar m'achmhainn a thuiscint.
a height to which my mind cannot attain.

37 Curfá
Má deir-im go bhfo-lóidh an dor-a-chacht mé___ is go mbeidh so-las an lae in-a oí-che liom,
39
_ ní dor-a-cha leat-sa an dor-a-chacht___ is comh-sho-las duit lá a-gus oí-che.___
2
2
41 Bhéarsa
Scrú-daíonn tú mé, a Thiar - na, a - gus is eol duit mé;
42
más luí dom, más suí dom, is eol_ duit é; is eol duit mo rún is mé i bhfad uait.___

5.6 Peadar Ó Riada: *Aifreann Eoin na Croise, Salm 139* (bars 37–51)

As we have seen, neither of Seán Ó Riada's mass settings, *Ceol an aifrinn* or *Aifreann 2*, contains a psalm setting.[31] *Aifreann Eoin na Croise* provides the first encounter with this pre-eminent textual form, whose distinctive rhythms beat continuously within the heart of the sung liturgy of the Roman rite.[32] An orally based form, which makes use of the compositional device of parallelism, generally consisting of a single idea expressed with the help of two complementary or contrasting utterances,[33] Hebrew psalmody is expressed most essentially in the Christian musical tradition by means of the standard two-phrase plainchant psalm-tone.[34]

Salm 139, with its markedly mystical emphasis on God's all-encompassing knowledge of man, and man's eternal quest for union with God, was the text suggested to Ó Riada by the Carmelite Community of St Teresa's who commissioned the mass. The portion set by Ó Riada combines a four-line refrain (comprising verses 11 and 12) with a rather substantial eleven-line verse portion (verses 1–6 of the psalm). The higher tessitura of the verse follows closely on the Gregorian gradual tradition, and the ample dimensions of this through-composed psalmodic text prompt comparisons with the tracts of psalmody selected and set by chant composers for use during the period of Lent, as replacements for the Alleluia.

Refrain

Set in the tonal region of *D* major over a combination of tonic and dominant pedals, the refrain has a plagal melodic disposition, taking in the area a fifth above and a fourth below the final. Ó Riada's melodic composition of the refrain's four lines plays on the structural potentialities within these tonal limits to reveal a fascinatingly symmetrical weave of intervallic relationships based on fourths and fifths:

5.7 Peadar Ó Riada: *Aifreann Eoin na Croise, Salm 139*, tonal structures

The melodic structure of the refrain might be defined in thematic terms as ABCD, with traditional practice reflected in the climactic third phrase (bar 39), but an equally plausible reading might be ABBA, a tessitura-based approach which accords well with the rhetorical properties of the psalm couplets.

In view of the considerable richness of melodic expression already built up in the extended opening chant, it seems prudent to ascertain whether the refrain melody is entirely new or builds on some pre-existing ideas. The situating of the refrain in *D* major reminds us of the brief turn towards that tonal centre at the beginning of *Admhaím do Dhia mhóir*, and thematic comparison reveals striking similarities between the opening couplets of both pieces:

5.8 Peadar Ó Riada: *Aifreann Eoin na Croise, Admhaím do Dhia mhóir* (bars 24–25) and *Salm 139* (bars 37–38)

The visual similarities of the melodies, however, belie the significant difference in aural perception brought about by a change of drone from A in the opening chant to *d* in the psalm. This conceptual reframing of the above melody, then, seems to represent a following-through in the psalm of what was only hinted at in the earlier piece. A is still extremely prominent structurally, but the choice of *D* as accompanimental drone and final note provide another tonal given.

Verse

In formal terms, the opening four lines (bars 41–44) of this eleven-line verse broadly follow an ABA1B pattern, with A1 representing a modified repeat of A at the higher octave, and the exact repeat of B suggested by the structural and rhetorical similarities of the lines. In melodic terms both the A and B elements of the verse correspond very closely to the opening two lines of the refrain, built as they are on the tonality's constituent perfect fourths, *A-d* and *e-a*. Phrase B is of particular interest, since its roots seem to reach back beyond the psalm refrain, to the litanic motif from bars 26–28 of *Admhaím do Dhia mhóir*. The phrase-end notes so far are A, *f#*, *a*, *f#* and already by the third line (bar 43) the piece's range has been extended upwards by a fifth.

The fifth line of the verse (bar 45) establishes a new melodic tessitura based on the high *a*, which provides the tonal foundation for a self-contained melody spanning the five lines up to line nine of the text, and following the form CDEFF (bars 45–49). The first two of these lines alternate the flattened and sharpened seventh as they build up to the climactic E phase, which has a number of interesting structural and thematic features. It begins with a repetition, up an octave, of the concluding motif of bar 42, now dramatically 're-framed' as a strongly rhetorical opening gesture on the phrase 'A Thiarna' (bar 47). This line, continuing with 'is eol duit ar fad é' ('you know it all through and through') has obviously been chosen by Ó Riada as the expressive climax of the psalm setting, and it is interesting to note as the musical 'meat' of the line, the presence of the significant concluding *doh-ta-lah-soh* motif from the *Opening Chant*.[35] This dramatic melodic expression of phrase E is balanced at a lower level by two statements of F, an *a*-based phrase which reinstates the sharpened seventh.

Parallelism

There is an interesting structural counterpoint at work in Ó Riada's setting of the above five-line section (CDEFF) which appears to pit a textual pattern of 1+2+2 (line/couplet/couplet) against a musical pattern of 2+1+2 (couplet/line/couplet). As we shall now see, this phenomenon seems to have at its origins the conflicting demands of textual and musical parallelism. The compositional technique of parallelism is one of the defining characteristics of oral literature.[36] We have already noted its centrality within the tradition of Hebrew psalmodic texts. It also pervades the almost exclusively symmetrical text structures of Irish traditional song,[37] where it tends to produce couplet-based musical responses characterised variously by melodically incremental or antithetical expression. Albert Lord sees the device of parallelism as vital to the art of the oral epic singer/composer whose problem is 'to construct one line after another very rapidly' and whose 'need for the "next" line is upon him even before he utters the final syllable of a line'.[38] The dynamic pull of the musical couplet, then, exerts a strong influence on the oral composer, one which sometimes may prove difficult to resist as he moves forward sequentially, phrase by phrase, through the given text.[39] The textual structure of the five-line segment in question is presented here in translation:

> You know all my ways;
> before a word is heard on my mouth,
> O Lord, you know it through and through.
> You fence me around, behind and in front,
> and you continually keep your hand on me.

As already summarised, this section follows immediately on two very clearly defined textual-musical couplets. Ó Riada, dealing sequentially with the text,[40] seizes, it would appear, on the structural ambiguity of line 6 ('Before a word is heard on my mouth') and, without looking further ahead, treats it as the concluding line of a couplet, instead of an opening line, which in fact it is. In this way he sustains unbroken composition by couplet into six lines of verse text, unaware, presumably, that he may have to 'face the asymmetrical music' very soon.

The potency of pre-existing systemic musical structures and their application in psalm text setting is re-echoed in the context of Emma Hornby's recent study of text/music relationships in eighth-mode psalm tracts from the medieval chant tradition, where she states that 'within an oral genre, once a phrase is begun, the rest is inevitable, unless there is a strong textual cue'.[41] In this case, it would appear, the textual cue in line 6 of this psalm extract was either not strong enough, or was too ambivalent to prevent the continuation of a couplet-driven melodic flow.

So what happens in the climactic 'isolated' line 7 (bar 47), given that the two succeeding lines clearly suggest a self-enclosed couplet? Ó Riada's instincts compel him to persist with a musical couplet dynamic, which he manages to fashion very convincingly within the rhetorical structure of a *single* line by providing two clearly defined melodic gestures: 'A Thiarna, / is eol duit ar fad é.' The final two lines of the verse, which might be described in melodic/formal terms as G and G1,[42] bring the melodic movement back down to triad-based activity over *d* (bars 50–51), and leave the bottom fourth of the *Salm*'s range clear to facilitate a fresh return of the refrain.

AILILIÚIA

Ailiiliúia, Ailiiliúia, ó Ailiiliúia.
Solas Críost, a ruaigeann an oíche,
oích'ár n-anama. Ailiiliúia.

Alleluia, Alleluia, O Alleluia.
The light of Christ, which dispels the night,
the night of our souls. Alleluia.

5.9 Peadar Ó Riada: *Aifreann Eoin na Croise, Ailiiliúia* (bars 52–58)

As we have already seen in our discussion of Seán Ó Riada's mass settings, *Ceol an aifrinn* did not include a setting of the gospel *Alleluia*. Neither did the Ó Canainn-published version of the Glenstal-commissioned *Aifreann 2*, which provided Peadar with the only access to his father's second mass and the only basis for his 1979 recording of it with Cór Chúil Aodha. As far as Peadar was concerned, then, this *Ailiiliúia* was the first Ó Riada attempt at this liturgical genre.[43] It features a triple-acclamation (of the congregational type first promoted in the Vatican II post-conciliar popular chant compendium, *Iubilate Deo*)[44] with a verse 'Solas Críost' which continues and Christianises the darkness versus light theme of the preceding Old Testament psalm refrain.

Peadar Ó Riada's understanding of the *Aililiúia* is as a 'joyful, celebratory acclamation', and it is in this sense that he feels free to include an uplifting 'ó' as a lead-in to the final acclamation.[45] A rhythmic spring and arpeggio-based melodic setting characterise this major-mode (*D*-based) *Aililiúia* and its ensuing verse. The melodic composition of the three successive 'Aililiúia's is ingenious in its identifying and mixing of the three distinctive pitch areas marked out by the notes of the major arpeggio, following the balanced pattern, middle-top-bottom. There is also a directional variety built into the principal gestures, which themselves may be summarised in the melodic form ABC.

The *verse* takes the component elements of this form and recombines them[46] to suit a four-line shape which incorporates a three-line verse and a concluding 'Aililiúia'. For the verse beginning 'Solas Críost' ('The light of Christ'), Ó Riada selects a declamatory opening (B) followed by two mid-range (AA) deliveries and concludes with a low-range (C) 'Aililiúia' which echoes the close of the acclamation itself.[47] The overall composition, then, follows the motivic form ABCBAAC, with the mid-range motif (*a*-based) carrying the most textual weight.

The keyboard accompaniment features a *D* drone for the first two 'Aililiúia's (complete with right-hand thirds and sixths and the trademark added ninths) and a I–V–I, already latent in the acclamation's upper-part movement, is repeated carillon-like in the tenor register before the rhyming I–V–I 'Aililiúia' cadence returns to conclude the piece.

From a liturgical point of view, the most significant aspect of the form of this *Aililiúia* is the non-return of the full acclamation itself. Why did Ó Riada eschew a direct and full repetition, opting instead for a more elegant but perhaps apparently less congregation-friendly solution? Ó Riada's answer to this question reveals much about the composer's instinctive understanding of the specific purpose of various liturgical elements, and of music's power to genuinely engage and prepare people for important ritual moments:

> The reading of the Gospel is for me by far the most important happening in the first half of the mass. After all, these are the words of the man himself ... The purpose of the *Aililiúia* is to prepare people for that moment ... That's why I have a more open-ended form ... A self-enclosed *Aililiúia* form doesn't work half as well, in my opinion. It becomes an end in itself ...[48]

GUÍ AN PHOBAIL

S. A Thiarna, éist linn. *Lord, hear us.*
P. A Thiarna, bí ceannsa's éist linn. *Lord, graciously hear us.*

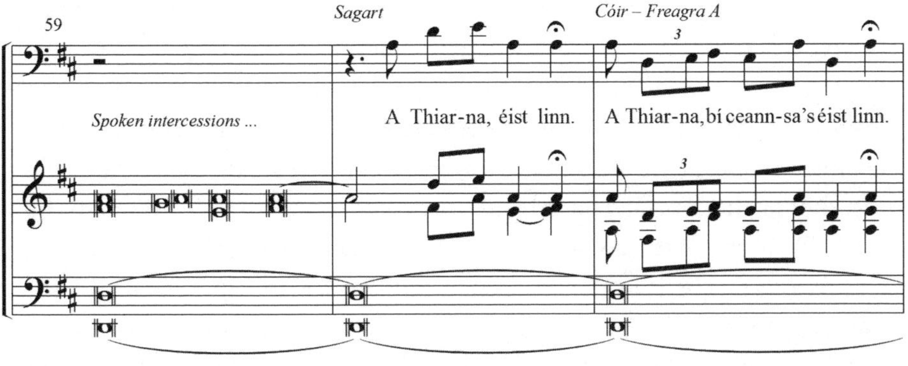

5.10 Peadar Ó Riada: *Aifreann Eoin na Croise, Guí an phobail* (bars 59–64)

In another new development along the three-mass liturgical continuum, Ó Riada offers musical settings for the invitation and responses to the prayers of intercession, and also for the concluding prayer together with its 'Amen'.[49] In the audio recording the intercessions are spoken over a *D* pedal, with limited and discreet upper-part movement. The organ part, then, acts as a unifying element throughout the rite. The main musical protagonists are identified as 'sagart' (priest) and 'cóir' (choir), the latter intended as an aid to the people's involvement. The variation element present in the 'people's' responses (*Freagra* A, *Freagra* B above), suggestive of the necessity for a leading group of some description, is the most interesting musico-liturgical feature of this setting. Its rolling, developing nature has illustrious antecedents in some of the earliest congregation-oriented responsorial forms of the Gregorian tradition,[50] and, in a contemporary liturgical climate where congregations are often rather poorly viewed in musical terms and provided for accordingly, Ó Riada's setting raises provocative questions about how music might more fruitfully integrate with a repetitive ritual like the prayers of intercession. His concept is simple: an alternation of tonally open (*a*) and closed (*d*) endings to the same basic response. The response itself is a type of mirror image of the preceding invitation (ascending *a-d'* opening answered by descending *a-d* motif; answering fifth intervals held together by the central *a* pitch) and the people are further connected to the priest by means of the continuous *D* pedal, which straddles both invitation and response. The priest's part, unlike similar elements in Seán Ó Riada's music, is fully even if discreetly accompanied, a concept that is further developed in the shifting harmonic backdrop to the *a*-centred chanting of the concluding prayer.[51]

IS NAOFA

Is Naofa, Naofa, Naofa thú, *Holy, Holy, Holy are you,*
A Thiarna, Dia na Slua. *Lord, God of Hosts.*
Tá neamh agus talamh lán de do ghlóir.
Heaven and earth are full of your glory.
Hosanna sna harda. *Hosanna in the highest.*
Is beannaithe'n té 'tá ag teacht in ainm an Tiarna.
Blessed is he who is coming in the name of the Lord.
Hosanna sna harda. *Hosanna in the highest.*

5.11 Peadar Ó Riada: *Aifreann Eoin na Croise, Is Naofa* (bars 65–70)

Peadar Ó Riada's starting point for this setting seems almost certainly to have been the version most frequently used for mass in Cúil Aodha, that of Seán's *Aifreann 2*. Although the generally lower tessitura and different directional pull of Peadar's version give a different context to the musical expression, a straightforward melodic comparison of the two openings provides compelling evidence of a link. The following are the first two lines of both settings, with the second example transposed up a fourth, to facilitate comparison:

5.12 Seán Ó Riada: *Aifreann 2*, Is Naofa (bars 98–103)
Peadar Ó Riada: *Aifreann Eoin na Croise, Is Naofa* (bars 65–66, transposed)

Although the descending *d-c#-A* movement (bar 65) of the opening motif (recalling both the opening of the earlier *Admhaím do Dhia mhóir* and the verse opening of *Salm 139*) sets out in an apparently different direction, the rhythm, static repetitions and tonal dynamic of the *Aifreann 2* setting seems to have won out as early as the end of the first line (bar 65), so that the younger composer is forced to take dramatic steps at the beginning of the second line to avoid being further pulled into its slipstream (bar 66). With line three, however, he manages to break free of the rhythmic template by means of a melisma prompted, not inappropriately, by the word 'lán' ('full'). This slows the syllabic movement down towards a distinctively coloured intermediary cadence on the other keyword 'ghlóir', at the lower flattened seventh pitch (bar 67).

Ó Riada's approach to the fourth 'Hosanna' line is notable for its rather free treatment of the text, and yet within the music there are again distant echoes of its Cúil Aodha precursors. In dispensing with the phrase 'Hosanna sna harda' and replacing it with three successive 'Hosanna's, Ó Riada seems to be mirroring the opening threefold 'Is Naofa', perhaps responding to the very similar phonetic make-up of both phrases. This similarity is musically encapsulated in the two-note neumatic gesture which delivers the accented syllables of Is *Nao*fa and Hos*anna*.[52] The musical expression of the threefold 'Hosanna', with its dramatic leaps and deliberate melodic build-up, comes to a climactic cadence on *d'*, the melodic apex of the piece. Notwithstanding the modifications in the text, this highly declamatory delivery of the first 'Hosanna' line of the text may be seen as a further, more developed example of a rhetorical approach already established by *Ceol an aifrinn* and *Aifreann 2*.

Following the climactic 'Hosanna', the Benedictus text 'Is beannaithe …' is used to change the melodic centre of gravity from *d'* back down to *a'*, a pitch which, in its higher and lower forms, has never been far away from the melodic action. In a device which features elsewhere in his liturgical compositions,[53] Peadar Ó Riada uses the tonal affinity between this high and low *soh*-type pitch to effect an immediate change of tessitura. The final 'Hosanna' line begins at this latter pitch, A, with the composer following the concept of triple repetitions through to its logical conclusion (although this time the 'Hosanna' repetitions are completed with a closing, melodically discreet 'sna harda') to a melodic motif (*ac#d*) which presents an elegant mirror-image answer to the *dc#a* motif of the piece's opening triple invocation.

Ó Riada's rather free treatment of the text is probably the most noteworthy feature of this setting. On the evidence of the mass so far, he seems unlikely to have been hampered by any technical deficiency in grappling with an irregular text such as *Is Naofa*; he has already more than adequately displayed his command of asymmetrical forms. Ó Riada has, then, chosen freely to adapt the text of *Is Naofa*, by introducing the extra repetitions of the 'Hosanna' acclamation. Why? When asked this question, the composer responded as follows:

> Well, I suppose it is in keeping with the meditative spirit of the mass. As well as that, I have always been interested in the idea of a 'mantra', and the pagan in me has always been drawn to this idea of triple repetition! You'll see that I often conclude psalm settings, for instance, by a triple repetition of the final phrase … My father first did something like this in the hymn 'A Íosa bháin' from his second mass …[54]

RÚNDIAMHAIR AN CHREIDIMH

S. Fógraimís rúndiamhair an chreidimh.	*Let us proclaim the mystery of faith.*
P. A Íosa, fuair tú bás ar ár son;	*Jesus, you died on our behalf;*
d'éirigh tú ó na mairbh;	*you rose from the dead;*
tiocfaidh tú 'rís.	*you will come again.*

5.13 Peadar Ó Riada: *Aifreann Eoin na Croise, Rúndiamhar an chreidimh* (bars 71–74)

The inclusion of this setting from the pre-existing *Aifreann 2* is an interesting one. What were the determining factors? A deliberate link with tradition? Pragmatism or lack of time? Could it be that the composer particularly admired this setting and felt that it could not be improved on? When questioned on this point in May 2007, Peadar Ó Riada's reply revealed that over the years he had come to think of A *Íosa, fuair tú bás ar ár son* as his own composition, and he had forgotten that it was his father's. His comments reveal much about the nature of tradition and orality.

At any rate, the inclusion of A *Íosa* seems well justified on aesthetic grounds. Its *D*-based tonality and structurally prominent *a* link it with the preceding *Is Naofa* and the succeeding conclusion to the eucharistic prayer, while its own distinctive tonal turn towards the subdominant *g* brings here, just as it did in the earlier setting, a musical freshness to the mass setting in general and to this ritual moment in particular. As in the earlier *Guí an phobail*, Peadar Ó Riada departs here from the liturgically traditional unaccompanied approach to parts involving the priest (adhered to in spirit, as we saw, in his father's *Ceol an aifrinn*), and chooses a more fully supportive harmonic backdrop (characterised by tonal stability and minimal part movement) to carry the ritual invitation.

IS TRÍD/AMEN MÓR

S. Is tríd, agus leis, agus ann,	*Through him, and with him and in him,*
a thugtar gach onóir agus glóir duitse,	*all honour and glory are given to you,*
a Dhia, an tAthair uilechumhachtach,	*God, the almighty Father,*
mar aon leis an Spiorad Naomh	*one with the Holy Spirit*
trí shaol na saol.	*forever and ever.*
P. Amen.	*Amen.*

5.14 Peadar Ó Riada: *Aifreann Eoin na Croise, Is tríd/Amen mór* (bars 75–76)

The practice of accompanied presidential chanting comes even more to the fore in the concluding doxology, a more extended and liturgically self-contained text (it requires only an 'Amen' for its conclusion). Ó Riada adopts the same tonally stable harmonic approach, supporting and discreetly enriching the recited *a* which carries the prayer. The underlying *D* pedal functions, as at other such times in the mass, as a bridge into the people's response. In keeping with the leaning toward text repetition which has so far characterised the mass setting, Ó Riada opts for a four-fold *Amen mór*,[55] following the form AAAB. The two musical elements which constitute this form bring us back in contact with certain givens of the major diatonic scale, founded as it is on two structurally identical tetrachords.[56] The melodic motif which sustains the 'Amen' repeats the *d'c#a* movement already noted in the openings of *Is Naofa*, *Salm 139* and *Admhaím do Dhia mhóir*, a motivic shape which may eventually be traced back to its first appearance, albeit at a different pitch, at the end of the first prayer of the *Opening Chant* (bars 4–5).

ÁR NATHAIR–SÍOCHÁIN

P.	Ár nAthair atá ar neamh,	*Our Father who art in heaven,*
	go naofar tAinm,	*hallowed be your name,*
	go dtaga do ríocht,	*your kingdom come,*
	go ndeántar do thoil ar an dtalamh	*your will be done on earth*
	mar a dhéantar ar neamh.	*as it is in heaven.*
	Ár n-arán laethiúil tabhair dúinn inniu,	*give us this day our daily bread,*
	agus maith dúinn ár bhfiacha,	*and forgive us our debts,*
	mar a mhaithimidne d'ár bhféichiúna féin.	*as we forgive our own debtors.*
	Agus ná lig sinn i gcathú,	*And lead us not into temptation,*
	ach saor sinn ó olc.	*but deliver us from evil.*
S.	Saor sinn ó gach olc … Críost.	*Deliver us from every evil … Christ.*
P.	Óir is leatsa an ríocht	*For yours is the kingdom,*
	agus an chumhacht agus an ghlóir,	*the power and the glory,*
	trí shaol na saol.	*forever.*
S.	A Thiarna, Íosa Chríost …	*Lord, Jesus Christ …*
P.	Amen.	*Amen.*
S.	Síocháin an Tiarna libh i gcónaí.	*The peace of the Lord be with you always.*
P.	Agus leat féin.	*And also with you.*
S.	Cuirigí síocháin in iúl dá chéile.	*Show that there is peace amongst you.*

5.15 Peadar Ó Riada: *Aifreann Eoin na Croise, Ár nAthair–Síochain* (bars 77–84)

We have already noted how, in liturgical terms, Seán Ó Riada's *Aifreann 2* represented a significant development over its predecessor.[57] Noted also was the involvement in the process of the religious community who commissioned the mass. Peadar Ó Riada's decision to musically set the Communion Rite of *Aifreann Eoin na Croise*, from the Ár *nAthair* introduction right through to the end of the A *Uain Dé*, represents a further musico-liturgical development, one which brings this mass setting much closer to the principles of the 'missa cantata' of the Roman rite.

Ár nAthair–Síocháin

For the delivery of the lengthiest of the fixed mass texts, the *Ár nAthair*, Ó Riada returns to the low A recitation device of 'An marnabh'. As in the earlier piece, the bass A keyboard drone which sustains the delivery is set off by fourth- and fifth-degree melodic alternation in the tenor part. Though not indicated in the original score, in the recording this additional part movement develops upwards during the ensuing embolism 'Saor sinn...', chanted on high *a* by the priest, fashioning a type of musical preparation for the proclaiming of the lesser doxology 'Óir is leatsa' (bar 79). This is formed melodically around the recited *a*, but a telling melodic shift to *d'* on the word 'ríocht' prompts a similar shift of bass drone to the same pitch. It is worth noting Ó Riada's omission of the phrase 'agus an ghlóir' ('and the glory') from this doxology.[58]

The new *D*-drone will underpin the remaining elements of the musical sequence. These consist of the prayer for peace, chanted on *a*, and a three-part exchange which introduces the sign of peace. The melodic material for the opening of the latter is the same as for the preceding 'Óir is leatsa', and for the concluding 'Cuirigí in iúl ...' (this rare ritual moment which involves a presidential command *not* verbally responded to by the people) the celebrant is for once granted the privilege, not to say pleasure, of a full melodic close, represented by a descending *D* major arpeggio.

A UAIN DÉ

A Uain Dé, a thógann peacaí an domhain, déan trócaire 'rainn.
A Uain Dé, a thógann peacaí an domhain, déan trócaire 'rainn.
A Uain Dé, tabhair dúinn síocháin.
Lamb of God, who takes away the sins of the world, have mercy on us.

Lamb of God, who takes away the sins of the world, have mercy on us.
Lamb of God, grant us peace.

5.16 Peadar Ó Riada: *Aifreann Eoin na Croise, A Uain Dé* (bars 85–87)

By contrast with the earlier mass part *Is Naofa*, which, as has been suggested, owes much to the existence of *Aifreann 2*, the conceptual starting point for this setting of *A Uain Dé* seems to reach back to the beginnings of what we may now call the Cúil Aodha tradition and the version found in Seán Ó Riada's *Ceol an aifrinn*. In that earlier setting, the repeated litanic invocations of the prayer were grafted on to a melodically incremental structure typical of traditional song construction, imbuing the text music composition with a certain dramatic quality. The final mass part from *Aifreann Eoin na Croise* takes the same general approach, but includes some significant developments and modifications.

The *D*-based tonality, maintained fairly consistently since *Salm 139*,[59] is retained for this final mass part, underpinning a melodic setting which contains important musical elements from earlier on in the mass. The main body of the first invocation recalls one of the mass's central musical gestures (noted earlier in our discussion of the *Amen*), as presented at the beginning of *Admhaím do Dhia mhóir*:

5.17 Peadar Ó Riada: *Aifreann Eoin na Croise, Admhaím do Dhia mhóir* (bar 24)

In the second invocation, the flattened seventh, already noted in the more large-scale *Opening Chant* and *Salm 139*, and in the inherited *Rúndiamhair an chreidimh*, returns in classic modal form, as a decoration of the fifth (bar 86).[60] This invocation also includes in its final phrase 'déan trócaire orainn', an integration of a distinctive motif, *f#gba*, already noted in relation to the opening and closing prayers of the *Opening Chant* (bars 2 and 34–35) and last employed as the central gesture of the *Síocháin* sequence (bar 83).

The brief final invocation is notable for Ó Riada's elision of the central portion of the text. The gathering tension of the whole piece, which reaches a melodic climax in the final 'A Uain Dé', is released and resolved in the unprecedented downward octave plea 'tabhair dúinn síocháin' ('grant us peace'). As with other such points in the mass, Ó Riada's decision to modify the given text is one which can certainly be justified on musical grounds: the results are artistically convincing and, in this case, even compelling. The impetus of this final modification would appear to be of a rhetorical nature: Ó Riada seems to have arrived at the crucial point in the final invocation and, judging that a full repeat of the text would serve only to weaken his case, bypasses the central portion and moves on immediately to the distinguishing and culminating textual element of the piece.

A final observation concerns the three repetitions of the phrase 'A Uain Dé', on which the structure of this piece is hung. The developmental melodic approach has its general roots in traditional Irish melodic construction, and the use of this device has already been noted in the *Ceol an aifrinn* setting of the same text. In that setting the phrase in question was delivered in a recitational manner, and so musical development was linked solely to the choice of pitch region for each successive repeat. In *Aifreann Eoin na Croise*, however, the successive repetitions feature not only melodic but also motivic development, the latter going beyond anything previously encountered in litanic passages throughout the whole Cúil Aodha continuum, at the same time challenging, from an oral perspective, received understandings as to what might constitute a 'motif':

5.18 Peadar Ó Riada: *Aifreann Eoin na Croise, A Uain Dé*, repetitions

AN COSÁN DRAÍOCHTA

Curfá (Bhéarsa 1)	***Chorus (Verse 1)***
A Chríost, a Rí, scaip síol inár gcroí,	*O Christ, O King, in our hearts sow seeds,*
as a bhfásfaidh aníos fíorbhláthanna spioradálta.	*from which will grow true mystic flowers.*
Go scéithfidh amach a ndraíocht, go cumhra	*Whose magic will emanate, with fragrance*
thar dhroim an tsaoil,	*o'er earth's face,*
draíocht Eoin na Croise céasta,	*the magic of John of the Cross unveiled,*
is Treasa Naofa ó Aville.	*and Holy Teresa of Avila.*

Bhéarsa 2	***Verse 2***
A Rí, impím, cuir do dhréimire síos,	*O king, I plead, lower your ladder,*
nó báfar sinn gan bhrí i dtonnta tuile.	*or we shall drown meaninglessly in the waves of the deluge.*
Tuile amplach an chraois, na sainte 's na baoise,	*The deluge of greed, of gluttony and deceit,*
a scuabfaidh gan trócaire síos sinn	*which will sweep us without pity*
go leacaibh Ifrinn.	*down to the flags of Hell.*

88
Curfá
A Chríost, a Rí, scaip síol in - ár gcroí,
89
as a bhfás - faidh a - níos fíor - bhlá - than - na spio - ra - dál - ta.
90
Go scéith - fidh a - mach a ndraíocht, go cumh - ra thar dhroim an tsaoil,
91
draíocht Eoin na Croi - se céas - ta's Trea - sa Nao - fa ó A - ville.

5.19 Peadar Ó Riada: *Aifreann Eoin na Croise, An cosán draíochta* (bars 88–95)

At the early stages of planning for this mass, Ó Riada asked local poet Joan Kelly to provide a hymn text based on the theme of St John of the Cross. He felt confident that she would be able to respond, based on the kinship he had noticed between the spirituality of the local area and that expressed in the writings of the Carmelite saint: 'The *Cosán draíochta* arrived because my friend Joan Kelly and I had spent many nights going through all that country and she expressed a wish to try a poem in that area. I asked her to complete it then as a communion hymn for the mass.'[61] The full text which she produced contains four verses and is addressed to Christ the King. In the first verse, Christ is asked to sow seeds in believers' hearts, which will blossom forth with the fragrant spirituality of St John of the Cross and 'Holy Teresa of Avila'. The second and third verses are concerned with the fate of humanity, in danger of being submerged beneath the waters of its own weakness or beneath the weight of life's trials. The King is asked to lower his ladder and save his people from hell, clasping them close to his heart. In the final verse, the example of John and the Carmelite spirituality are held up as guiding lights on 'the magic path to the door of Heaven'.

The four-line verses are not concerned with absolute metrical strictness but follow a general pattern of two shorter lines followed by two longer ones. Rhyme agreement at line ends is consistently maintained, with line two of the first verse providing the only exception. Ó Riada makes this opening verse the central element of the composition, treating it as a recurring refrain which introduces and follows the three remaining verses. In its form and its proportions, but also in its melodic range, tonality and thematic content, *An cosán draíochta* most closely resembles *Salm 139*. A comparison of the second line of the refrain with that of *Salm 139*'s first verse indicates a clear reworking of melodic material from the earlier composition:

5.20 Peadar Ó Riada: *Aifreann Eoin na Croise, An cosán draíochta* (bar 89)
Peadar Ó Riada: *Aifreann Eoin na Croise, Salm 139* (bar 41)

The refrain of *An cosán draíochta* differs melodically from that of *Salm 139* in its markedly dominant dynamic (e.g. opening A-based arpeggio, phrase-end notes *A-e-e'-d*) which resolves to the tonic only on the final word of the text. This inherent tonal dynamic is underlined throughout all repetitions of the refrain by the presence of a dominant pedal which resolves with the last note.[62] The refrain melody of *Salm 139*, on the other hand, while containing a strong *a*-based element, is more clearly biased towards the tonic *d*, and this also is expressed in its drone activity.

The melody for the refrain of the communion hymn is remarkable for its extremely wide range of two octaves and a minor second. Noteworthy also is the way in which the opening of the third line of the melody thematically answers that of the second at a higher pitch:[63]

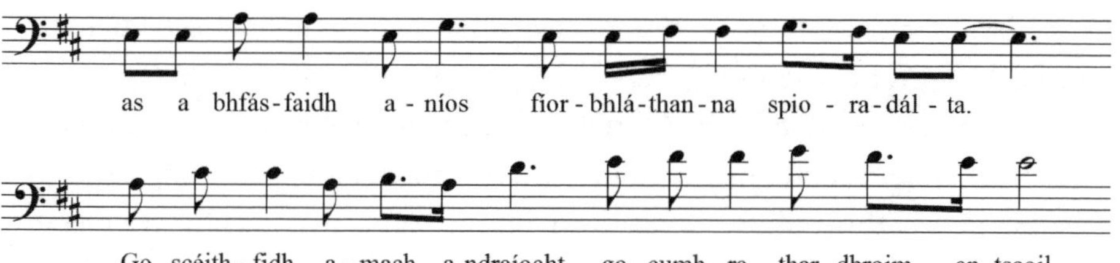

5.21 Peadar Ó Riada: *Aifreann Eoin na Croise, An cosán draíochta* (bar 89, bar 90)

It may be noted, however, that the arpeggiaic build-up of the first three phrases is entirely in accordance with traditional Irish melodic practice, even if the distances covered by Ó Riada tend to be larger and the build-ups more dramatic:[64]

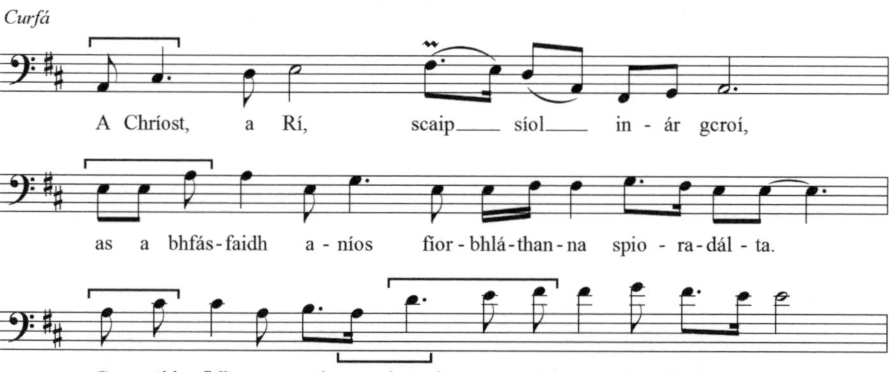

5.22 Peadar Ó Riada: *Aifreann Eoin na Croise, An cosán draíochta* (bars 88–90)

The fourth and concluding line of the refrain serves to release gradually the preceding build-up of melodic tension. Its unremittingly stepwise octave descent consists of two successive tetrachords of a perfect fourth, an interval which has never been far from the heart of the mass's musical proceedings, and which in stepwise form will once more feature significantly at the end of the verse melody.

Before considering the final melodic journey of *Aifreann Eoin na Croise*, it is worth noting that the musical architecture of the foregoing refrain, with its incremental melodic build-ups, climactic third line and descending final phrase, sums up very well the characteristic melodic aesthetic of traditional song which governs Ó Riada's compositional approach, from the three-phrase *Aililiúia* refrain through to the larger-scale melodic structures found in the *Opening Chant* and *Salm 139*.

The Communion verse, also governed by the principle of the 'melodic curve', begins by reaffirming the final descending fourth of the refrain, this time over a newly established tonic pedal, bringing the phrase to rest on *a* (bar 92). The second line consolidates *a* as a tonal base, venturing a fourth below and a third above. The third line is more melodically energetic, featuring at its end a disjunct melodic path consisting of intervals of the fifth, sixth and fourth, but ending also on *a* (bar 94). The melodic make-up of the final phrase presents an early *d* cadence halfway through the text, on the tonic (bar 95).[65] The tonic *d*, presented at the verse's beginning as a firm tonal foundation, is revealed now as a false bottom, providing not a tonal end, but a mere first step down Ó Riada's final 'secret ladder' presented here in the distinctive *doh-ta-lah-soh* configuration which portentously concluded the *Opening Chant* of his 'mystical mass'.[66]

6

Aifreann *Eoin na Croise*: Motivic Analysis

Introduction

The analysis of *Aifreann Eoin na Croise* contained in chapter five maintained the more general approach already adopted for *Ceol an aifrinn* and *Aifreann 2*, and allowed for a consideration of textual and liturgical aspects as well as musical questions. In terms of the continuum of the three mass settings under discussion, we saw earlier how the prose settings of *Ceol an aifrinn* were largely sustained by the recitational principle, with very few instances of thematic migration. *Aifreann 2*, which drew primarily on the sustaining power of a particular modal structure, relied more on motivic repetition, but mainly *within* individual pieces where it was frequently employed in a static manner to accompany litany-type text repetitions. The scale and pervasive nature of motivic repetition observed in *Aifreann Eoin na Croise*, however, signal a new departure and a markedly different compositional approach, the significance of which will ultimately be seen to be applicable to the larger generative questions pertaining to the possible development of a modern-day 'vernacular chant'.

Following an introduction to some relevant aspects of the term 'motif', and with the aid of a motivic chart of the mass setting, this chapter proceeds with a detailed examination of the musical nature, distribution and categorisation of its constituent motifs. The overall compositional picture emerging from this initial analysis is first of all interpreted through the lens of orality as applied in the disciplines of literature, ethnomusicology and plainchant scholarship. A second line of inquiry returns to John Stevens' concept of the 'non-relationship' of words and music, as it considers the free nature of the interplay between melodic motifs and the accentual and syntactic properties of the text. As a means of summarising the findings of both lines of inquiry (motivic composition and text/music relationships) in the analysis of *Aifreann Eoin na Croise*, a specific chant setting from within the Roman liturgical tradition, Gloria VIII, is advanced as an aesthetically and structurally cognate example of music/text composition. A final section in this chapter, devoted to motivic analysis, brings the discussion beyond the more purely utilitarian aspects of motifs and their composition and application, to questions surrounding the nature, content, origins and ultimate meaning of these culturally grounded, elemental musical 'sayings'.

Motivic Analysis

> A motif may be of any size, and is most commonly regarded as the shortest subdivision of a theme or phrase that still maintains its identity as an idea. (William Drabkin)[1]

In his *New Grove* article, Drabkin proceeds to draw attention to the 'elemental' and 'incomplete' nature of the motif, and also to its consequences for the shape and structure of the larger composition in which it functions. Peter Jeffery, writing from the combined perspectives of plainchant and ethnomusicology, and using the parallel term 'formula', begins by focusing on the question of repetition:

> The most obvious attribute of formulas – their stereotyped character which is the reason for calling them 'formulas' – was captured in one way by a scholar who opted for a strictly notational definition, defining a formula as 'a recurrent sequence of neumes, i.e. a string of signs which occurs several times in the material'.[2]

Having identified repetition or recurrence of a pattern of notes as a basic characteristic of formulas or, as we shall call them, 'motifs', Jeffery goes on to develop his attempted definition in terms of motivic *flexibility*, not just in purely melodic terms (i.e. straddling the gamut from motivic adaptation to motivic 'transformation'),[3] but also in the chant-related context of application of motifs to the liturgical text: 'One type of flexibility, of course, is seen when the "same" formula is applied to different texts, with different numbers of syllables or patterns of accentuation …'.[4] This text/music relationship question is further developed in a section which relates melodic motifs with the broader considerations of textual syntax: 'The most venerable approach to the study of melodic formulas in Christian chant … involves cataloguing them according to their apparent function in marking syntactical divisions in the text.'[5]

My initial analysis of *Aifreann Eoin na Croise* revealed a total of seven distinct motivic categories. In trying to assess the relative importance of each motif, given that recurrence is the *sine qua non* of the genre,[6] Jeffery's broader focus on motivic adaptation, but perhaps more importantly on questions surrounding motif-text relationships, has proven particularly useful. The application of these principles, along with one specifically relating to the presence or absence of motifs in the hugely significant (in its size as well as its primary position within the liturgical sequence) *Opening Chant*, has resulted in a division of motivic content into two hierarchically ordered categories (primary and secondary), as will be outlined below.

To be kept in mind throughout the analysis, however, is Guido d'Arezzo's principle of 'double-melody', by which we are reminded of the compositional integrity of the music itself. The following passage from the medieval musician/composer describing the art of monophonic composition has been recently described by Theodore Karp as an explicit acknowledgement of the importance of a motif-based approach.[7] In it, Guido advises the musician:

> ... that the phrases be of the same length, like lines of verse, and be sometimes repeated, either the same or modified by some change, even though slight, and, if they are particularly beautiful, be duplicated, with their 'parts' not too diverse: and let those occasional phrases that are the same be varied as to intervals [*per modos*], or, if they retain the same intervals, let them be heard transposed higher or lower. Also a neume, turning back on itself, may return the same way it came and by the same steps.[8]

Compositional devices such as duplication, modification, transposition, even palindromic configurations will be clearly seen to feature in the motivic analysis of *Aifreann Eoin na Croise* which now follows.[9]

AIFREANN EOIN NA CROISE – MOTIVIC ANALYSIS

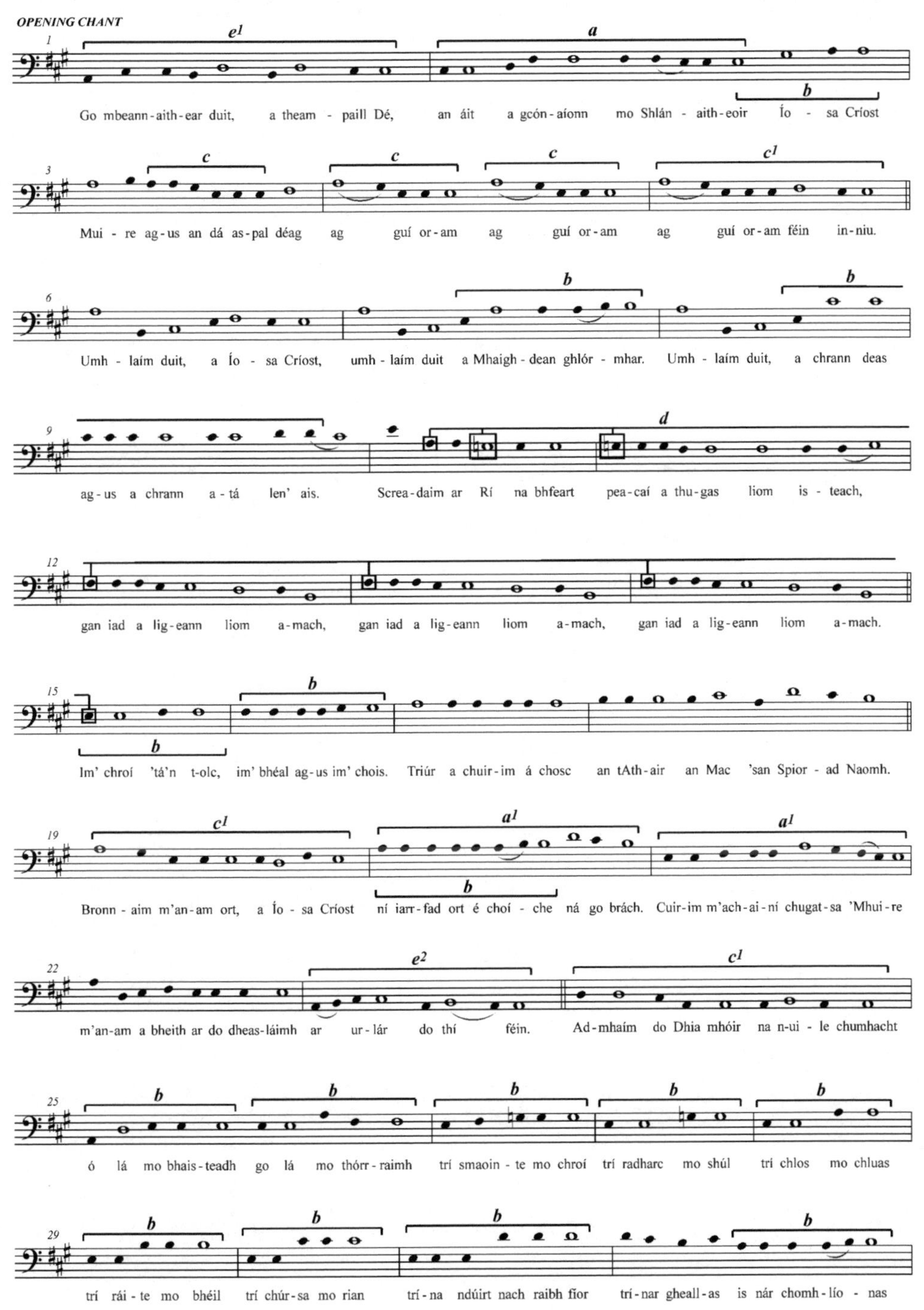

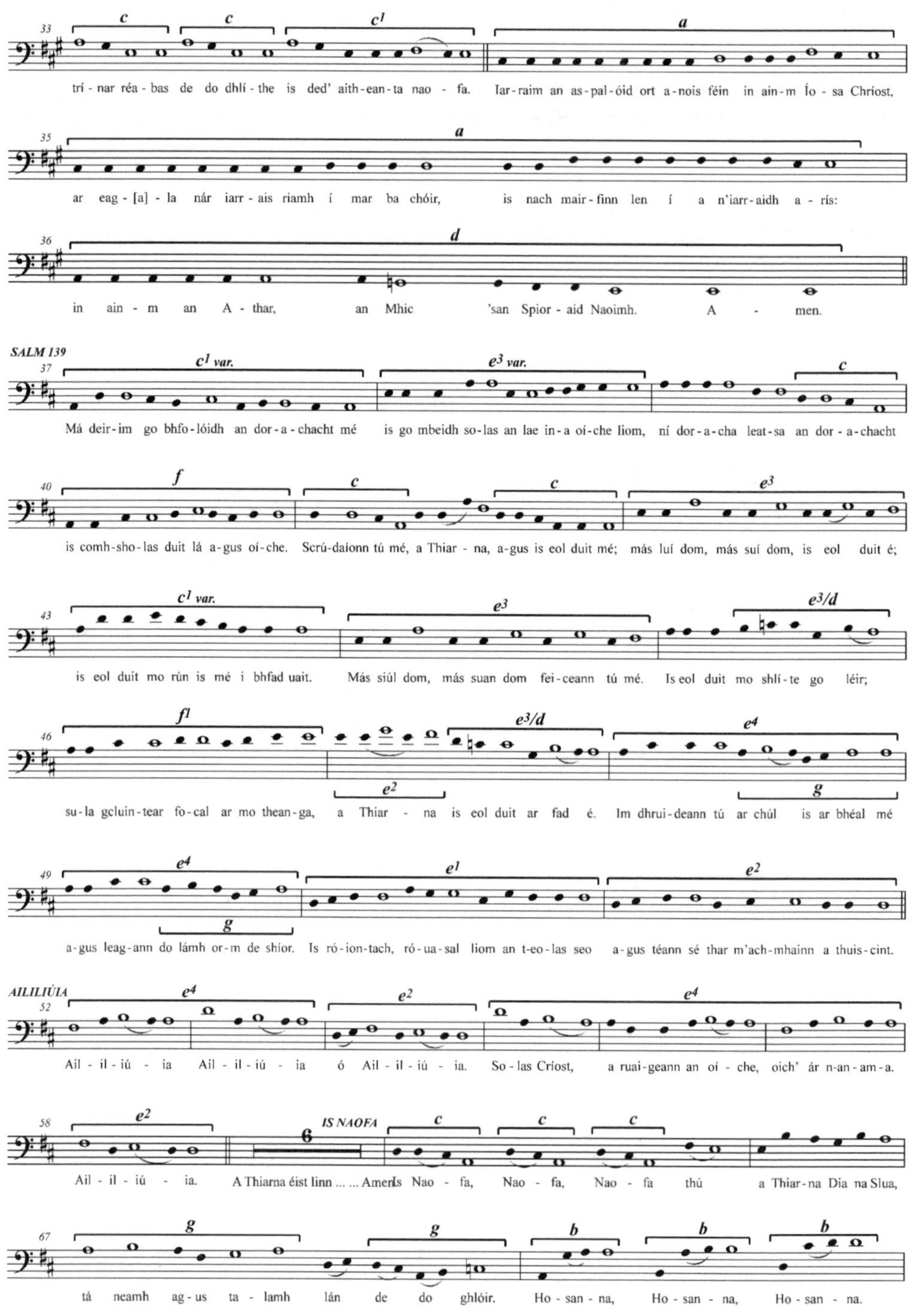
33
c c c1 a
trí - nar réa - bas de do dhlí - the is ded' aith - ean - ta nao - fa. Iar - raim an as - pal - óid ort a - nois féin in ain - m Ío - sa Chríost,
35
a
ar eag - [a] - la nár iarr - ais riamh í mar ba chóir, is nach mair - finn len í a n'iarr - aidh a - rís:
36
d
in ain - m an A - thar, an Mhic 'san Spior - aid Naoimh. A - men.
SALM 139
37
c1 var. e3 var. c
Má deir - im go bhfo - lóidh an dor - a - chacht mé is go mbeidh so - las an lae in - a oí - che liom, ní dor - a - cha leat - sa an dor - a - chacht
40
f c c e3
is comh - sho - las duit lá a - gus oí - che. Scrú - daíonn tú mé, a Thiar - na, a - gus is eol duit mé; más luí dom, más suí dom, is eol duit é;
43
c1 var. e3 e3/d
is eol duit mo rún is mé i bhfad uait. Más siúl dom, más suan dom fei - ceann tú mé. Is eol duit mo shlí - te go léir;
46
f1 e3/d e4
e2 g
su - la gcluin - tear fo - cal ar mo thean - ga, a Thiar - na is eol duit ar fad é. Im dhrui - deann tú ar chúl is ar bhéal mé
49
e4 e1 e2
g
a - gus leag - ann do lámh or - m de shíor. Is ró - ion - tach, ró - ua - sal liom an t-eo - las seo a - gus téann sé thar m'ach - mhainn a thuis - cint.
AILILIÚIA
52
e4 e2 e4
Ail - il - iú - ia Ail - il - iú - ia ó Ail - il - iú - ia. So - las Críost, a ruai - geann an oí - che, oich' ár n-an - am - a.
58
e2 IS NAOFA c c c
6
Ail - il - iú - ia. A Thiarna éist linn ... ... Amen Is Nao - fa, Nao - fa, Nao - fa thú a Thiar - na Dia na Slua,
67
g g b b b
tá neamh ag - us ta - lamh lán de do ghlóir. Ho - san - na, Ho - san - na, Ho - san - na.

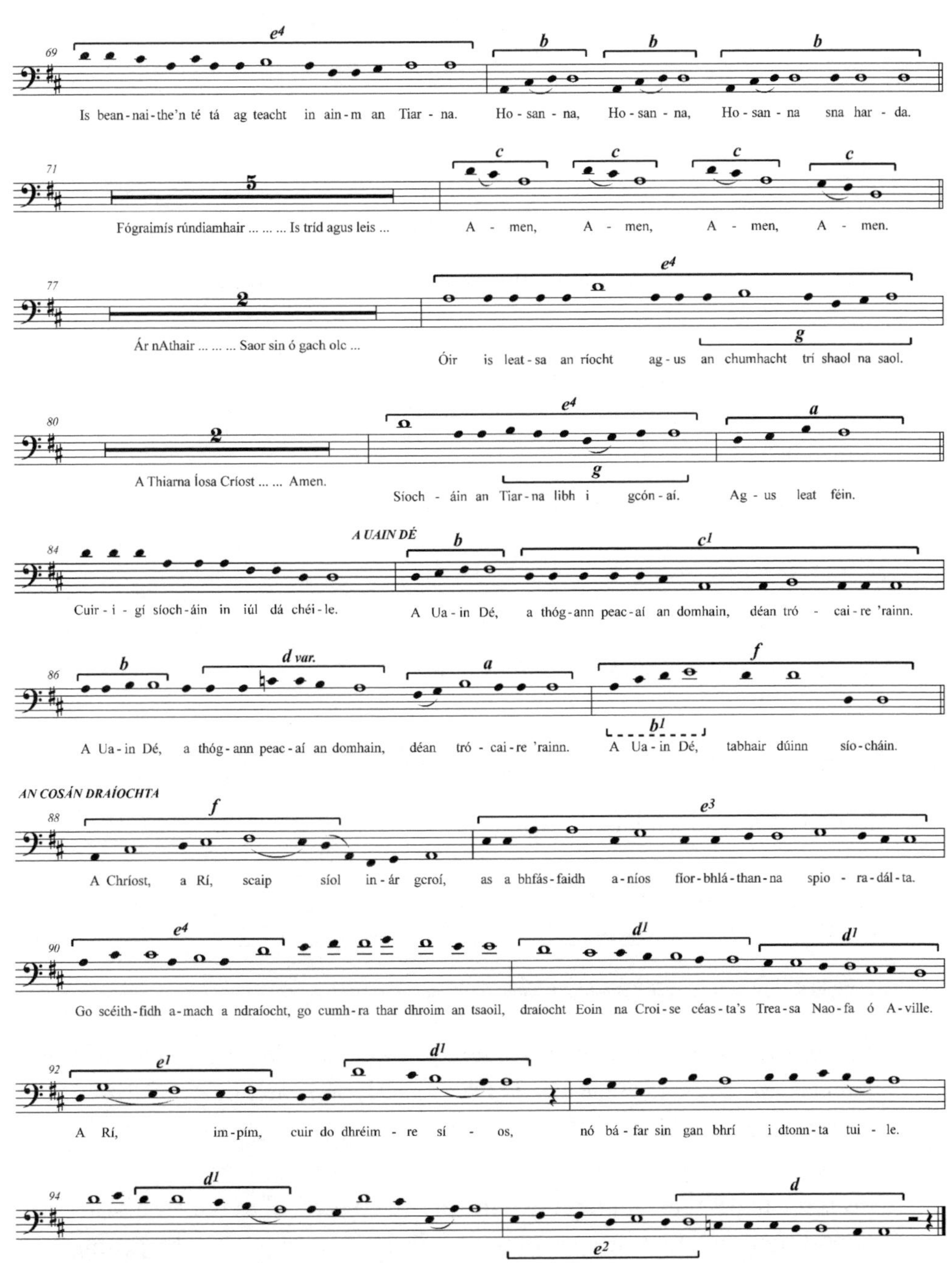

6.1 Peadar Ó Riada: *Aifreann Eoin na Croise*, Motivic Analysis

Primary Motifs (*a*, *b*, c and *d*)

These four motifs have been designated as primary for the following reasons:

1. They are characterised by a distinctive melodic contour.
2. Their reappearances are multiple and well-distributed throughout the mass setting.
3. They are flexibly used in a variety of textual contexts, both syntactic and accentual, and often mark ritually significant moments.
4. They are presented during the course of the *Opening Chant*.

MOTIF *a*

Motif *a*: mid-range *mi–fah–lah–soh* structure

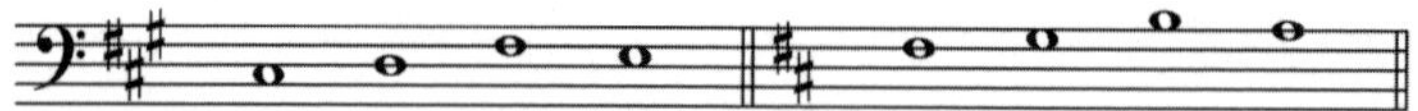

Motif *a1*: *doh-* and *soh-*based versions of *a*

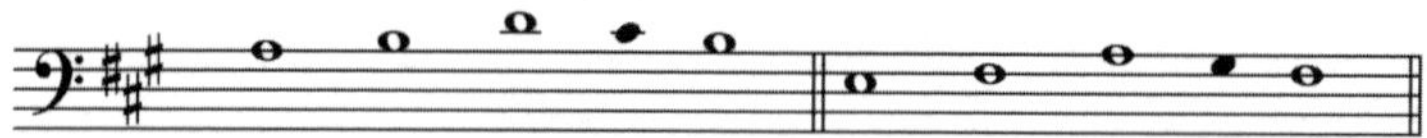

6.2 Peadar Ó Riada: *Aifreann Eoin na Croisc*, motif *a*

Five repetitions across four movements: three in *Opening Chant* (*Go mbeannaíthear duit* and *Admhaím do Dhia mhóir*); one each in *Ár nAthair – Síochái*n and *A Uain Dé*.

This is the motif that can most definitively be connected to the Irish sean-nós tradition, in which it appears as the distinctive *mi-fa-lah-soh* opening gesture of the Múscraí song *Aisling gheal*, a melody much admired by Ó Riada.[10] The composer had earlier employed it as the starting point for his setting of the Hail Mary, *Go mbeannaítear duit*.[11]

In *Aifreann Eoin na Croise* it is employed on three occasions in varying text-related capacities during the *Opening Chant* (bars 2, 34 and 35), as a short communion-rite congregational response (bar 83) and as the closing melodic gesture of the second 'A Uain Dé' invocation (bar 86). Transposed versions of the motif (a^1) operating from the primary structural pitches of *doh* and *soh* may be observed in bars 20 and 21 of the *Opening Chant*.

MOTIF *b*

Motif *b*: rising, accent-driven litanic cell, with broad range of melodic applications

6.3 Peadar Ó Riada: *Aifreann Eoin na Croise*, motif b

Twenty-four repetitions: fifteen throughout the *Opening Chant*, six in *Is Naofa* and three in *A Uain Dé*.

Motif *b* is a rising gesture capable of multiple adaptations and defined to a significant extent by its culminating pitch repetitions. In its initial configuration at the end of bar 2, it represents a mirror image of motif *c*, a kinship which is later summarised in the triple text repetitions which begin and conclude the *Is Naofa* setting:

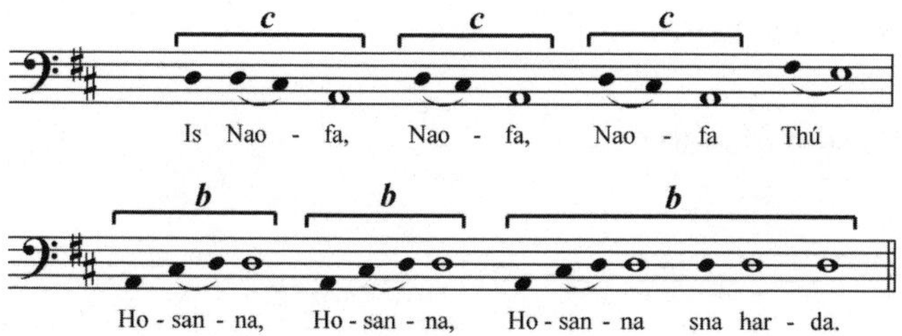

6.4 Peadar Ó Riada: *Aifreann Eoin na Croise*, bars 65 and 70

More typical, however, is its use in a melodically incremental way, as a carrier of various litanic sections contained in the *Opening Chant* (bars 7–9, 15–16, 25–32). The internal rising 'Hosanna's of *Is Naofa* (bar 68) maintain this litanic approach, and the rising repetitions of A *Uain Dé* (bars 85, 86 and 87) bring the process even further, as already suggested in the general analysis of the mass, from motivic adaptation towards 'transformation'.

MOTIF c

Motif *c*: descending *doh-ti-soh*-type cell, largely associated with litanic repetitions

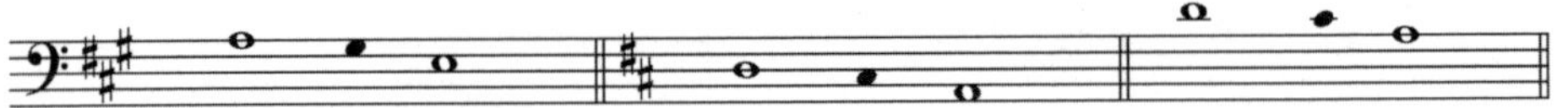

6.5 Peadar Ó Riada: *Aifreann Eoin na Croise*, motif *c*

Fifteen repetitions across five movements: five in the *Opening Chant* (*Go mbeannaíthear duit* and *Admhaím do Dhia mhóir*); three in *Salm 139*; three in *Is Naofa* and four in *Amen mór*.

The importance of this motif in the overall context of the mass may be seen in the composer's employment of it for the liturgically significant triple 'Is Naofa' and quadruple 'Amen' repetitions (bars 65 and 72). A characteristic Irish melodic gesture (*doh'-ti-soh*),[12] it also features prominently in *Salm 139*, in both refrain and verse. It first appears in passing in bar 3 of the *Opening Chant* (more fleeting appearances may be found in bars 67 and 69 of *Is Naofa*), before being properly announced and developed as part of the repeated cadential sequence *c* + *c* + c^1 (bars 4–5 and bar 33). Motif c^1, while undeniably derived from c, goes on to have an independent life of its own and its influence is considered below.

Motif c^1: melodic expansion of motif c

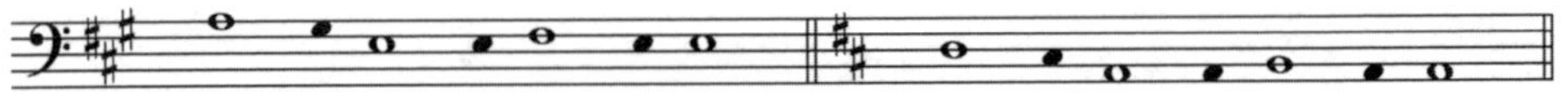

6.6 Peadar Ó Riada: *Aifreann Eoin na Croise*, motif c^1

Six repetitions across four chants: four in the Opening Chant (*Go mbeannaíthear duit*, *Bronnaim m'anam ort*, *Admhaím do Dhia mhóir*), one each in *Salm 139* and A *Uain Dé*.

First appearing in bar 5, and reprised in bar 33 as a cadential-type development of **c**, it is subsequently employed independently as a melodic opening for *Bronnaim m'anam ort* and *Admhaím do Dhia mhóir* (bars 19 and 24). A further application sees it woven in with the second and third phrases of the opening 'A Uain Dé' invocation (bar 85). The intonation-type motif c^1*var.* which begins the *Salm* (bar 37) and returns six bars later (bar 43) may be seen as a 'filled-in' version of c^1.

MOTIF *d*

Motif *d*: descending *doh–ta–la–soh* tetrachord

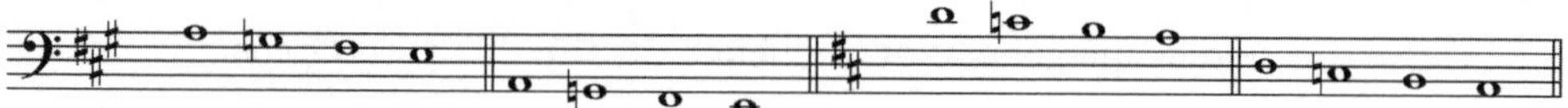

6.7 Peadar Ó Riada: *Aifreann Eoin na Croise*, motif *d*

Including modifications, ten repetitions across four chants: two each in *Opening Chant* (*Umhlaím duit / Im' chroí 'tá'n t-olc* and *Admhaím do Dhia mhóir*) and *Salm 139*; one in A *Uain Dé*; five in *An cosán draíochta.*

This four-note descending motif, characterised by the use of the flattened seventh (*doh-ta-lah-soh*) can also be identified in Seán Ó Riada's *Ceol an aifrinn*, in the hymn *Ag Críost an síol* (where it characterises three of the four phrases), and as the concluding melodic gesture of the *Agnus Dei* ('tabhair dúinn síocháin'). Though alluded to in the course of bars 10–15 of *Aifreann Eoin na Croise*, its first clear statement in this mass setting is reserved as a dramatic (in range as well as melodic content) conclusion to the large-scale *Opening Chant* (bar 36). It is used in an almost identical fashion at the conclusion of the verse of the mass setting's final piece, *An cosán draíochta*, another considerably weighty setting, throughout which the motif also appears (for the first time in the mass and to striking effect) transfigured into the d^1 sequence (*doh-ti-lah-soh*) (bars 91 (twice), 92 and 94). It appears in modified form (*soh-ta-lah-soh*) in the preceding A *Uain Dé* (bar 86), and closer to the middle of the mass setting, *Salm 139* (bars 45 and 47) contains further references of a passing nature (see discussion of motif e^3 below).

Distribution of Primary Motifs

Opening Chant:	a, a^1, b, c, c^1, d
Salm 139:	c, c^1, d
Aililiúia:	none
Is Naofa:	b, c
Amen mór:	c
Ár nAthair–Síocháin:	a
A Uain Dé:	a, b, c^1, d *var.*
An cosán draíochta:	d, d^1

The overall picture shows a well-balanced 'cento' or patchwork arrangement, with the primary motifs appearing fairly regularly throughout the composition. The appearances of motifs *a* and *d* in the *Opening Chant* are balanced by the recurrences towards the end of the mass setting. Motif *b* exerts a significant generative influence on the five-part *Opening Chant*, one which is resumed in the composition of the concluding mass ordinary movements, *Is Naofa* and *A Uain Dé*. Motif *c* and its development c^1 are the most pervasive, covering between them five of the eight movements.

Secondary Motifs (e^1, e^2, e^3, e^4, *f* and g)

The motivic categories e^1, e^2, e^3 and e^4 are united in their reliance on a basic pattern of melodic oscillation so elemental and variable as to be best described in terms of a motivic or formulaic 'system'.[13] Taken individually, however, none of the four motifs manages to fulfil all the requirements which would allow them to be included in the previous category of primary motifs. Motifs e^1 and e^2 will be seen to be limited both in distribution and text application. Motif e^3, while more varied, as we shall see, in its textual applications, does not make its first appearance until the *Salm*, thirty-eight bars into the composition. Motif e^4 appears as late as bar 48 and its incidences tend to be solely of an intonational/declamatory nature. Motifs *f* and *g* both provide examples of interesting textual application, some of which will be discussed later, but independent distribution of the motifs is relatively limited; and again, neither makes an appearance during the opening chant.

MOTIF e^1

Motif e^1: intonational oscillating structure

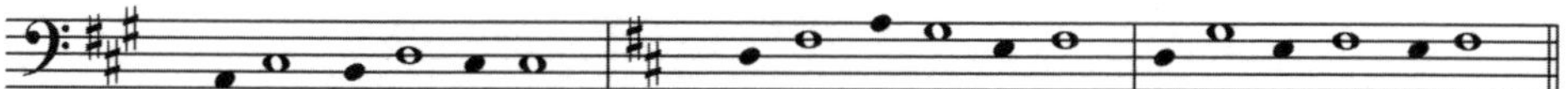

6.8 Peadar Ó Riada: *Aifreann Eoin na Croise*, motif e^1

Three statements: one in *Opening Chant (Go mbeannaíthear duit)*, one in *Salm 139* and one in *An cosán draíochta.*

This intonation-type phrase, centring on the movement between *mi* and *doh*, begins the mass setting (bar 1) and appears on two other occasions, at the beginning of the final couplet of the *Salm* verse (bar 50), and in a further modification at the beginning of the verse section of the communion hymn *An cosán draíochta* (bar 92).

MOTIF e^2

Motif e^2: cadential oscillating structure (*mi–doh*)

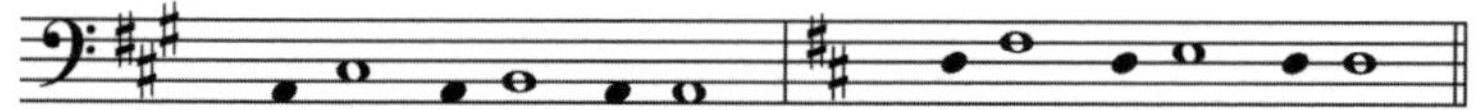

6.9 Peadar Ó Riada: *Aifreann Eoin na Croise*, motif e^2

Four repetitions across four chants: one each in *Opening Chant* (*Bronnaim m'anam ort*), *Salm 139*, *Aililiúia* and *An cosán draíochta.*

This typically traditional cadential figure appears as a tonal full-close to mark a structural division in the *Opening Chant* (bar 23),[14] and to conclude both the *Salm*-verse and *Aililiúia* (bars 51 and 54). In terms of melodic structure, it most closely resembles the tonally dynamic e^4 (bars 48–49) to which, it could be suggested, it presents a tonic resolution:

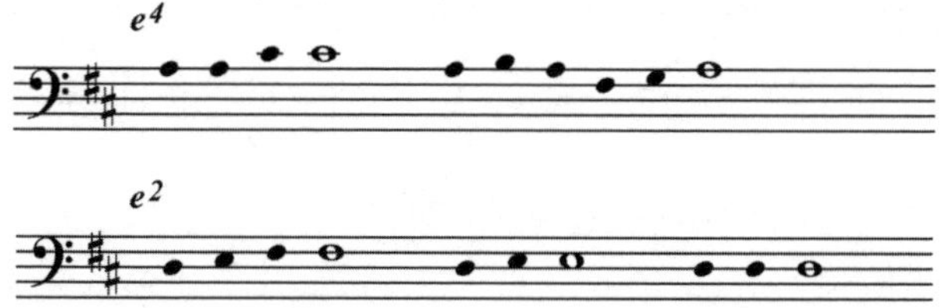

6.10 Example 6.9 – Peadar Ó Riada: *Aifreann Eoin na Croise*, Salm (bars 49 and 51)

MOTIF e^3

Motif e^3: intermediary oscillating structure (based on *ray*)

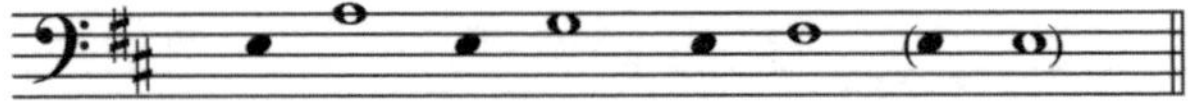

6.11 Peadar Ó Riada: *Aifreann Eoin na Croise*, motif e^3

Five repetitions across two chants: three in *Salm 139*; two in *An cosán draíochta*.

Foreshadowed in line two of the *Salm* refrain (bar 38), this *ray*-based oscillating motif appears in its most characteristic form in the second and fourth litany-style lines of the *Salm* verse (bars 42 and 44). It also appears in an answering/continuing context as the second line of *An cosán draíochta*, where its ending is tonally adapted down a step (bar 89). In this latter modification, e^3 most clearly reveals its structural indebtedness to motif *d*:

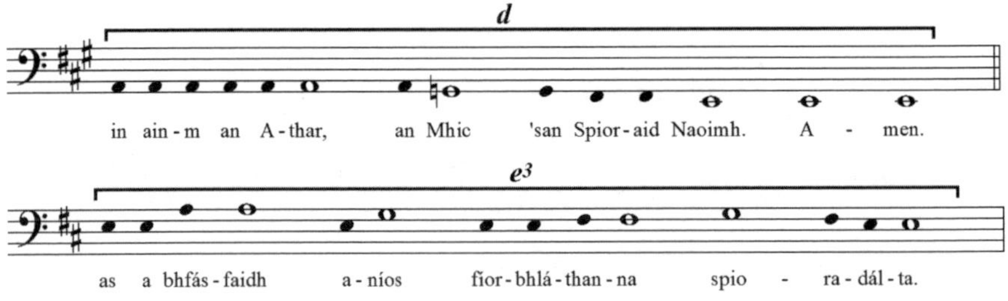

6.12 Peadar Ó Riada: *Aifreann Eoin na Croise* (bars 36 and 89)

The structural closeness of *e* and *d* is further highlighted in bars 45 and 47 of the *Salm* verse, where the two motifs seem to merge, to the point where it is difficult to designate in favour of one or the other.

MOTIF e^4

Motif e^4: intermediary oscillating structure (based on *soh*)

6.13 Peadar Ó Riada: *Aifreann Eoin na Croise*, motif e^4

Seven repetitions: two each in *Salm 139*, *Aililiúia* and *Ár nAthair–Síocháin*; one in *An cosán draíochta*.

Motif e^4 is a *soh*-based oscillating structure around whose foundational pitch a number of intermediary phrases operate. It exerts a considerable influence throughout a number of movements, appearing in litanic repetition later on in the *Salm* verse (bars 48 and 49), and in modified form in the *Aililiúia* (bars 55–57), *Is Naofa* (bar 69) and the *Ár nAthair–Síocháin* sequence (bars 79 and 82). A further adaptation appears in line three of *An cosán draíochta* (bar 90), taking the form of a transposed repetition (it preserves the directional changes) of the e^3 motif structure of the previous phrase.

MOTIF *f*

Motif *f*: cadential, *soh*–based rising fifth structure

6.14 Peadar Ó Riada: *Aifreann Eoin na Croise*, motif *f*

Four appearances across three chants: two in *Salm 139*; one each in *A Uain Dé* and *An cosán draíochta.*

Motif *f* is exceptional amongst all the motivic categories identified in relation to *Aifreann Eoin na Croise*, in that it is the only melodic figure to break through the natural tetrachordal structures within which the composer seems to habitually operate.[15] The motif, built around a rising dominant arpeggio, first appears in cadential form as the final phrase of the *Salm* refrain (bar 40). Its second such appearance occurs an octave higher, at the end of *A Uain Dé*, where it carries the textually modified final invocation (bar 87). This concluding musical gesture of *A Uain Dé* seems to have provided the inspiration for the immediately-ensuing *An cosán draíochta* which begins with the motif, adapted melodically and cadentially to suit the length and 'opening' nature of the phrase (bar 88). An earlier statement, modified to sustain a dominant tonal thrust, occurs as a preparation to the intense melodic climax of the psalm's verse (bar 46).

MOTIF g

Motif *g*: turn-like component of motif e^4

6.15 Peadar Ó Riada: *Aifreann Eoin na Croise*, motif *g*

Independently of e^4, of which it is a constituent part, two statements: both occur in *Is Naofa*.

Appearing throughout as the concluding melodic gesture of motif e^4, which is built on the dominant pitch A, this turn-like motif briefly gains its independence in *Is Naofa*, firstly re-framed as an opening gesture, and immediately re-stated in a transposed form incorporating the flattened seventh (bar 67). The characteristic configuration of the motif bears a fascinating palindromic resemblance to motif *a*, of which it might be described as a type of 're-combination':

6.16 Peadar Ó Riada: *Aifreann Eoin na Croise*, motifs *a* and *g*

The relationship between these motifs seems to find an echo in the following recommendation regarding the art of melodic composition, by Guido d'Arezzo, whose thoughts on the subject introduced this section:

> Diversity is reasonable if it creates a measured variety of neumes and phrases, yet in such a way that neumes answer harmoniously to neumes and phrases to phrases, with always a certain resemblance. That is, let the likeness be incomplete, in the manner of the outstandingly lovely chant of St Ambrose.[16]

Distribution of Secondary Motifs

Entrance Chant:	e^1, e^2
*Salm 139:**	e^1, e^2, e^3, e^4, f^1, g
Aililiúia:	e^2, e^4
Is Naofa:	e^4, g
Amen mór:	none
Ár nAthair/Síochháin:	e^4, g
A Uain Dé:	f
*An cosán draíochta:**	e^1, e^2, e^3, e^4, f

* The similarities in scale and tonality between these pieces have been noted earlier.

While none of its constituent motifs, as we have already noted, fulfilled all the necessary criteria for inclusion into the primary motivic category, the *e*-based motivic system, absent only from *A Uain Dé*, exerts a significant generative influence throughout the work, producing some twenty-six lines of music, and featuring strongly in the larger-scale compositions of *Salm 139* and *An cosán draíochta*.

Motivic Composition of *Aifreann Eoin na Croise*

The textual scale of *Aifreann Eoin na Croise* is of a different order to that of its predecessors in the Cúil Aodha tradition.[17] Leaving aside the pre-existing memorial acclamation and prayer of the faithful and those texts delivered on a monotone, the textual canvas chosen by the composer comprises some seventy-seven lines of unmetred prose, cast in a variety of mainly asymmetrical forms. The task of providing a solution which would render such a text (a) musically meaningful, and (b) possible for traditional singers to memorise and perform, called forth from the composer a response which may be termed 'traditional' in the widest sense of the word, in that it employs compositional procedures characteristic not just of Irish traditional music, but also observable in the broader field of oral literature and, by virtue of recent scholarship, the various repertories of western liturgical chant.

This section will consider the compositional make-up of *Aifreann Eoin na Croise* from a number of scholarly perspectives. These include the so-called 'oral-formulaic' theory advanced by Parry and Lord, the related questions of 'centonisation' and 'thrift' as interpreted by scholars of liturgical chant such as Willi Apel, Leo Treitler, Edward Nowacki and Paul Cutter, and, finally, the generative processes of folk music, in particular the Irish melodic tradition, viewed primarily through the work of James Cowdery.

THE ORAL: FORMULAIC THEORY: DISTRIBUTION AND CATEGORISATION OF MOTIFS

> It is most significant that there is no line or part of a line that did not fit into some formulaic pattern ... In other words, the manner of learning described earlier leads the singer to make and remake phrases, the same phrases, over and over again whenever he needs them. The formulas in oral narrative style are not limited to a comparatively few epic 'tags' but are in reality all pervasive. There is nothing in the poem that is not formulaic. (Albert Lord)[18]

So reads part of Lord's analysis of the Yugoslavian oral epic poem 'The Song of Baghdad' in his classic work *The Singer of Tales* (1960). Building on the work of his teacher, Milman Parry, on the question of orality in Homer's epic poetry, Lord confirmed Parry's discoveries through analysis of a surviving tradition of oral epic poetry, and from their combined scholarly work arose the so-called oral-formulaic theory. The above-quoted passage might well be applied to the music of *Aifreann Eoin na Croise*, the vast bulk of which, as we have seen, may be explained in terms of repeated melodic motifs operating at various levels and with varying degrees of significance.[19]

On this last point, and relating to the concept of a motivic hierarchy, Lord states that in oral epic 'the phrases for the ideas most commonly used become more securely fixed than those for less frequent ideas, with the result that the singer's formulas are not all of the same degree of fixity'.[20] His analyses further reveal that there are usually *four* principal, more stable formulas which carry 'the most common ideas of the poetry'.[21] This primary category of commonly used and therefore widely distributed formulas accords very well with the hierarchy of motifs which naturally emerged from the musical analysis of *Aifreann Eoin na Croise*, and which, most interestingly, also yielded an upper stratum of four primary motifs, so designated because of their pervasive influence throughout the work.

MOTIVIC ADAPTATION/TRANSFORMATION

> We shall see that the formulas are not the ossified clichés which they have the reputation of being, but that they are capable of change and are indeed frequently highly productive of other and new formulas. (Lord)[22]

Lord is referring here to the phenomenon of motivic adaptation which is intrinsic to oral narrative epic, and by which the singer/composer makes or re-makes traditional phrases to fit 'the idea of the moment, on the pattern established by the basic formulas'.[23] Observable throughout the motivic spectrum of *Aifreann Eoin na Croise*, this practice is most elementally evident in the *e* group – described earlier as a motivic 'system' – and in the multiple realisations of motif *b* which is continually adapted to suit emerging textual situations and surrounding melodic contexts.

Describing the traditional singer/composer's flexible relationship with the formula, Lord states further on in his work: 'The formulaic technique was developed to serve him as a craftsman, not to enslave him.'[24] Ó Riada's consistently flexible and free treatment of his motivic material would seem to bear this out. Another compositional phenomenon described by Lord (albeit in the context of larger-scale 'themes') is that whereby 'the singer is carried from one major theme to another by the demands for further action that are brought out in the developing of a theme'.[25] This process is mirrored very tellingly in Ó Riada's treatment of motif *b* from the triple 'Hosanna' repetitions which conclude *Is Naofa*, through the developing *A Uain Dé* invocations, eventually resulting in a thematic 'breakthrough', 'transformation', or 'crossing' to motif *f* on the final statement, and the subsequent maintaining of that theme for the opening of the following movement.

In attempting to explain the phenomenon of motivic transformation in Gregorian and other chant traditions, Theodore Karp, in his major work on orality in plainchant, draws on the insights of Lord and others in the field of oral literature: 'In various oral literatures there are tales that share one or more motifs. On occasion, narrators reaching a point common to two themes may suddenly switch from one framework to another. This is known as "crossing" or "mixing".'[26]

Having touched on specific questions concerning motivic hierarchy, distribution, adaptation and transformation observable in *Aifreann Eoin na Croise*, which, as we have seen, concur very closely with similar processes observable in oral literature, we now turn to the world of chant scholarship in search of further phenomenological parallels which may help to explain why Ó Riada's mass setting took the form that it did. In doing so, we will take some time to consider the related concepts of 'centonisation' and 'thrift', beginning with the first of these.

CENTONISATION

In observing the overall compositional picture of *Aifreann Eoin na Croise* the visual concept of 'cento' or 'patchwork' is one which is difficult to ignore. Pressed into musical service (having been borrowed, interestingly, from poetry) by chant scholar Paulo Ferretti in his book *Estetica gregoriana*,[27] it may be defined as a technique of 'composition by the synthesis of pre-existing musical units'.[28] This definition would seem to accord well with what we have already determined regarding the nature and origin within the Irish song tradition of Ó Riada's primary motifs. Willi Apel defines centonisation succinctly as a 'unified aggregate of … elements variously selected and combined'.[29] A more recent, more detailed definition has been suggested by Theodore Karp:

> … we might define centonisation as a creative procedure based on traditional methods of utilizing multiple formulaic systems. These may belong to one or more families; they have distinctive surface features and are used in a sufficient multiplicity of ways that in a panoramic survey of the pertinent genre a kaleidoscopic effect results.[30]

In an address to the 1983 International Symposium on Gregorian Chant, held in Washington DC, the Abbot of Solesmes, Dom Jean Prou, explains the phenomenon of centonisation in terms of a compositional response to the requirements of certain types of texts, in this case referring to material from the office antiphon repertoire:

> Next we find a new layer of composition, called *centonisation*, which freely makes use of the accentual formulas previously identified in the stereotyped melodies, together with other new connecting formulas. This enabled the preparation of custom-made musical garments for texts of less conventional size which could not be fitted to any of the ordinary fixed melodic patterns.[31]

The textual make-up of *Aifreann Eoin na Croise* certainly comes under the heading of 'less conventional size', albeit on a much larger and even more disparate scale than the more highly unified office antiphon repertory which Dom Prou is describing.

Reflecting on further possible causal factors for the existence of centonisation within the Gregorian tradition, Apel suggests the following: '... wherever encountered, it is obviously rooted in, or, at least, strongly influenced by a practical consideration, that is, to facilitate the task of the singer by reducing the melodies to a limited fund of formulae that can be memorized and applied according to the requirements of the texts'.[32]

Considering the challenges facing Ó Riada regarding the textual canvas of his mass, and the orally based nature of his choir, it is not entirely surprising that he should adopt a similar compositional technique, in the light of the challenges faced historically by oral composers of liturgical chant.

Apel's attempt to go beneath the surface of centonisation, and to explore the underlying reasons for its existence, is based on an instinctive grasp of the processes of oral composition and of the practicalities of liturgical performance, and it brings him in touch with the closely related phenomenon of 'thrift', which we shall now explore.

THRIFT

> Once a singer has solved a particular problem in verse-making, does he attempt to find any other solution for it? In other words, does he have two formulas, metrically equivalent, which express the same essential idea? (Lord)[33]

The above questions (to which his own studies provide the answer 'no') summarise Lord's application of the phenomenon of thrift, first identified by Milman Parry in his study of Homer's epic poetry.[34] Thrift, in the generally understood sense of economic and telling use of a limited fund of materials (usually in an ongoing, duration-extended context), would seem to be an appropriate term to use in relation to Ó Riada's musical setting of the extended textual tapestry which comprises *Aifreann Eoin na Croise*. This broader understanding of the term is implicit in Edward Nowacki's description of the compositional approach to the extensive body of Old Roman office antiphons which 'give the impression of a limited amount of material that is simply used over and over again'[35] and more explicit in his summary of Paul Cutter's application of the concept, also in relation to the strongly oral Old Roman repertoire. Cutter, he says 'accepts the characterization of the Old Roman versions as uniform, but attributes it to thrift, the tendency of singers asserting itself afresh in each performance, to rely on familiar patterns and avoid novelty'.[36]

Implicit in the discussion of any genre of plainchant, such as those referred to above, is the concept of an 'extended textual tapestry' demanded by the ongoing nature of liturgical celebration. Leo Treitler, taking his cue from the theories of James McKinnon, which suggest the creation of significant portions of the Gregorian repertoire in relatively concentrated and highly unified 'bursts', applies the Parry-Lord concept of thrift in the following terms:

> I have thought to recognize such a phenomenon in the tendency to sing [compose?] again what one has just sung in the same chant, in the office or mass, in antiphons for the same day, in the same cycle of feasts, and I have interpreted it in the light of the exigencies of oral performance. In his book, *The Advent Project*, James McKinnon has interpreted such clustering of melody-types within the same feast cycle as the musical counterpart, in a large-scale compositional project, of the narrative continuity – and therefore unity – of the liturgical texts.[37]

The notion of thrift, arising out of the 'exigencies of oral performance' and providing musical unity within the texts of a 'large-scale compositional project' brings us even more in touch with the type of concrete liturgical model which might provide the conditions for the emergence of a composition such as *Aifreann Eoin na Croise*.

The foregoing two sections have in some sense tried to interpret the broader artistic and cultural significance of *Aifreann Eoin na Croise*, through its undoubted connections with the processes of oral formulaic literature, and also through the lenses of centonisation and thrift, as applied to the study of western liturgical chant. Ó Riada's composition, however, exists within the very specific cultural context of Irish oral-tradition music, and it uses as its raw material the melodic heritage of that tradition. The third part of our reflection on factors governing the compositional make-up of *Aifreann Eoin na Croise* will focus on the question of formularity in Irish traditional music, primarily through the work of James Cowdery.

The Irish Melodic Tradition

'Formulae appear in most genres of folk music, although in some they are primarily responsible for the generation of overall form.'[38] So writes Philip Bohlman at the outset of his book *The Study of Folk Music in the Modern World*. Further on in his opening chapter Bohlman acknowledges the influence of the Parry–Lord oral-formulaic theory on folk music studies:

> This theory recognizes tremendous stability in small formulae, with wide-ranging variation and creativity in the performance of the entire epic … The long Yugoslav epics … illustrate the dual role formula plays as a mnemonic device and a catalyst for creativity. So important is this role that some scholars measure the extent of orality in folk music by the prevalence of formulaic structures.[39]

Referring specifically to the Irish melodic tradition, in a section entitled 'Motivic aspects of Irish music', Tomás Ó Canainn considers the phenomenon in the following terms:

> Some Irish music displays such an apparent unity in its musical design that one is forced to ask whether it is the result of a conscious attempt

> on the part of a composer to build up a piece of music from a short motif or it is due to an unconscious musical philosophy which dictates that development takes place by building on what already exists and letting the material expand homogenously.[40]

In his book *The Melodic Tradition of Ireland* James Cowdery considers in some depth the various processes at work in the creating, maintaining and developing of that tradition. Building on the work of Bayard and Bronson in the area of folk tune and repertoire analysis, Cowdery suggests that 'If we wish to understand this process, we must look for *principles* – the overlapping and flexible ways in which musicians work with their materials – rather than looking for categories to impose from the outside.'[41] Of the three principles identified by Cowdery as providing the most comprehensive explanation for the repertoire as it exists, the first two are as follows: (a) the *outlining principle*, in which melodies are analysed and compared primarily in terms of contour; (b) the *conjoining principle*, in which 'tunes grouped … have sections in common, while other sections differ'.[42]

The third principle observable in the Irish melodic tradition, and the one which is the most significant in terms of explaining the musical make-up of *Aifreann Eoin na Croise*, Cowdery calls the *recombining principle*, arising out of his contact with the work of Bertrand Bronson who states: '… the materials of folk-melody are common property to be *combined and recombined in ever-shifting ways*' [my italics].[43] Following this principle, Cowdery says that in our attempts to discover the unifying elements of the tradition by means of melodic analysis and comparison, 'we may compare sections to sections *and* wholes to wholes without requiring a fixed overall contour'. He then goes on to give an example from the tradition, comparing two apparently 'different' tunes:

> The two song tunes … sound like entirely different melodies; their general outlines do not correspond. However when we line them up in this way we can see that they are built from the same melodic moves or motifs which tend to be ordered in specific ways … all of the moves correspond one way or another, but their order is completely different. Thus we can begin to see the importance of the recombining principle. Through it,

> we may start to understand more completely the processes by which folk music continues to thrive and replenish itself. Of course, a given culture may be predisposed to certain kinds of melodic contours, but the actual *process* of composition is suggested by complex permutations based on melodic pools.[44]

Both Bronson's statement and Cowdery's elaboration of the principle of 'recombining' are based on material drawn from considerably large bodies of individual tunes, the composition of which gradually emerged over a considerable period of time by means of successive generations of musicians. In the light of this, the significant achievement of Ó Riada's composition, brought about undoubtedly by the considerable textual demands of *Aifreann Eoin na Croise*, is its apparent distillation of the tradition's melodic processes in order to meet those textual demands.

Text-Motif Relationships in *Aifreann Eoin na Croise*

The foregoing reflections have tried to concentrate on the more compositionally related, purely musical aspects of *Aifreann Eoin na Croise*, exploring questions of form and the use of formulae throughout the work and interpreting the evidence through scholarly work on orality, plainchant and Irish traditional music. However, as we saw, the question of textual influence on the music was rarely far away, featuring as it did in all three categories of discussion. This should not surprise us, because, over and above questions of formulaic construction, compositional process or choice of musical language is the fact that we are dealing with liturgical music, defined in the introduction to this study as 'a combination of music and words'. Edward Nowacki's important work on syntactical analysis of plainchant starts out from the premise that chant is a musical language with its own 'purely musical' rules of syntax, which he attempts to define. However, as his work progresses, he becomes increasingly aware of the equal significance of text in moulding and determining the final musical result:

> In this preliminary study, I have sought to describe pitch organization as an aspect of the theory of plainchant separate from questions of text

> declamation. As the theory is expanded to include rules for mapping the pitches generated by the syntactical system onto texts, it may be discovered that textual determinants interlock with rules of pitch organization in a complex way.[45]

Nowacki's acknowledgement of the complexities of the relationships between pitch and text evident at the heart of the Old Roman repertoire reminds us once more of Guido's 'double-melody' concept and John Stevens' question concerning the at times apparent 'non-relationship between music and words'. The following section, then, in focusing on certain aspects of text/music relationships in *Aifreann Eoin na Croise*, brings us back in touch with the essential nature of Christian liturgical music as a combination of music and words,[46] and with it, to one of the central concerns of this thesis, the nature of the relationship between the two.

The first part of this section will systematically trace the textual application of all seven motivic categories throughout the mass setting. The second part will concentrate in particular on relationships between musical motif and *textual syntax*, and between musical motif and *textual accentual pattern*, exploring both questions in the light of relevant academic scholarship. Of central interest here is evidence, following Peter Jeffery, for the flexible application of melodic motifs to the words, in a manner free from the constraints of both textual syntax and textual accent.[47]

PRIMARY MOTIFS

The appearance of motif *a* in a variety of different textual contexts, at line beginnings (bar 2) and endings (83, 86), and as carrier of extended complete lines (34, 35), has already been noted above. Text applications range from the purely syllabic (bar 83) right through to the fully 'recitational' (bars 34–35). The third, upper pitch of the melodic sequence is normally associated with a textually accented syllable, but the motif is judged flexible enough by the composer to carry the short four-syllable response 'agus leat féin' (bar 83), where the textual accents fall naturally on the first and last syllables.

Motif *b* is quite clearly an accent-driven cell, whose essential musical urge arises from the rhythmic characteristics (in this case defined by the concluding pattern: long-short-long) of certain word-groupings. Its free engagement with a broad range of syntactical elements, however, is clearly evident throughout the *Opening Chant*.

The textual applications of motif *c* display a variety of approach which is encapsulated in the opening line of *Salm 139*'s verse (bar 41). Here *c* is used to both open and close the line and, by being robust enough to recite on *either* the upper or lower notes of the motif, it is able to accommodate phrases of a markedly different accentual character.[48]

Motif c^1 likewise demonstrates variety of application, being flexibly used in the *Opening Chant* as both opening (bars 19, 24 and 37) and closing (bars 5, 33) gesture. Both functions appear to come together simultaneously towards the end of the mass, in A *Uain Dé*, where it is ingeniously re-cast, Janus-like, at the central 'hinge'-point of the opening three-part invocation (bar 85):

6.17 Peadar Ó Riada: *Aifreann Eoin na Croise*, bar 85

In its characteristic form (*doh'-ta-la-soh*), motif *d* invariably appears at phrase-endings. The most structurally and symbolically significant of these occur, as we have seen, at the end of the lengthy opening and closing movements of the mass. As in the case of motif *a*, we contrast the strongly 'recitational' opening statement (bar 36) with the more syllabic application of the motif which occurs at the end of the mass (bar 95). Returning to the question of structural positioning of the motif, we note that in its modified versions, e^3/d (compare bars 45 and 47) and d^1 (the *doh'-ti-lah-soh / fah-mi-re-doh*) sequence of bar 91, the motif functions equally in opening and concluding contexts.

The distinctive sequence $c + c + c^1$ appears twice, towards opposite ends of the *Opening Chant* (bars 4–5, bar 33), each time at the conclusion of a section of prayer. The textual applications, however, seem on the face of it to be completely different. Its first appearance accompanies the concluding rhetorically driven text repetitions 'ag guí orm, ag guí orm, ag guí orm féin inniu', while in the second case it is wedded to an unmodified line 'trína réabas de do dhlíthe is ded' aitheanta naofa'. However, when the context preceding the second (i.e. an extended urgent litany supported by short musical utterances) is considered, the composer's choice of musical expression seems to be a particularly apt means of bringing this impassioned litany in to land.

SECONDARY MOTIFS

The consistently cadential use of motif e^2 has already been noted. Consistent also are the four three-accent phrases in which it is employed. The intonational motif e^1 exhibits more potential for phrasal adaptation, as demonstrated by the four- (bar 1), three- (bar 50) and two-accent (bar 92) structures which it carries. Motif e^3 in its characteristic *e*-based form is largely associated with the 'answering' phrases of textual couplets. Initially connected with lines containing litanic elements (bars 42, 44), it re-emerges in the final movement, this time moulded to a non-litanic line (bar 89). The A-based motif e^4, on the other hand, normally appears in a 'setting-out' context (bars 55, 69, 81, 90), though the *Salm* contains one example (bar 48 followed by bar 49) where it fulfils both structural functions.

Motif *f* is used in both intonational and cadential contexts (compare bars 88 and 40), roles which it appears to fulfil simultaneously in the final invocation of *A Uain Dé* (bar 87). Motif *g* demonstrates a consistent accentual profile when it appears as an ancilliary component of e^4, but a notable exception occurs when, as an independent phrase-opening statement in bar 67, the accentual weight is distributed differently throughout the notes of the motif.

MELODIC MOTIFS AND TEXTUAL SYNTAX

> A number of chants employ the same motive at separate places for the close of different periods or sections, a phenomenon known as musical rhyme ... Occasionally the musical rhyme corresponds to, and is obviously prompted by, a 'textual rhyme' ... Usually, however, it is a purely musical device of structural organization and unification. (Apel) [49]

The structural use of special cadential and also initial formulae is a recognised feature of the Gregorian repertoire. One only has to recall certain 'typical' openings associated with mass or office antiphons of modes

1 and 7, for instance, or of typical cadential figures associated equally with the endings of chants in modes 1 and 5, or in modes 3 and 4. Apel makes mention above of the occasional appearance of internal musico-textual rhyme, but concludes that the formula is largely independent of the sound or content of the text and that its overriding function is as 'a purely musical device of structural organization and unification'. This last remark provides a useful starting point for some reflection on the nature of the distribution of musical motifs throughout the textual tapestry of *Aifreann Eoin na Croise*.

In establishing the primacy of each of the melodic motifs identified as *a, b, c*(1) and *d*, one of the clinching characteristics which marked them out was their association with a variety of textual situations. These ranged from couplet/line openings and closings, to complete couplets/lines and even occasional mid-stream appearances. The following passages involving *c*1 provide a relevant reminder of this variety of approach:

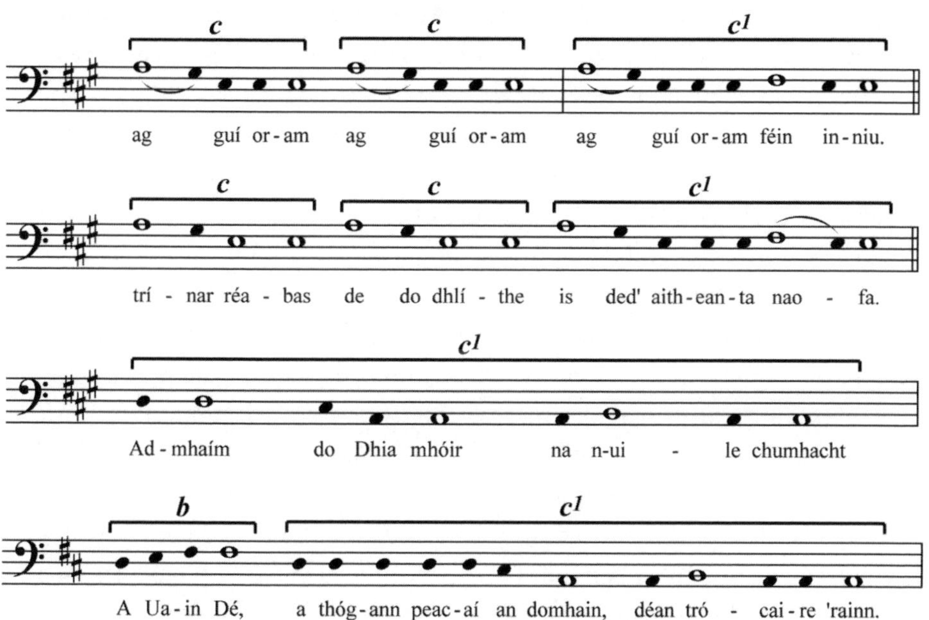

6.18 Peadar Ó Riada: *Aifreann Eoin na Croise*, bars 4–5, 33, 24, 85

We note first of all the way in which c^1 first emerges, as a natural response to the emphatic word 'féin',[50] to conclude a cluster of rhetorically driven repetitions. The resultant melodic cluster $c + c + c^1$ is next applied to a passage which features no elements of textual repetition. In these first two examples, c^1 appears as the conclusion, not just to a line or couplet but to a major section of text. Contrast this with its next appearance as the opening gesture of the extended, concluding prayer of the *Opening Chant*. Finally, and most intriguingly, we observe the introduction of the motif in mid-text flow, extended in the manner of a musical enjambement across a clear text division.

The apparent freedom of association, as evidenced by the above example, between primary melodic motifs and varied components of textual syntax brings us quite a distance, however, from the stereotyped and melodically distinct opening and closing formulae of, for instance, the Gregorian introit repertoire. Research into melody text relationships in other chant genres provides us with more helpful models. Apel refers to Ferretti's study of the tract repertoire in *Estetica gregoriana* for instance, which he says gives 'several examples showing how the standard phrases are modified according to the exigencies of the text, either by the interpolation of recitation passages or, occasionally, by splitting a neume into two shorter neumes'.[51] While this certainly demonstrates the adaptability of the musical formula to different text structures, the 'standard phrases' in question are limited to those from within a single liturgical genre, one in which the formula appears in musical sequence as a pre-determined element in a type of 'model melody'.[52] A similar situation obtains in the more stylistically related, mainly syllabic repertory of office antiphons where, in the case of fully centonised compositions, the motifs or set phrases tend to be syntactically determined.[53] A more helpful model of textually flexible formula has emerged from a recent doctoral study of the Old Roman offertory repertoire by Rebecca Maloy,[54] whose identification of the phenomenon was a crucial discovery enabling her to untangle the melodic structure of the offertories. The phenomenon, which she terms 'syntactical homonymity', is one 'which often operates in Roman formulas: some segments can serve more than one melodic function in the syntax. The multiple functions of a melodic segment are clearly differentiated by their position in the phrase and their occurrence in typical combinations with other segments.'[55] The musico-textual phenomenon of 'syntactical homonymity' more closely describes the behaviour of, for instance, motif *c*[1] above, and it is interesting that it should be identified within the context of the Old Roman tradition, a plainchant repertoire which possesses more pronounced oral characteristics.

MELODIC MOTIF AND TEXTUAL ACCENT

We can see how certain melodic cells are closely associated with repeated accentual patterns such as obtain in concentrated form in litanic passages (e.g. the beginnings of bars 6, 7 and 8), or, as has been noted in the case of motif *c*, for instance, are dispersed throughout the textual canvas. However, in contrast to this, we have also observed, at both upper and lower levels of the motivic hierarchy (specifically, motifs *a*, *b* and *g*), instances of melodic motifs engaging with radically different accent-patterns. The following examples involving *a* and *g* will serve as reminders. In the case of both, the motif is presented first in a more 'typical' accentual configuration, then in an 'adapted' form. The accented text syllables are italicised:

6.19 Peadar Ó Riada: *Aifreann Eoin na Croise*, bars 86, 83, 79, 67

This free association of the same melodic pattern with accentually varied textual phrases has a huge bearing on the question of the relationship between words and music as understood by a traditional composer. It demonstrates the resilience, adaptability and, to borrow a term from Albert Lord, 'usefulness' of the musical pattern, and, moreover, its independence of any previous or other rhythmic relationships with text structures. This phenomenon is highlighted in a medieval context by John Stevens in his comparison of the sequences 'Fulget dies' and 'Concelebremus' which are shown to feature different patterns of textual accent wedded to identical melodic phrases.[56] Reflecting further on the question, through analysis of the prose sequences of Notker, Stevens concludes:

> That Notker should permit such variation of verbal accent suggests strongly that he did not regard this melodic phrase as having a marked and inviolable rhythmic character of its own. This confirms the tentative conclusion reached above that in the prose sequences words and melody are reconciled to each other in an unforced recitatory or narrative manner.[57]

What we have observed thus far in our analysis of *Aifreann Eoin na Croise* (in textual essence, itself an extended 'prose sequence') would seem to suggest a strong link with the compositional aesthetic of medieval prose sequences, and further confirm Stevens' comments on the flexible nature of the relationship between melody and the rhythms of prose as observed in those sequences. In such an aesthetic, the melodic content of the motif tends to predominate, being judged resilient enough to receive multiple rhythmic realisations. Each new rhythmic 'spin' of the motif confers something new, both on the motif and on the text it is being newly applied to. The 'renewed' versions of *a* and *g* above certainly tell us much about the compositional aesthetic of *Aifreann Eoin na Croise*, and about the composer's flexible use of his materials. In considering the causal factors relating specifically to both of the above 'adapted' versions of *a* and *g*, however, one further observation needs to be made.

The above-quoted adaptation of the four-note motif *a* to the four-syllable 'agus leat féin', and of the six-note motif *g* to the six-syllable 'tá neamh agus talamh' brings the question of music/text relationships beyond considerations of representation, rhetoric, and even word accent, back once more to Stevens' basic reality of number, i.e. 'counting your syllables' and, in this case presumably, notes.[58]

We cannot leave the question of accentual/rhythmic adaptation of melodic motifs without first placing it back within the broader compositional framework of *Aifreann Eoin na Croise*. Staying with motifs *a* and *g*, we note that each 'adaptation' tends to occur after a number of repetitions of the motif in its 'standard' rhythmic form, suggesting the introduction of an element of 'variation' on the part of the composer. That this can be done without compromising the melodic shape of the motif is testament to the musical flexibility of the patterns that have been selected, and to the resourcefulness of the composer/craftsman. The crucial factor, however, is the decision to 'vary' or, more properly, 'adapt', instead of to 'invent'. Ó Riada's instinctive avoidance of new material at these points, well into the overall composition, and his reworking of pre-existing material, give us an insight into the mind-set of the oral composer, while at the same time bringing us back into contact with the associated phenomena of 'centonisation' and 'thrift'. As Leo Treitler states, (echoing Apel): '… performers [composers] in oral traditions tend … towards an economy in the number of constituent elements that need to be managed, such as the melodic formulae of chant'.[59]

Gloria VIII – A Compositional Parallel?

The preceding motivic analysis of *Aifreann Eoin na Croise* has focused primarily on three important questions: (a) the motivic composition of the mass, (b) the so-called 'free association' of melodic motif with textual syntax, and (c) the flexible relationship between melodic motif and textual accent. In relation to the question of motivic composition, insights were sought from the disciplines of oral literature and Irish traditional music studies. An overall backdrop, however, and a persistent framework against which to refer the various analytical findings lay in the pre-eminent and musically cognate liturgical repertoire of plainchant. While the characteristics of various chant genres and associated practices were used to shed light on certain compositional and aesthetic questions, no one category provided anything approaching a complete, pre-existing artistic model for *Aifreann Eoin na Croise*. Such an overall model would need to have the following characteristics: an extended, asymmetrical text; pervasive use of a limited fund of melodic motifs to sustain and unify that text and, finally, a free and flexible interaction of those melodic motifs with textual accent and syntax. Something approaching such a model, I believe, exists in the musical setting of Gloria VIII,[60] a later accretion to the core chant repertoire of mass ordinary movements. The following is the text, complete with motivic identifications:

6.20 Gloria VIII

Like *Aifreann Eoin na Croise*, Gloria VIII is built on four primary motifs: *a*, *b*, *c* and *d* (in this case there are no secondary motifs). Invoking Lord's proof of oral provenance, we note that there is nothing in the piece that is not formulaic.[61] The motivic phrases are combined, 'recombined' (Cowdery) and 'adapted' (Lord),[62] all according to the demands of the text. Motifs constantly operate independently of syntactical constraints and, crucially, of accentual considerations (compare for instance the first two appearances of motif *a* and motif *b*). In short, Gloria VIII appears to provide a notably comprehensive and concentrated liturgical parallel for the compositional processes at work in *Aifreann Eoin na Croise*.[63] By the same token, then, we may say that in terms of the nature of its composition the 'neo-Gregorian' Gloria VIII bears within itself many of the hallmarks of an orally based approach to the setting of liturgical texts.

Motivic Composition and Text-Motif Relationships: Summary

One of the principal aims of the overall analysis of *Aifreann Eoin na Croise* has been to observe the way in which music and text, as individual entities, relate to one another. The textual element of the mass is a pre-given entity, even if the composer has had some degree of choice in the selection of certain items (e.g. *Opening Chant*). The motivic analysis merely confirms that already instinctively known by Ó Riada and his singers (otherwise it would simply not work), i.e. that this is unified, coherent music, based on traditional material and methods of composition. Aspects of the nature of the music/text relationship, such as freedom of association between melodic motifs and syntactic and accentual aspects of the text, confirm to a certain extent the conceptual independence of the two in the composer's mind. That they work so successfully together brings us back to Guido's concept of 'double-melody' and to its application in the work of John Stevens on medieval monophonic song.[64] Referring in *Words and Music* to the musico-textual aesthetic of the medieval *lai*, Stevens describes the relationship in the following terms: 'Parallel to these [extremely varied] verbal patterns, and coinciding with them in their larger structures, are musical patterns: they have their own relations, echoes, contrasts, building up to a "net" of sounds that fits perfectly over the "net" of words but has a different mesh …'.[65]

This extremely effective, if not inspired image of complementary but distinctive layers seems a particularly apt description of the relationship of music and text in *Aifreann Eoin na Croise* together with its suggested compositional corollary, Gloria VIII, and it is one which is strongly echoed in the following description by Albert Lord of a similar relationship implicit in the art of the oral epic poet:

> In studying the patterns and systems of oral narrative verse we are in reality observing the 'grammar' of the poetry, a grammar superimposed, as it were, on the grammar of the language concerned … The formulas are the phrases and clauses and sentences of this specialized poetic grammar. The speaker of this language, once he has mastered it, does not move any more mechanically within it than we do in ordinary speech.[66]

Having thus considered various aspects of the motivic composition of *Aifreann Eoin na Croise* and the nature of the relationship of the constituent motifs with the liturgical texts, a final area of focus in this motivic analysis brings us back in touch with the melodic motifs themselves and to questions concerning their nature, content and origins.

Nature and Content of Melodic Motifs

Referring to the 'emic' reality of a culture of oral composition/ transmission in which the musical intentions of the composer must be fully in harmony with the sensibilities and capabilities of the performer, Leo Treitler suggests in relation to melodies in oral chant traditions that 'the same melodic properties that would have facilitated composing the chants would have facilitated remembering them'.[67] In another context Treitler refers to a third, related consideration, that of 'reception by the religious communities for which they were intended'.[68] In the case of the work under discussion, we might ask: what are the properties of the motifs selected (consciously or unconsciously) by Ó Riada to sustain this lengthy composition, at the same time ensuring its memorisation by the singers and reception by the community? We have already explored aspects of the motifs' musical flexibility and adaptability under different textual conditions, in other words their 'usefulness' to the composer, who seems to have adapted and manipulated them naturally and skilfully. But what of their musical and cultural content and origin? Warning against the dangers of a purely technical analysis of such orally based material, Lord states:

> … it seems to me that in confining ourselves to this method we tend to obscure the dynamic life of the repeated phrases and to lose an awareness of how and why they came into being. Are we not conceiving of the formula as a tool rather than as a living phenomenon of metrical composition?[69]

Further on in his study of oral epic composition, Lord contends that formulae were selected and retained not out of considerations of mere compositional usefulness, but because of their content, their 'traditionally intuitive meaning'.[70] These views are echoed in a more specifically musical context by Leo Treitler, who says the following of motivic formulae:

> For the features that had mnemotechnical utility were not marked as such. That is they were the very stuff itself, not some attached handholds for the memory … If a particular corpus in oral tradition has an arsenal of formulae that arose in response to mnemotechnical needs, that says something about their genesis. But as sayable or singable groups they must have had a sensible function within the context of an epic or song that went hand in hand with their mnemotechnical function.[71]

In the case of *Aifreann Eoin na Croise* we can clearly see that the melodic motifs not only contribute to the unity and oral performability of the music, they are indeed 'the very stuff' of the music itself. As to their content, we have already identified the primary motifs as being drawn from a living, meaningful tradition of song embedded in the distinctive culture of an Irish-speaking community. In relation to the question of 'reception' by the Cúil Aodha choir and community, we have, coupled with the testament of the ongoing liturgical tradition, observations such as the following from Mícheál Ua Duinnín, distinguished sean-nós singer and native son of the area, concerning the musical content: 'You sense that this thing has come straight up out of Loch Uí Bhogaigh.'[72] This mirrors Peadar Ó Riada's own understanding of the shared musical-cultural framework within which he and his singers operate: 'You don't teach them songs or hymns: you draw it out of them.'[73] Ó Riada's selection of these culturally organic, inherently repeatable and adaptable musical gestures or 'sayings', and his free application of them to liturgical texts, is given a more universal framework in this concluding reflection by Dom Jean Prou on the nature, content and purpose of melodic motifs within the Gregorian chant tradition:

> The melody thus seems to translate not word colours (and indeed how could it do so since in the stereotyped melodies the same melodic formula is used for entirely different texts?), but the sapiential character of the text. The 'wisdom of nations' has always liked to condense its experience into sayings in which under the impact of clashing words, an idea sparkles. And God's Wisdom has seen fit to have recourse to the same process, using dense and striking expressions, apparently stereotyped, but, in actual fact, sources of inexhaustible vitality. The schemes (which are at once rhythmical and logical) of these 'sayings' were 'canonised', so to speak, and came to constitute an arsenal of ready-made formulas, a collection of tested and approved *moulds* [my italics], the product of natural selection, placed at the disposal of sages and ready to serve as the receptacles of their thought. The melodies of our stereotyped antiphons are the musical equivalent of these literary formulas; they have all the exactness, elegance and conciseness of maxims easy to memorise; they constitute the classics of the repertory and one can hear them again and again without ever growing tired of them.[74]

7
Vernacular Chant: Models, Modes and Motifs

Introduction

The essential definition of Christian liturgical music as a combination of music and words has underpinned this study from the outset.[1] The words underpinning the compositions of the combined Ó Riada corpus under investigation may be categorised under the following broad headings: scriptural, liturgical and devotional. Apart from a relatively small number of metrically crafted texts associated with the last category (though by no means comprising the whole category), the overriding textual reality has been that of prose. In this first and crucial respect, then, may the subject material of the study be proposed as a genuine continuation of the traditions of Roman rite liturgical music.

In chapter two, attention was focused on the aesthetic similarities of the relationship between music and words within the monophonic traditions of plainchant, medieval song and traditional Irish song. The nature of the relationship revealed placed music at the service of textual *structure* and, to an even greater extent, *number*, while at the same time remaining free of any overtly emotional or referential obligations to textual *content*. This general aesthetic backdrop formed a useful lens which, when later applied to the altogether new musico-textual reality underlying the Ó Riada corpus, revealed a similar set of relationships at work.[2] At the heart of the enterprise lay the inescapable reality of number, as expressed in the random patterns of scriptural, liturgical and native prose, which provided the textual given for the composers. Fidelity to the physical form of the traditional text is a noteworthy feature of the Ó Riada collection, thus providing another foundational link with Roman liturgical practice: that of *through-composition*. The traditional musical language employed by both men in accommodating the constantly changing structural and numerical realities was shown to be extremely flexible, subtle and responsive to the patterns of word-boundary. More than that, however, as the language of a living tradition it may be said to uphold the words in a positive and, above all, musically convincing way. Nothing less would, in fact, be tolerated by the native singers charged with delivering this music on an ongoing liturgical basis. As John Stevens suggests in relation to the melodic architecture supporting the large-scale and textually irregular courtly chansons of the Middle Ages: 'In the last resort, we have to feel it *as music* …'.[3]

The duality of purpose inherent in liturgical music which requires it to be true to the nature and demands of the text on the one hand, and true to itself as music on the other, puts into context the challenge facing those who would compose for the liturgy. This duality is echoed in the Guidonian concept of 'double-melody', a concept which has received multiple applications during the course of this thesis, because of its enduring usefulness as a metaphor for monophonic music text relationships. The concept, arising out of a flourishing medieval context of liturgical chant, attests to the close structural connection which must exist between music and text, but also to the demands of artistic unity, balance and wholeness which apply to the musical composition itself.[4]

Models

In the mass ordinary of Seán Ó Riada's *Ceol an aifrinn*, which as we have seen, corresponded closely in compositional intention with the through-composed models of Gregorian chant, musical unity was achieved across a broad range of asymmetrical forms, largely by the effective use of the elemental chant-related device of recitative. Employed almost exclusively to carry litanic sections (including, as we saw, those found in the native *Iontróid* text), recitative was shown to function in a tonally dynamic way, interspersed with more purely melodic elements and integrated into the broad melodic frame, typical of Munster traditional song, selected from the outset by the composer.

Over the past fifty years liturgical recitative has been most characteristically employed as a means of carrying the rich and compositionally challenging multiplicity of psalmodic texts which now form part of the Roman Lectionary. An early post-Vatican II publication, *The Simple Gradual for Sundays and Holy Days*,[5] reveals a link with the past in its inclusion of two-line chant-style recitation formulae by Dom Gregory Murray, and signals a new way forward in the four-line recitative-based tones of Joseph Gelineau, which, to this day, remains the pre-eminent model for vernacular chanted psalmody.[6] Such melodic formulae, while offering a practical and liturgically viable solution, remain at the level of pre-cast musical moulds into which words are poured, and their use of recitative therefore differs from the more flexible and dynamic approach which works so successfully in *Ceol an aifrinn*. In terms of compositional affinity, a close and successful recent parallel to the Ó Riada combination of the principle of 'dynamic recitative' with large-range, melodically developmental forms may be found in the through-composed English vernacular psalm settings of Ronan McDonagh, a contemporary liturgical composer also working consciously within a traditional Irish musical aesthetic. The following is his setting of Psalm 64 (melody line and text only):[7]

7.1 Ronan McDonagh: *Psalm 64*

McDonagh's natural sensitivity to phrase boundary and textual accent, exhibited above, extends also the broader arena of textual form, and his Irish vernacular setting of the *Sanctus* provides a worthy successor to the through-composed model first established in *Ceol an aifrinn*:[8]

7.2 Ronan McDonagh: *Sanctus*

Through-composition, without alteration, of given mass ordinary texts is established in the earliest syllabic examples of Roman-rite liturgical chant and it accords well with the foundational Christian liturgical concept of *logike latreia* or 'rational praise'.[9] This concept, which informed the deliberations of the Council of Trent on the purpose of liturgical music,[10] was invoked once again for the church of the twentieth century in clear and forceful terms: 'The liturgical text must be sung just as it stands in the authentic books, without changing or transposing the words, without needless repetition, without dividing the syllables, and always so that it can be understood by the people who hear it.'[11] By this principle is not only the content of the texts, but also their form and character preserved from the undue influence of purely musical considerations. The text-driven approach instinctively adopted by Seán Ó Riada and, subsequently, by Ronan McDonagh raises important questions about contemporary vernacular musical approaches to given liturgical texts such as the 'Holy, Holy'. In recent decades it has become acceptable to use text-repetition as a means of evening out irregular, asymmetrical ordinary texts into a shape that readily fits into a pre-cast musical song form, in effect changing the essential nature of the liturgical element.[12] This approach, which may be viewed positively by some as making certain liturgical elements more accessible to assemblies,[13] has been critiqued by Gelineau in the following terms: 'There is always the temptation, however, to judge a song for the liturgy by its music first. This approach risks blurring other ritual and communal aspects of the piece. This may explain why, since the council, we have generally neglected the broader field of chant and have, instead, emphasized songs.'[14] Gelineau goes on to argue that the standardising of the formally distinctive liturgical texts of the mass ordinary by means of a 'one-size-fits-all' musical approach represents a serious impoverishment to both music and liturgy, and signals a significant fracture with the Church's musical tradition. By contrast, the combined Ó Riada corpus investigated in this study convincingly demonstrates the benefits of a strong contact with tradition, proven in the absolute ease and flexibility with which the native musical language can accommodate a multitude of textual forms, so that, in the words of Vatican II, 'the new forms … grow organically from forms that already exist'.[15]

Modes

> When you hear what can be done, people haven't realized the possibilities of melody at all. (Seán Ó Riada)[16]

In Seán Ó Riada's *Aifreann 2*, we saw the composer selecting and committing to a particular and potentially fruitful scalar structure, and going on to inventively explore, according to the nature and requirements of the liturgical texts, the varied modal possibilities presented within that structure. Thus was musical unity maintained and at the same time variety achieved. A striking characteristic was the composer's freedom in the choice of final notes. This freedom had already been hinted at in Ó Riada's varied use of upper and lower tonic and middle fifth degrees as concluding pitches in *Ceol an aifrinn*, and the concept of modal ambiguity involving tonic, dominant and subdominant degrees has also been noted in relation to Peadar Ó Riada's *Aifreann Eoin na Croise*, a composition distinguished by its sensitivity to the natural tetrachordal divisions of the scale. The tetrachordally based Gregorian modal system of *D*, *E*, *F* and G finals, representing a type of distillation of the theoretical possibilities available within the diatonic scale, itself presents a tonal horizon going far beyond our more limited received contemporary notions of major and minor keys. The true nature of chant modality, however, is even more varied and elusive. The evidence presented in chapter two attested to the presence of modal fluctuation within individual compositions (bi-modality) and recent chant studies in the area of 'archaic modality' have questioned the importance of the role of the final in the minds of those involved in creating the repertoire before the age of written transmission. This attitude is given credence by studies in the oral transmission of folk music, which stress the importance of contour over final. All of this serves to underline the enormous and enduring potential of the diatonic scale placed at the service of monophonic composition for the liturgy. Composers who maintain a strong contact with either Gregorian chant or monophonic traditional song gain access to this world of subtle and sophisticated tonal relationships and become more aware of the potential they contain. Consider the elusive and extremely effective modal relationships inherent in the following recent setting by Ronan McDonagh traditional musician and organist of one of a number of Irish churches which maintain a regular commitment to the performance of Gregorian chant:[17]

7.3 Ronan McDonagh: *Come, adore this wondrous presence*

The notion of 'open-ended' tonality frequently associated with the modes of plainchant and having obvious symbolic implications within the ongoing and inherently incomplete nature of liturgical worship (either as a totality or as expressed in any given ritual gesture) is probably most clearly paralleled in the Irish musical tradition by the existence of the *soh*-mode. This mode is calculated by Breandán Breathnach as accounting for approximately fifteen per cent of our native melodies, being second only to that of the major-oriented *doh*-mode. This *soh* tonality, effectively distilled in the very first mass ordinary movement of the Ó Riada corpus, the *Kyrie* from *Ceol an aifrinn*, has since proven a fertile ground for Irish liturgical composers. It appears in its most characteristic form in Fintan O'Carroll's classic Irish-language setting of Psalm 23 '*Sé an Tiarna m'aoire*, the refrain of which appears below:

7.4 Fintan O'Carroll: *'Sé an Tiarna m'aoire*

O'Carroll utilises the distinctive properties of the *soh*-mode in a different and more declamatory way in his *Mass of the Immaculate Conception*,[18] where it concludes, at the fifth *above* the tonic, his settings of the Gloria and memorial acclamation:

7.5 Fintan O'Carroll: *Memorial Acclamation*

Motifs

O'Carroll's finely crafted mass setting, which also employs upper and lower *d* as final, is even more interesting for its consciously *referential* use of melodic motifs expressing the contrasting textual dynamics of declamation and petition. Thus, for example, the triple Kyrie and Agnus Dei litanies make use of the same succession of concentrated melodic figures, while the Alleluia, 'Hosanna' (Sanctus) and memorial acclamation are characterised by a rising arpeggio shape (see previous musical example).

The use of motifs in a less textually referential and more traditional manner may be observed in Seóirse Bodley's *Mass of Peace*,[19] a setting whose manner of construction recalls the frequent use of limited materials identified earlier in relation to the compositional processes of Old Roman chant.[20] The composer's ingenious re-use of complete motifs and motivic fragments in his setting of the Gloria results in a highly unified and convincing composition, prompting comparisons with the plainchant Gloria VIII, discussed in the preceding chapter.[21] Most of the motivic material is contained in the music of the opening couplet:

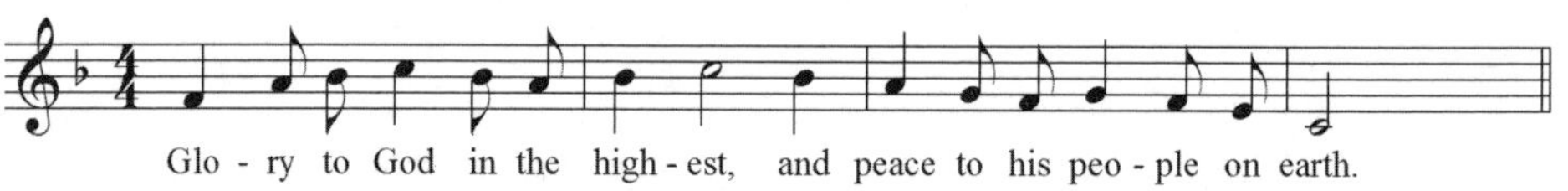

7.6 Seóirse Bodley: *Gloria* (bars 1–4)

Even more liturgically potent, however, is Bodley's monophonic setting of the Sanctus from the same mass, a composition which presents in model form a positive distillation of all the major questions associated with this thesis – prose, number, through-composition, motivic construction, modality and the aesthetics of text/music relationships:

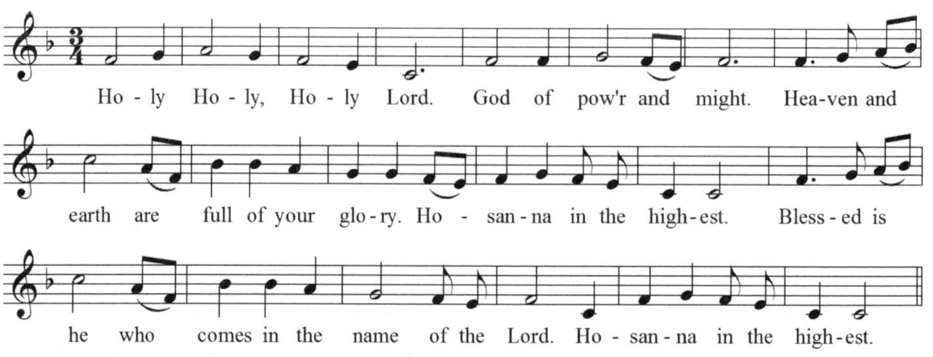

7.7 Seóirse Bodley: *Mass of Peace, Holy Holy*

The asymmetrical nature of the text is obvious, and its prose rhythms are articulated by the numerically random pattern 4, 3, 4, 2, 5, 2. Bodley adopts a through-composed approach, avoiding any text repetition or adaptation. The opening two lines duplicate material from the mass's Alleluia and Amen sections, and the remainder of the setting is built on ascending and descending motifs found earlier in the Gloria. The second of these motifs, an 8-7-5 melodic pattern, articulates the natural textual division and the conclusion, placing the music clearly in an open-ended *soh*-mode tonal dynamic. Most interesting of all, perhaps, is the referentially free use of this descending motif to carry the repeated phrase 'Hosanna in the highest'.[22] In this setting of the Sanctus the character of the text's accentual 'music' is sensitively maintained, while running alongside it is a melody possessing its own closely aligned, yet independent, musical integrity. To borrow once more the significant phrase from Guido d'Arezzo, we are 'doubly charmed by a twofold melody'.[23]

The raw material (characteristic Irish phrases), modal flexibility (oscillating between *doh* and *soh* modes) and thrifty compositional approach of Bodley's *Mass of Peace* combine in a natural and unforced manner with the liturgical texts of the mass ordinary to produce a number of model settings which retained a validity and currency in Irish liturgical celebrations right up to the advent of the 2011 *Roman Missal*, with its revised translations.[24] Its style, aesthetic and, above all, compositional make-up place it as the native mass setting which stands in nearest relationship to the culminatory work of this thesis, Peadar Ó Riada's *Aifreann Eoin na Croise*. The sheer scale of the latter, however, places it in a somewhat different position. The huge textual canvas of Ó Riada's mass demands by its very nature a more richly patterned musical response, one in which, it may be said, a broader array of motifs is more freely combined and adapted to take account of the simultaneous demands of textual structure and overall melodic architecture. In *Aifreann Eoin na Croise*, a mass composed for a specific occasion and in honour of a specific personage, we note a distinct shift of textual emphasis away from the mass ordinary (the mass, for example, lacks settings for the Kyrie and Gloria) towards the notion of the proper, as expressed in the John-oriented communion hymn, the apt responsorial psalm and above all in the series of spiritually 'appropriate' native prayers woven together by the composer to form the epic opening chant.

The Challenge of the Roman Proper

The care taken by early Christians in the selection of appropriate texts for specific liturgical celebrations was another expression of the concept of 'rational praise' which lay at the basis of their worship.[25] This principle would find ultimate expression in the full-blown repertoire of Roman proper antiphons, selected in accordance with the kaleidoscopic, constantly changing thematic nature of Christian liturgical celebration, and constituting by far the more significant and more characteristic feature of the heritage of western plainchant. An early and clear preference for scripture, in both its content and in its sober, non-metrical form, also lay the foundations for future Roman-rite practice, as acknowledged by Josef Jungmann in his masterly work *The Mass of the Roman Rite: its origins and development*:

> … hymnody, composed on the principles of metre and strophe, which was introduced about the time of St. Ambrose, was not admitted to the Roman Mass for over five hundred years. At Rome a strict rule was observed in the face of the wild and crafty song-propaganda of Manichean and Gnostic groups: We use only the songs dictated by the Spirit of God himself.[26]

The extremely rich theological basis from which the Roman proper antiphon tradition emerged has recently been explored by the Hungarian musicologist László Dobszay, who notes the centrality of psalmody at the level of content (the Book of Psalms is the direct source for the majority of antiphon texts) and structure (the Roman antiphon normally alternates with carefully selected psalm verses). Dobszay's reflections also dwell on the question of the received textual *form*, from which, he argues, textual content cannot be easily separated, without significant loss to the liturgy and those who participate in it. Selecting examples from the introit repertoire of Ascension, Easter, Advent and Lent he goes on to make the following observations:

> All these examples have one thing in common. Someone *speaks* in them. Now, when we listen to a strophic hymn, this precise effect of *locution directa* is diminished, in fact disappears completely. When we sing even

> the finest hymns, we feel they are the compositions of a poet – it is the poet who speaks in these chants. And that difference is a consequence of the *form*. There, the flow of thoughts, the length and linkage of phrases, the selection of words is defined and determined by the poetic form, by its rhythmic structure and rhyme. The strophic poem is *artefactum*, an artificial construct, an artistic opus. And when the result is not of the highest quality either as regards its theological or poetical dimension, then we sense even more vividly that the necessities of the poem direct the thought, rather than *vice versa*. One does not need at all to despise sung poetry in hymns, even those of extra-liturgical origin, in order to recognise that hymns can never be such speech-like texts as one finds in free biblical prose.
>
> Since the chants of the Mass proper, with but few exceptions, are based upon biblical texts, they are, again with but few exceptions, manifestations of a 'spiritual speech' rather than 'poems'. Finding their own pleasant articulation, they proceed with the naturalness of speech: the singer can take it on his lips as speech delivered in a special way. This is what Ewald Jammers meant when he affirmed that 'Man does not "compose" music to God's word; instead, he pronounces it. And he does so at worship by speaking not in the language of the everyday, the language of the marketplace, but rather in a solemn singing voice.' Psychologically, the prose form always approximates speech more closely; when pronouncing a text of this kind, we feel more easily that we are *praying*. This is not to say that prayers in strophic form cannot be uttered with a prayerful mentality. But even then, there always remains something that reminds us: we are speaking 'in quotation marks.'[27]

Dobszay's description of the above antiphons as a series of prayer-oriented prose texts set to music underscores the significance of the concept, apparently independently and instinctively arrived at by Peadar Ó Riada in setting the series of native prayers which constitute the *Opening Chant* of his *Aifreann Eoin na Croise*. The Hungarian church musician's observations, published some forty years after the Vatican II *Sacrosanctum concilium*, and following a lifetime of engagement with chant scholarship and practice at the highest level, provide useful and timely reminders of the richness at the heart of the Roman-rite liturgical music tradition.[28]

An awareness of this richness amongst English-speaking musicians, poets and liturgists, combined with critical appraisal of patterns of vernacular musical worship which had become established in the intervening decades since Vatican II, informed and inspired a major project undertaken in the 1990s by the International Commission for English in the Liturgy (ICEL). Commission member Margaret Daly-Denton sets the context for us. In a 1998 article entitled 'Psalmody as "Word of Christ"' she notes:

> Recent years have seen a considerable change. The singing of the Roman psalm-based chants is confined mainly to monasteries. In Catholic parish worship, psalmody has, to a great extent, been eclipsed by hymnody. During the early stages of the liturgical movement, Roman Catholics looked to the experience of the Christian churches which had long since established a vernacular musical repertory, notably the Anglican and Lutheran communions. From them they adopted vernacular hymns. In the days when singing of the people was barely tolerated, as it were, on the fringes of the liturgy, the 'four-hymn' pattern evolved – entrance, offertory, communion, and recessional hymns. One of the side effects of this was to establish a presupposition that the hymn should comment on the liturgical action during which it is sung. Thus we had a proliferation of gathering songs for the entrance, offering songs for what was then called the offertory, 'eucharistic' songs for the communion procession, and missioning songs for the recessional ... Something valuable has been lost – the breadth, the biblical richness, the capacity of an unexpected entrance or communion antiphon to challenge and stretch us beyond our presuppositions. The Roman entrance and communion antiphons were, of course, translated for the Missal of Paul VI [dating from 1974], but, shorn of the psalm verses to which they should have been refrains and frequently rendered in musically unworkable translations, they did not inspire significant numbers of composers. Consequently the directive in the *General Instruction* that the entrance or communion antiphon should be regarded as the first choice was 'more honour'd in the breach than the observance.'[29]

ICEL's response was to include, within the broader context of the preparation of a *Revised Sacramentary*, an *Antiphonary*, newly translated from the Latin, containing over six hundred entrance and communion antiphons with recommended psalm verses to be sung with them. While ICEL's overall proposal was ultimately rejected by the Roman Congregation for Divine Worship, the spirit which animated the *Antiphonary* project, i.e. that of making the liturgical propers more musically and liturgically accessible, had much to recommend it. The re-translated propers eventually ratified by Rome and published in the 2011 *Roman Missal* constitute a huge repertoire of prose texts functionally oriented towards song. Now that such a large body of vernacular, multiform and metrically random material has once more been made available and presented to composers, what type of musician is likely to be equipped for such a challenge, and what type of musical approach may be expected to yield success on a large scale?

Vernacular Chant: Limited Understandings

One possible starting point for those attempting to undertake this challenge might be that exemplified by the following passage from Vatican II's *Musicam sacram*, from a section entitled 'Preparing Melodies for Vernacular Texts': 'In composing these, musicians will consider whether the traditional melodies of the Latin liturgy ... can inspire the melody to be used for the same texts in the vernacular.'[30]

While this passage in fact refers primarily to ritual texts involving priest and people, and its principles were carried through with a certain amount of success in the Paul VI *Roman Missal* of 1974, the practice of using the melodies of Gregorian Latin propers as starting points for settings of their vernacular counterparts has for many years had a certain currency among monastic and religious communities.[31] This compositional paradigm may be seen as early as Rev. George Herbert Palmer's 1926 publication *The Diurnal Noted from the Salisbury Use*, compiled with the intention of making the riches of the chant proper tradition accessible to his companions in the Anglican 'Community of the Resurrection'.[32] The following example, from a later publication, illustrates the approach:

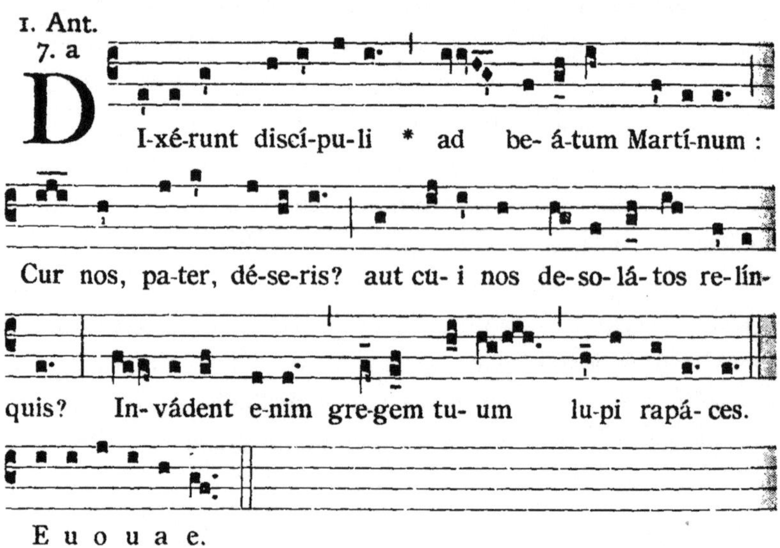

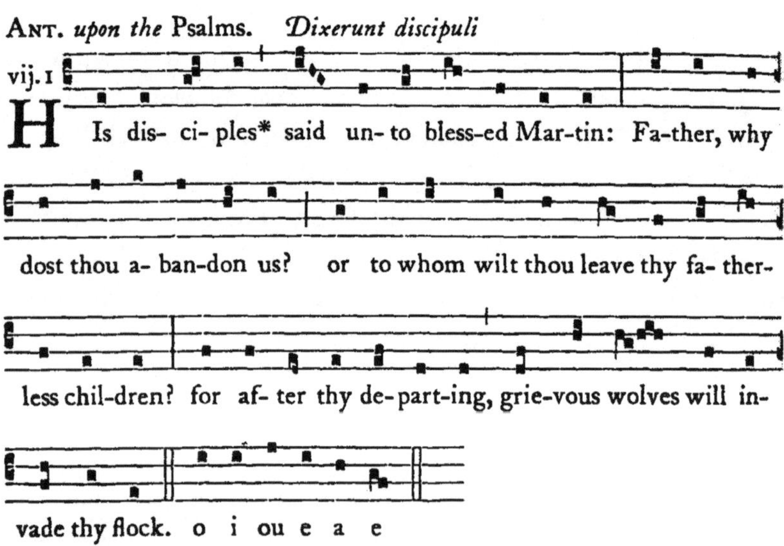

7.8 'Dixerunt discipuli' from Roman *Antiphonarium pro diurnis horis* (1924).
'His disciples said' from Rev. G. H. Palmer's *The Order of Vespers throughout the Year* (1947).

The paradigm underpinning the Wantage publication, which continues to exert a significant governing influence on received notions regarding the concept of 'vernacular chant', is undoubtedly the model for Bruce E. Ford's *American Gradual*, a major collection of vernacular propers for the church year, in which, crucially, specific *melodic* examples from the Gregorian tradition are taken as the compositional starting point.[33] The foreword to a similarly inspired collection of vernacular propers, *By Flowing Waters*,[34] acknowledged by the composer, Paul F. Ford, as an attempt at a vernacularised *Graduale simplex*,[35] clearly states the position: '*By Flowing Waters* attempts to make it possible for an American congregation to sing English words which fit easily into the old chant melodies.'[36] In the Introduction to his book, Paul Ford goes on to state regarding the proper elements that: '… its whole aim is to allow the music which expressed the meaning of the original words to try to convey the same meaning to those who speak English.'[37] Ford's broader intentions regarding the restoration of the sung vernacular proper are laudable. His introduction acknowledges the pre-eminence of the scriptural words and the melodic richness of the plainchant tradition. His compositions display a competent knowledge of the melodic structures of that tradition. Yet, by comparison with the vernacular chant compositions discussed in this study, the result seems markedly unconvincing.[38] This, in spite of the fact that all the necessary ingredients for a potential 'vernacular chant' seem to be in position. But are they, in fact? At this point it is worth recalling the essential definition of Christian liturgical music maintained throughout this thesis as a *combination* of music and words. Applying this to the liturgically pre-eminent compositional reality of the western plainchant tradition is to acknowledge that the real value of this orally derived tradition lies in the instinctive sensitivity of melodic expression to the subtlest manifestations, not necessarily of textual content (Ford's 'meaning') but of text structure, word-boundary, word accent and inflection. To achieve this with any degree of success Ford, or indeed anyone pursuing this line of exploration, would, surely, have to have an *insider*'s knowledge of plainchant composition in Latin to a degree equaling that of Nowacki's Old Roman cantor, whose '... command of tonal syntax was so pliable that he could always declaim a text in a manner that was at once unique and idiomatic, innovative and traditional'.[39] Even if that were possible, which is hardly likely, he would then have to see whether such knowledge and expertise could be applied in the context of a wholly new reality of vernacular text structures and relationships. It is important here to stress the crucial difference between the Old Roman cantor and the composer who would attempt a modern-day pastiche of plainchant, which is that, unlike the latter musician, the first one moved freely and naturally (albeit with expert craftsmanship) within a rich and *living* cultural nexus of orally derived, monophonic text/music relationships.[40]

That the Ó Riada corpus examined here emerged from a broadly similar musico-cultural matrix has, one hopes, been established consistently throughout this thesis. It is a view implicit in Harry White's assessment of Seán Ó Riada's mass settings, where, he says, 'the idiom and syntax of the ethnic repertory are "recomposed" so as to provide a musical vocabulary answerable to the text of the mass ordinary in Irish'.[41] This summarises Seán Ó Riada's principal achievement in the area of Irish liturgical music: he provided potent native models for future settings of the ordinary. The achievement of Peadar Ó Riada in his proper-oriented *Aifreann Eoin na Croise*, however, suggests something no less significant, having to do with the deeper creative processes of oral composition which make possible the organic development of repertoires vast in scale and variety. The younger composer's mastery of a large-scale and varied tapestry of liturgical, scriptural and devotional prose, by means of the manipulation and adaptation of melodic motifs, is a musical achievement of profound significance, particularly in the context of the emergence of a newly translated body of Roman propers.

Envisioning Future Musical Cultures: Homer, Gregory, Ó Riada

At the conclusion of his ground-breaking study of the art of the twentieth-century Yugoslav oral epic singer, *The Singer of Tales*, Albert B. Lord turns his attention to the work of the Greek poet, Homer. Applying to the *Iliad* and the *Odyssey* the tests of orality (pervasiveness of formulas, 'thriftiness' of formulaic systems, repetition of themes) distilled from his analysis of a living art of oral epic, Lord concludes as follows:

> First, this knowledge places Homer inside an oral tradition of epic song. He is not an outsider approaching the tradition with only a superficial grasp of it, using a bit here and a bit there, or trying to present a flavour of the traditional, yet ever thinking in terms essentially different from it. He is not a split personality with half of his understanding and technique in the tradition and the other half in a Parnassus of literate methods … He is the tradition; he is one of the integral parts of that complex … His vividness and immediacy arise from the fact that he is a practicing oral poet … he has none of the artificiality of those who use traditional themes or traditional devices for non-traditional purposes … And so we see Homer as the men of his own time saw him, a poet singer among poet singers. The tradition in which he belonged was a rich one. He heard many good singers, and he himself had great talent, so that he was well known wherever songs were sung. The singer who performed the *Iliad* and the *Odyssey* was obviously no novice in the art. Both poems are too well done, show too great a mastery of technique (and by this I mean oral technique) to be by a young man in the stages of learning. To attain such mastery, Homer must have been a singer with a large repertory of songs … He was not a two-song man … (Albert B. Lord, *The Singer of Tales*)[42]

In terms of his immersion, sustained contact (since childhood) with, and ongoing creative contribution to the living expression of his native musical culture in Múscraí, Peadar Ó Riada may indeed be described as a composer working from within an oral tradition. His recorded vocal and instrumental compositions and arrangements, both secular and religious, betray nothing of 'the artificiality of those who use traditional themes or traditional devices for non-traditional purposes' but instead demonstrate the greatest of respect for the essential elements of that tradition.[43] On the other hand, his intimacy with, and freedom within, the tradition allows him to recognise and harness the untapped potential of some of these elements and to project them forward in traditional yet radically innovative ways.[44] The deeply and pervasively formulaic nature of the composer's large-scale *Aifreann Eoin na Croise* presents the most comprehensive evidence of oral compositional technique, according to the following definition advanced by Albert Lord: 'An *oral* text will yield a predominance of clearly demonstrable formulas, with the bulk of the remainder "formulaic", and a small number of nonformulaic expressions. A *literary* text will show a predominance of nonformulaic expressions, with some formulaic expressions, and very few clear formulas.'[45]

That such a definition identifies Peadar Ó Riada as the more deeply oral of the two liturgical composers studied in this thesis is not something to be wondered at when one considers the intimate nature and extent of his involvement with the musical traditions of Múscraí since his childhood years.[46] The process of enculturation into such an orally based artistic tradition, which relies to a large degree on the device of formula for its propagation and organic development, is here described by Lord:

> The formula is the offspring of the marriage between thought and sung verse. Whereas thought, in theory at least, may be free, sung verse imposes restrictions, varying in degree of rigidity from culture to culture, that shape the form of the thought. Any study of formula must therefore begin with a study of metrics and music, particularly as confronted by the young singer first becoming aware of the demands of his art. Later we shall have to consider the question of why story becomes wedded to song and verse, to ask ourselves what kind of tale finds its expression in these very special methods of presentation. These are not problems that the contemporary singer of tales faces; for he has inherited the answers. The fact of narrative song is around him from birth; the technique of it is the possession of his elders, and he falls heir to it … he absorbs into his own experience a feeling for the tendency towards the distribution of accented and unaccented syllables and their very subtle variations caused by the play of tonic accent, vowel length, and melodic line. These 'restrictive' elements he comes to know from much listening to the songs about him and from being engrossed in their imaginative world. He learns the meter ever in association with particular phrases, those expressing the most common and oft-repeated ideas of the traditional story. Even in pre-singing years rhythm and thought are one, and the singer's concept of the formula is shaped though not explicit. He is aware of the successive beats and the varying lengths of repeated thoughts, and these might be said to be his formulas. Basic patterns of meter, word-boundary, melody have become his possession, and in him the tradition begins to reproduce itself.[47]

The textual demands of *Aifreann Eoin na Croise* drew forth from Peadar Ó Riada his accumulated knowledge of the tradition at both immediate levels of response and deeper currents of artistic creativity, and the result provides a unique and distilled insight into some of the compositional processes governing the continuation of the Irish melodic tradition, such as is rarely available to scholars of this discipline. As one such scholar, James Cowdery, attests: 'folk composition can seldom be studied directly'.[48]

A rare opportunity to observe the 'live' process of oral composition was provided at a seminar on liturgical composition given by Peadar Ó Riada as part of a weekend course held in Cúil Aodha in May 2006.[49] Two years earlier, I had interviewed him on the subject.[50] On the question of text selection, his comments revealed a liturgical practicality ('selecting texts that you'd get mileage out of') and also a sense of personal engagement with the words ('I picked that psalm out because the words are wonderful') and their structure ('I was looking at that one recently and seeing how I might divide it up').[51] Regarding the moment of musical composition itself, however, a more striking picture was painted by the composer in the following series of observations:

> When I'm putting music to something new, I never prepare it beforehand, because it works better when you're under pressure … I'm with the choir, there … 'and this is the line', and it just comes out … With an eight-line form, when I start the first line, I haven't the foggiest idea of what's coming next. I don't think about it; it's purely instinctive.[52]

During the course of the 2006 seminar, Ó Riada asked if someone would suggest a liturgical text for him to set in English, as he had never done one before.[53] The opening line of the following psalm text was one of a number suggested orally from the floor, and, responding to it, the composer asked if the body of the text could be quickly provided. This, then, was the content *and structure* of the written text given to him:

> My soul is longing for your peace,
> near to you, my God.
>
> Lord, you know that my heart is not proud
> and my eyes are not lifted from the earth.

Lofty thoughts have never filled my mind;
far beyond my thoughts all ambitious deeds.

In your peace I have maintained my soul,
I have kept my heart in your quiet peace.
Israel, put all your hope in God,
place your trust in him now and evermore.

It was quickly established that the first two lines would act as a refrain. The church musicians present expected that, given such a structure, the response would return twice during the course of the psalm, but things did not turn out this way. In fact Ó Riada elected to deal with a larger eight-line tract of psalmody instead of the now-conventional four-line portions established by the Gelineau model, earlier referred to in our discussion of recitative. He did not signal this, but merely dealt with the phrases in succession, and returned to the response in the end. Having held down a bass A on the harmonium, he proceeded as illustrated here:[54]

7.9 Peadar Ó Riada: *Psalm 131*

The entire process lasted approximately twenty minutes. Apart from one structural decision, taken with a view to facilitating a 'fresh' return of the refrain, and the melodic alternative offered by the composer to the listeners in the second last line, each phrase arrived in fully finished form: there were no revisions.[56] Once the phrase came, the composer noted the pitch-letter name above the textual syllables, if necessary went back a phrase or two to regain melodic bearings and momentum, and then proceeded forward again. By and large, it may be said, and this may be observed in the written structure, the musical expression moves forward in couplets by means of a series of balances characteristic of the parallelisms of oral style. These may be incremental, as in the case of the opening textual couplet, but are more normally antithetical in their use of discrete and separate pitch areas. The overall, tetrachordally derived structure, with its carefully regulated musical balances and its motivic repetitions, transpositions and adaptations, presents a text book example of the Guidonian ideals of melodic composition.[57] The 're-framing' as an opening gesture (verse, line four) of the closing turn-like motif which appears in line one, provides evidence of a freedom of association of motifs with textual *structure*, and a similar independence of motif from textual *accent* may be seen by comparing the opening gestures of lines one and two of the refrain.

The freedom of music from any referential obligations towards textual *content* is epitomised by the composer's positive ambivalence in relation to the melodic setting of the key word 'hope' in the second last line of the text.[58] There is admittedly a structural 8-7-5 motivic repetition at the beginning of each quatrain of the verse, but other than that, the variety and aptness of the melodic expression is quite impressive.[59] This variety may be further observed in the palindromic structure articulated by the phrase-end notes:[60]

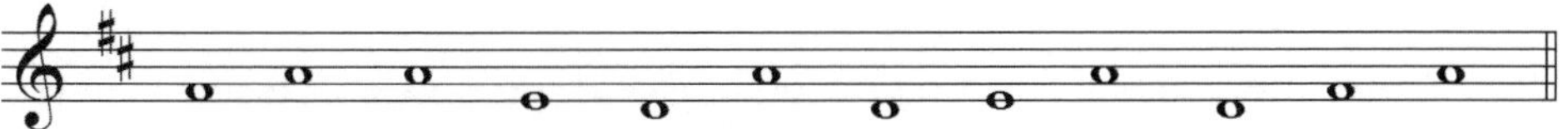

7.10 Peadar Ó Riada: *Psalm 131*, phrase-endings

From the historical perspective of Christian monophonic liturgical music, the above composition could be described as a suitable 'combination of words and music' and, from the more purely artistic point of view, in Guidonian terms, as 'a unified, polished work'.[61] In relation to the compositional *process*, however, an even more compelling parallel is provided by the following passage from Leo Treitler's highly significant 'Homer and Gregory' article, in which, combining his knowledge of plainchant repertoire with insights gained from Lord's *The Singer of Tales*, Treitler speculates as to the compositional method of plainchant composers ultimately responsible for generating such a vast body of varied, yet artistically unified and coherent monophonic liturgical music:

> Any account of the oral invention of plainchant, to be realistic, must look to the practical, recognizing that in composition through performance the primary, pervasive, and controlling condition is the continuity of the performance. The singer does not make sketches, he does not consult a catalogue of formulas and deliberate about which ones he will string together, he does not have before him a skeleton outline of the melody that he is to elaborate, and he does not go back and make revisions. He will have planned before beginning, and he will have paused at moments of articulation quickly thinking what should come next as he scans the next phrase of the text.[62]

In undertaking a 'live' setting of Psalm 131 within the context of a public seminar, Peadar Ó Riada was expressing a singular confidence in the ability of the native tradition (through his intimate contact with it) to provide what would be required for a worthy and coherent composition. The remarkable thing for this observer was not that a setting was produced so quickly, but, crucially, that it was of such a high quality.

From 'Singer of Tales' to '*Psaltes*'

> The traditional oral epic singer is not an artist; he is a seer. The patterns of thought that he has inherited came into being to serve not art but religion in its broadest sense. His balances, his antitheses, his similes and metaphors, his repetitions, were not intended to be devices and conventions of Parnassus, but were techniques for emphasis of the potent symbol. (Lord)[63]

In a paper given at the inaugural gathering of representatives of Higher Institutes of Church Music Education held in Budapest in November 2006, László Dobszay traced the development of Catholic church music from its beginnings to the present day by focusing on five historical models of the church musician.[64] At the beginning of this development, hand in hand with the emerging Christian liturgy, he places the figure of the *psaltes*:

> The key-person in this liturgical chant culture was the singer of [the] psalm, the *psaltes*, the only one in [this] environment who can be called a professional musician, at least in the true sense, as they are present with their special knowledge in the living oral traditions. The memory of the *psaltes* was the storehouse of the repertory, not only as a fixed musical material, but also as one element of an overall liturgical custom. He was the trustee of the communal memory, the keeper of the tradition of the community. But the way that he used this communal knowledge, adapted the rigorously-set elements in the improvisation or ornate performance was, at the same time, very individual; it was an artistic production appreciated in the community. This twofold common and individual aspect of this activity is manifest, for example, in the cantor-artistry of Jewish synagogues. The *psaltes* took his knowledge from another *psaltes*; from childhood or youth he was the apprentice of a great master who passed onto him his repertory, his methods, the rules of adaptation, and introduced his successor into his function. The *psaltes* was a liturgical person, who entered his office blessed by the bishop. Much of his knowledge still lives – transformed, of course, over time – in the Gregorian chant as responsorial psalmody, the chant of the tract and graduale and the rich formulary of recitations.

Surrounded from childhood by the rich, orally derived musico-cultural traditions of Múscraí, and similarly formed by almost fifty years of unbroken service in a uniquely creative and fruitful liturgical context, Peadar Ó Riada, it could be suggested, fits the description of a twenty-first-century *psaltes*. Working at a crucial time in the initial and formative stages of an emerging vernacular liturgical practice, he is now indeed the keeper of an already rich oral tradition of liturgical music. To this continually evolving tradition, he himself has already supplied, in addition to the mass setting discussed in this thesis, a large (unpublished) body of individually wrought 'proper' psalm settings and Alleluia verses, hymns for national and local patron saints, and musical settings for special Roman rite rituals such as the Exsultet and the Litany of the Saints.[65] He inherited this tradition from a visionary musician, one who had confidence in the ability of a native cultural tradition of song to provide fittingly for the vernacular musical requirements of the Roman rite. This confidence, firmly expressed in the contents of the Christmas card sent by Seán Ó Riada to Glenstal Abbey in 1968, has been fully borne out, to the mutual enrichment of liturgy, and, precisely by means of its contact with the textual forms of that liturgy, the art of music itself.

ENDNOTES

Introduction

1 A region in which Irish functions as the primary vernacular language. 'The Gaeltacht covers extensive parts of counties Donegal, Mayo, Galway and Kerry – all along the western seaboard – and also parts of counties Cork, Meath and Waterford. There are also six populated offshore islands. The total population of the Gaeltacht is 100,716.' (Census 2011)

Chapter 1

1 The name of Seán Ó Riada (1931–1971) will need no introduction to Irish readers. The pre-eminent Irish composer of his time, he was the single most influential figure in the revival of Irish traditional music during the 1960s. See 'Seán Ó Riada' in Harry White and Barra Boydell (eds), *The Encyclopaedia of Music in Ireland* (Dublin: University College Dublin Press, 2013), pp. 803–6.

2 Paul McDonnell, 'Ó Riada at Glenstal Abbey', in Bernard Harris and Grattan Freyer (eds), *The Achievement of Seán Ó Riada* (Ballina: The Irish Humanities Centre, 1981), pp. 110–11.

3 *Musicam sacram* (Instruction on Music in the Liturgy), issued by the Roman Sacred Congregation of Rites (SCR), 5 March 1967. English translation in Austin Flannery (ed.), *Vatican Council II: the conciliar and post-conciliar documents*, revised edition (New York: Costello Publishing Company, 1988).

4 *Sacrosanctum concilium* (Constitution on the Sacred Liturgy), SCR, 4 December 1963. English translation in Flannery (1988).

5 Address of Pope Paul VI to the Consociatio Internationalis Musicae Sacrae, 12 October 1973. In Robert F. Hayburn, *Papal Legislation on Sacred Music 95 AD to 1977 AD* (Collegeville, MN: The Liturgical Press, 1979), pp. 567–8.

6 *Sacrosanctum concilium* 112, in Flannery, p. 31. The reader will note, in the Introduction and elsewhere in the thesis, my adoption of a more elemental expression of this definition, i.e. 'a combination of music and words'. The nature of the material being discussed, and the questions inherent in it, are best served by this approach.

7 *Sacrosanctum concilium* 121, in Flannery, p. 34.

8 *Tra le sollecitudini*, Hayburn, p. 224.

9 *Musicam sacram* 50, in Flannery, p. 93.

10 *Musicam sacram* 52, in ibid.

11 *Sacrosanctum concilium* 121, in ibid., p. 33.

12 *Musicam sacram* 59, in ibid., p. 95.

13 *Sacrosanctum concilium* 119, in ibid., p. 33.

14 *Musicam sacram* 61, in ibid., p. 95.

15 This choir constituted the beginnings of what would later come to be known as Cór Chúil Aodha. See 'Cór Chúil Aodha' in White and Boydell, pp. 242–3.

16 The acclamation was the 'Te decet laus' (*Antiphonale monasticum*, 1261), a doxological text associated with the office of Matins and until recently sung on a weekly basis in Glenstal. I am grateful to Dom Placid Murray for this information.

17 Harris and Freyer, p. 111.

18 Ibid., p. 171. Image reproduced with kind permission of the Estate of Tomás Ó Canainn, Ard Barra, Glanmire, Co. Cork.

19 The proceedings of the seminar, which also include contributions from other panellists Rev. Jeremiah Threadgold, Gerard Gillen, Seán McRéamonn and Phil Coulter, are recorded by Dom Paul McDonnell in 'Music: a supplement to *The Furrow*', no. 1, summer 1968 (*The Furrow*, vol. 19, nos 8/9).

20 Harris and Freyer, 111. McDonnell's reference to 'the Ó Riada mass' testifies to the popular, almost iconic status the work had already gained amongst Irish worshipping communities.

21 Son, and successor of Seán Ó Riada as director of Cór Chúil Aoidh, Peadar Ó Riada is an established composer, performer and arranger of traditional music. See Chapter Five, note 1.

22 Nicholas Carolan, 'Songs of Múscraí', *Ceol Tíre*, vol. 12, 1978, p. 2.

23 A collection of 120 local songs, some of the contents of which were later published in the 1923 and 1924 volumes of the *Journal of the Folk Song Society*.

24 A. Martin Freeman, 'Irish Folk Songs', *JFSS*, pt. 6, no. 23, Jan. 1920, pp. iii–xxviii, 95–205; no. 24, Jan. 1921, pp. 205–66; no. 25, Sept. 1921, pp. [265]–342.

25 Dáibhí Ó Cróinín, *The Songs of Elisabeth Cronin, Traditional Singer* (Dublin: Four Courts Press, 2000), p. 12.

26 Liam De Noraidh, *Ceol* ón Mumhain (Dublin: An Clóchomhar, 1965), p. 26. Of particular interest is De Noraidh's use of arrows to depict microtonal 'scoops' in the vocal delivery.

27 Ó Cróinín, p. 17.

28 Carolan, p. 2.

29 Interview with the author, 29 July 2004.

30 Interview with the author, 26 April 2007. Mícheál Ua Duinnín (1922–2007) was an acknowledged authority on the song traditions of Múscraí and Uíbh Ráthach (South Kerry). His recorded collection, *An Duinníneach: amhráin sean-nóis le Mícheál Ua Duinnín* (CD, Comhchoiste Ghaeltacht Uíbh Ráthaigh, 2004), contains songs principally related to his birthplace of Baile Mhúirne, among them one of his own compositions, 'Amhrán na bhFeirmeoirí'.

31 Interview with the author, 6 August 2004.

32 Ibid.

33 A fact which is not negated, as will be seen, by the use of the harmonium as an accompanying, unifying instrument to support the singing.

34 See note 14.

35 *Sacrosanctum concilium*, Art. 10: '... the liturgy is the summit towards which the activity of the Church is directed; it is also the fount from which all her power flows.' Flannery, p. 6.

36 In the mass, for example, there are the 'ordinary' or fixed portions of text, as opposed to the 'proper' elements, selected in accordance with specific feasts or seasons.

37 Willi Apel, *Gregorian Chant* (Bloomington, IN: Indiana University Press, 1958), p. 409.

38 Lucien Deiss, *Visions of Liturgy and Music for a New Century* (Collegeville, MN: The Liturgical Press, 1996), p. 80. For an authoritative treatment of the liturgical history of the Sanctus see Enrico Mazza, *The Celebration of the Eucharist: the origin of the rite and the development of its interpretation* (Collegeville, MN: The Liturgical Press, 1998), pp. 205–7, and Paul Bradshaw, *The Eucharistic Liturgies* (Collegeville, MN: The Liturgical Press, 2012), pp. 111–21.

39 *Itinerarium egeriae*, XXV, 4–5, quoted in James McKinnon, *Music in Early Christian Literature* (Cambridge: Cambridge University Press, 1987), p. 117.

40 Richard Crocker, *An Introduction to Gregorian Chant* (New Haven, CT: Yale University Press, 2000), p. 111.

41 Texts taken from the third edition of *The Roman Missal* (Dublin: Veritas, 2011), pp. 36, 50, 709.

42 Regina Randhofer, 'Oral versus Written: structural differences in Jewish and Christian psalms', paper read at *Cantus Planus 2004* (12th meeting of the IMS, Lillafüred, Hungary).

43 Peter Jeffery, *Re-Envisioning Past Musical Cultures: ethnomusicology in the study of Gregorian chant* (Chicago: The University of Chicago Press, 1992).

44 David Hiley, Review of P. Jeffery, *Re-Envisioning Past Musical Cultures: ethnomusicology in the study of Gregorian chant* (Chicago: University of Chicago Press, 1992), *Early Music History*, vol. 13, 1994, pp. 276–7.

45 *Sacrosanctum concilium* 121, in Flannery, p. 34.

46 Jeffery, p. 63. For more on the textual composition of plainchant propers see Christoph Tietze, 'The Use of Old Latin in the Non-Psalmic Introit Texts', in *Cantus Planus Lillafüred/Hungary, 2004: papers read at the 12th meeting of the IMS Study Group* (Budapest: Institute for Musicology of the Hungarian Academy of Sciences, 2006), pp. 259–85, and Jason McFarland, *Announcing the Feast: the entrance song in the mass of the Roman rite* (Collegeville, MN: Pueblo Books, 2012), pp. 47–50.

Chapter 2

1 John Stevens, *Words and Music in the Middle Ages: song, narrative, dance and drama, 1050–1350* (Cambridge: Cambridge University Press, 1986).

2 While Stevens' findings did not meet with universal uncritical acceptance at the time of the book's publication, no serious challenge has since been made to his 'non-relationship' (i.e. referential, emotional etc.) theory.

3 Elisabeth Aubrey, *The Music of the Troubadours* (Bloomington, IN: Indiana University Press, 1996), p. 75; Philip Bohlman, *The Study of Folk Music in the Modern World* (Bloomington, IN: Indiana University Press, 1988), p. 16; Tomás Ó Canainn, *Traditional Music in Ireland* (London: Routledge & Kegan Paul, 1978), p. 49; Hugh Shields, *Narrative Singing in Ireland: lays, ballads, come-all-yes and other songs* (Dublin: Irish Academic Press, 1993), p. 124.

4 Aubrey, p. 75.

5 Liam Mac Con Iomaire, 'Sean-nós', in Fintan Vallely (ed.), *The Companion to Irish Traditional Music* (Cork: Cork University Press, 1999), p. 336.

6 See Stevens, p. 69.

7 Based on a version sung by Sadie Bhreathnach of the Rinn Gaeltacht, Co. Waterford.

8 Aubrey, p. 75.

9 Ibid., p. 145.

10 Shields, p. 85.

11 Aubrey, p. 77.

12 Seán Ó Riada, *Our Musical Heritage* (Mountrath: The Dolmen Press, 1982), p. 26.

13 Nóirín Ní Riain, 'The Nature and Classification of Traditional Religious Songs', in Gerard Gillen and Harry White (eds), *Irish Musical Studies 2: music and the church* (Dublin: Irish Academic Press, 1993), pp. 191–6.

14 Aubrey Gwynn, *Anglo-Irish Church Life, Fourteenth and Fifteenth Centuries* (Dublin: Gill, 1968), p. 51, quoted in Ní Riain, p. 191.

15 Stevens, p. 46.

16 Ibid., p. 497.

17 Ibid., pp. 497–8.

18 Seán Ó Baoill, *The Irish Song Tradition* (Dublin: Gilbert Dalton, 1976), p. 25.

19 Annie Gilchrist, 'Lambkin: a study in evolution', *Journal of the English Folk Dance and Song Society*, vol. 1, 1932, p. 15, quoted in James Cowdery, *The Melodic Tradition of Ireland* (Kent, OH: Kent State University Press, 1990), p. 81.

20 Cowdery, pp. 40–1.

21 As Treitler observes, 'Medieval music was made and circulated in partnership with language, and medieval witnesses made no distinction between "speaking" and "singing" in reference to the execution of *cantus*.' Leo Treitler, *With Voice and Pen: coming to know medieval song and how it was made* (Oxford: Oxford University Press, 2003), p. 437.

22 Matthew 26:30; Mark 14:26. The cover image of *Ceol an aifrinn*, and of this book, taken from the *Book of Kells*, features the relevant text from St Matthew's Gospel, woven into a typically elaborate depiction of the 'Taking of Christ'.

23 Stevens, p. 269.

24 Ibid., p. 276.

25 In this regard the recorded work of chant performer/musicologist Marcel Pérès with traditional singers from Spain and Corsica is especially illuminating. Some of his views are set forth in *Les Voix du Plain-chant* (Paris: Desclée de Brouwer, 2001), a book co-written with Jacques Cheyronnaud.

26 Interview with the author, 6 August 2004.

27 Ibid.

28 *Tra le sollecitudini* 1, in Hayburn, p. 224. The Pauline principle of singing with the spirit *and with understanding* ('psallam spiritu et mente', I Cor. 14:15), strongly promoted in the Patristic era (see McKinnon), exerted a huge influence on the subsequent development of Christian liturgical music.

29 In this respect it is interesting to note Tomás Ó Canainn's account of Seán Ó Riada's early preparations with his choir for singing at Benediction: 'They learned "O salutaris" and "Tantum ergo" and Seán went to great pains to ensure that they all understood every word. Some of the time was spent in discussing a nice Irish turn of phrase to translate the Latin and all the experts joined in the discussion.' (Ó Canainn, in Harris and Freyer, p. 169).

30 A.M. Macdonald (ed.), *Chambers Twentieth Century Dictionary* (Edinburgh: Chambers, 1972), p. 218.

31 Stevens, pp. 268–9. An assessment confirmed, for instance, by Richard Crocker's description of the psalms as 'lyrical prose' and frequent use of the term 'sentence' in relation to the most numerous of all chant genres, the antiphon. Crocker, pp. 10 and 56. The 'floating' non-metrical nature of original Hebrew psalmodic structures is highlighted in Amnon Shiloah's article 'The Viewpoints of Two Medieval Jewish Philosophers on Music and Its Relation to the Old Testament and Cantillation' in *Cantus Planus Lillafüred/Hungary, 2004: papers read at the 12th meeting of the IMS Study Group* (Budapest: Institute for Musicology of the Hungarian Academy of Sciences, 2006), p. 19.

32 Rev. J. Chapman, quoted in V.S. Blankenhorn, *Irish Song-Craft and Metrical Practice since 1600* (New York: Edwin Mellen Press, 2003), p. 51. Chapman's definition constitutes a type of self-fulfilling prophecy, set as it is within a prose structure which would challenge the musical skills of any composer.

33 *Chambers Twentieth Century Dictionary* (ed. Macdonald), p. 75.

34 Hugh Shields, referring to the Ossianic poems, prefers the term 'lay', considering the term 'ballad' as a misleading description for such a large-scale epic form. Shields, p. 33.

35 Gerard Murphy, *Ossianic Lore* (Dublin: Cultural Relations Committee of Ireland, 1955), p. 59, quoted by Ní Riain in Gillen and White, p. 198.

36 Shields, p. 21.

37 *Catalogue of Hungarian Folksong Types*, ed. László Dobszay and Janka Szendrei (Budapest: Institute for Musicology of the Hungarian Academy of Sciences, 1992), p. 55.

38 Apel, pp. 201–45; David Hiley, *Western Plainchant: a handbook* (Oxford: Clarendon Press, 1993), pp. 47–69.

39 Stevens, p. 286. From within the central, neumatic stylistic category, the Introit may be also said to be strongly characterised by the presence of melodically static, recitational elements. (Hiley, pp. 109–16).

40 Helmut Hucke, 'Towards a New Historical View of Gregorian Chant', *Journal of the American Musicological Society*, vol. 33, no. 3, autumn 1980, pp. 437–67.

41 Treitler (2003), pp. 455–6.

42 Stevens, p. 7.

43 Edward Bunting, *A General Collection of the Ancient Music of Ireland* (London: Clementi & Co., 1809), Preface, p. i [republished as *The Ancient Music of Ireland: the Bunting collections* (Dublin: Waltons, 2002)].

44 Interview with the author, 29 July 2004.

45 Guido d'Arezzo, *Micrologus*, Art. 188, in Warren Babb and Claude Palisca (eds), *Hucbald, Guido and John on Music: three medieval treatises* (New Haven, CT: Yale University Press, 1978), p. 74.

46 Ibid., p. 72.

47 Stevens, p. 38. This is elaborated on by Elisabeth Aubrey in the following passage: 'This discrepancy between poetic and musical graphs is due at least in part to the superficial relationships between poetic verses and musical phrases. For example, poetic rhyme is rarely mirrored by musical repetition. Furthermore, the poetic devices for linking stanzas are not usually directly reflected in the music, since the melody is the same for all stanzas. Melodies are given structure by means of devices that are not found in poetry, including verse-length repetition schemes and repeated cadential patterns as well as smaller-scale motives that are repeated and manipulated, tonal centers, and direction and contour …' (Aubrey, p. 145).

48 Stevens, p. 90.

49 Apel, pp. 301–2.

50 Stevens, p. 45.

51 Ibid., p. 297.

52 See Michel Huglo, *Chant Grégorien et Musique* Médiévale (Aldershot: Ashgate, 2005, Variorum Collected Studies Series – CS814), p. 68. Willi Apel posits an explanation of the phenomenon as arising out of an aesthetic which seeks to 'counteract rather than over-emphasise' the given power of the accented syllable. (Apel, p. 289).

53 Dom Jean Prou OSB, 'Gregorian Chant in the Spirituality of the Church' a paper given at the 1983 International Symposium on Gregorian Chant held in Washington DC; reprinted in *Jubilus Review*, vol. 4, no. 4, 1987, p. 543.

54 Stevens, p. 409.

55 Timothy McGee, 'Music, Rhetoric and the Emperor's New Clothes', in John Haines, Randall Rosenfeld and Andrew Hughes, *Music and Medieval Manuscripts: paleography and performance. Essays dedicated to Andrew Hughes* (Aldershot: Ashgate, 2004), p. 259.

56 The independent rhetorical potential of unison melody is considered in a broader and more vivid context in the following passage concerning the act of chant composition: 'A melody embodies choices made from among the correct things that the [musical] grammar permits it to do. The musician must choose where to place a caesura or cadence, when to pose a modal contrast, how to open a phrase (with what intervals or formulae) and how to close it, and when to make associations between phrases. We might say that these things have to do with the rhetoric of the melody …' (Treitler, pp. 455–6).

57 Aubrey, pp. 87–8.

58 Stevens, p. 381.

59 Plotinus , VI.6.4.20–4, in Stevens, p. 13.

60 Ibid., p. 14.

61 István Fránk, *Repertoire Métrique de la Poésie des Troubadours*, Bibliotheque de L'École des Hautes Études, 303 and 308 (Paris, 1953 and 1957).

62 Stevens, p. 32.

63 Ibid., p. 40.

64 Ibid., p. 38.

65 Relationship between text and melody 'is syllabic (its basis is number in its most literal sense); and it is structural (words and music work together line by line, strophe by strophe)' (Ibid., p. 90).

66 'The chansons are evidently not in a regular and predictable metre ...' (Ibid., p. 46).

67 Of the *cantio* 'Veritatis veritatum' he says: 'The truths about "number" stand firm; I will not reiterate the arguments for believing that under the encrustations this is "syllabic melody" still and belongs to the centuries-old tradition of song-making in which counting your syllables, balancing your lines, weaving an harmonious fabric of units, was the all-important thing' (Ibid., p. 77).

68 Ibid., p. 47.

69 George Petrie, *The Petrie Collection of the Ancient Music of Ireland*, vol. I (Dublin: Gill, 1855, repr. Aldershot: The Scolar Press, 1978), p. xvi.

70 Petrie's assessment corresponds closely with Timothy McGee's reflections on the relationship between music and rhetoric prior to the sixteenth century (see note 55).

71 Following on the tradition of the Greek 'Academy', the recently established Acadamh Fódhla, based in Baile Mhúirne, is concerned with the preservation and promotion of the rich cultural heritage of the area.

72 The ritual text, adaptable to the various fields of knowledge identified by the Acadamh (music, history, poetry etc.) was composed, interestingly, by Peadar Ó Riada.

73 Stevens, p. 46.

74 Thomas A. McKean, *Hebridean Song-Maker: Iain MacNeacail of the Isle of Skye* (Edinburgh: Polygon, 1997), p. 123.

75 Ibid., p. 121.

76 Horst Brunner, 'Ton (i)', in Stanley Sadie (ed.), *The New Grove Dictionary of Music and Musicians (NG)* (London: Macmillan, 1980), pp. xix, 49.

77 Edward Nowacki, 'Studies on the Office Antiphons of the Old Roman Manuscripts', unpublished PhD dissertation, Brandeis University, 1980, p. 337.

78 Gilchrist (as note 19).

79 Petrie (as note 69), vol. II, pp. 42–3.

80 See Julie Hennigan, 'Sean-nós', in Vallely, p. 338, and Manuel Pedro Ferreira's study, 'Music at Cluny: the tradition of Gregorian chant for the proper of the mass. Melodic variants and microtonal nuances', unpublished PhD dissertation, Princeton, 1997.

81 Babb and Palisca, p. 63.

82 Edward Bunting, *The Ancient Music of Ireland, Arranged for the Pianoforte. To which is prefixed a dissertation on the Irish harp and harpers, including an account of the old melodies of Ireland* (Dublin: 1840; repr. Dublin: Waltons, 2002), p. 16.

83 From the popular guitar 'three-chord trick' to the contemporary orchestral compositions of John Adams. See for instance his 1985 *Harmonielehre*, final movement.

84 Anonymous, *Dialogus de Musica*; GS, I, pp. 251–264; part trans. O. Strunk, *Source Readings in Music History* (New York, 1950/R1965), p. 103 [attrib. Odo].

85 Harold Powers, 'Mode', in Stanley Sadie (ed.), *The New Grove Dictionary of Music and Musicians*, xii (London: Macmillan, 1980), p. 377.

86 Ibid., pp. 377–8.

87 Ibid., p. 384. Following in the tradition of Guido, the concept of plainchant finals as *intended* notes of destination is advanced in Fiona McAlpine's more recent study, *Tonal Consciousness in the Medieval West*, Varia Musicologica 10 (Bern: Peter Lang, 2008).

88 Babb and Palisca, p. 66.

89 'As there are eight tones, so also are there eight tenors …' (Chapter 11 of *De Musica*, Johannes Afflighemensis, Eng. trans. in Babb and Palisca).

90 Powers, p. 386.

91 Ibid., p. 379.

92 Dom Jean Claire, 'L'évolution Modale dans les Répertoires Liturgiques Occidentaux', *Revue Grégorienne*, 40, 1962, pp. 196–211 and 229–45.

93 Theodore Karp, *Aspects of Orality and Formularity in Gregorian Chant* (Evanston, IL: Northwestern University Press, 1998), p. 97.

94 Breandán Breathnach, 'Ireland II: Folk Music', *NG*, ix, 1980, p. 317. A similar, if more detailed approach, which acknowledges specific examples of E- and F-mode melodies, may be found in the Introduction to Aloys Fleischmann's *Sources of Irish Traditional Music c. 1600–1855*, vol. I (New York: Garland, 1998), pp. xxxii–xxxv. In the Irish tradition, modal designations such as C/*doh*, G/*soh* etc. are understood as transposable and not tied to any fixed pitches.

95 Annie Gilchrist, 'A Note on the Modal System of Gaelic Tunes', *JFSS*, vol. 4, 1910–13, p. 150.

96 Cowdery, p. 90.

97 Karp, p. 7.

98 Jeffery, p. 87.

99 Alfred B. Lord, *The Singer of Tales* (Cambridge, MA: Harvard University Press, 1960).

100 Bohlman, pp. 16–17.

101 Cowdery, p. 93.

102 Nowacki (1980), p. 337.

103 Ibid., p. 32.

104 Babb and Palisca, p. 71.

105 Ó Riada (1982), p. 35.

106 Ruth Finnegan, *Oral Poetry: its nature, significance and social context* (Cambridge: Cambridge University Press, 1980).

107 Karp, p. 59.

108 Lord, p. 4.

109 Jeffery, p. 92.

Chapter 3

1 Seán Ó Riada, *Ceol an Aifrinn mar a Chantar i nGaeltacht Chúil Aodha* (Baile Átha Cliath: An Clóchomhar, 1971). Literally 'Music of the mass as sung in the Irish-speaking area of Coolea'.

2 The supplementary hymns (11 and 12) 'for Communion or any other suitable time' stand outside of the main mass setting and are included by Ó Riada as part of an Aguisín (Appendix) to the collection.

3 The English translations of the texts of *Ceol an aifrinn* and *Aifreann 2* are those of the author, unless otherwise stated.

4 The first section of the text is quoted in Pádraig Ó Fiannachta and Desmond Forristal (eds), *Saltair: prayers from the Irish tradition* (Dublin: Columba Press, 1988), p. 25.

5 Outside the realm of mass ordinary texts, the brief, uplifting, *Iomann Iargomaoineach* text, *Réir Dé go nDeineam*, is treated in the same way.

6 Apel, p. 408.

7 The Irish vernacular translation, unlike the significantly modified English version (not included above) found in the 1974 *Roman Missal*, follows very closely the original Latin model in terms of phrase order and structure.

8 Guido d'Arezzo, *Micrologus*, in Babb and Palisca, pp. 66–67. Guido's final observation above is borne out in the tendency of traditional Irish singers to use phrase-end notes as significant points of repose, thus articulating an important part of the music's inherent structure. See Seóirse Bodley's 'Technique and Structure in Sean-Nós Singing', *Irish Folk Music Studies*, vol. 1, 1972–3, p. 46.

9 Apel, pp. 410–11.

10 *Liber usualis* (Tournai: Desclée, 1938), 17, 35, 38.

11 *Liber usualis*, 82.

12 See McGee, p. 259 and Stevens, p. 90.

13 *Liber usualis*, 32, 26, 19, 43.

14 See Huglo (2005), p. 68 and Prou, p. 546. Apel posits an explanation of the phenomenon as arising out of an aesthetic which seeks to 'counteract rather than over-emphasise the given power of the accented syllable' (Apel, p. 289).

15 Stevens, p. 78.

16 A relevant example, connected with the Irish oral epic *Laoi na Mná* Móire, is found in Breandán Breathnach, *Folk Music and Dances of Ireland* (Dublin and Cork: Mercier Press, 1971), p. 26.

17 *An Leabhar Aifrinn* (Má Nuad: An Sagart, 1973).

18 The imminent publication of a new Irish-language missal, complete with 'gregorianised' Irish preface texts, will go some way towards addressing these issues.

19 The textual layout at the head of this section should ideally combine lines 5 and 6 as one line.

20 Although there are no such instances of thematic repetition among syllabic Gregorian settings of the text, the neumatic Sanctus II and IV (*Liber usualis*, 21, 27) provide examples of corresponding re-deployment in the 'Hosanna' lines of material from the opening triple 'Sanctus'.

21 'Number exists before objects which are described by number. The variety of sense objects merely recalls to the soul the notion of number' (Plotinus, VI.6.4.20–24). Quoted in Stevens, p. 13. We recall also Petrie's observation regarding the numerical governing power of textual models:

'Melodies … in a general way expressive of … but always strictly coincident with, and subservient to, the laws of rhythm and metre which govern the construction of those songs, and to which they consequently owe their peculiarities of structure' (Petrie, p. xvi).

22 In terms of proportions, the opening pair of Latin lines, 'Pater … caelis' and 'sanctificetur … tuum', matches up perfectly. In the Irish translation, line 2, *in combination with* line 3, provides a better proportional match to the opening line.

23 *Liber usualis*, 18–88.

24 The setting is included in the *Liber cantualis* (Solesmes, 1978) as part of a composite collection which the editors have entitled 'Missa primitiva'.

25 Apel, p. 418.

26 This pattern, interestingly, represents a reversal of the musical approach adopted by the composer for a similarly structured litany in *An ghlóir* (bars 34–9) where the three invocations are held at the reciting pitch of *b-flat'* (*doh'*), while their respective petitions rise successively in a very declamatory and deliberate way.

27 'It was written by Michael Sheehan in 1916 as a poem, expressing sympathy to a friend whose twelve year old daughter had died. Sheehan (1870–1945) was a priest of the diocese of Waterford and was appointed professor of rhetoric at Maynooth in 1897.' (Paddy Jones, *Intercom*, November, 2009, p.33.

28 Tomás Ó Canainn, *Traditional Slow Airs of Ireland* (Cork: Ossian Press, 1995), pp. 87 and 49 respectively.

29 Fleischmann, vol. II, no. 4932.

30 See p. 74.

31 Versified translation from *Londubh an Chairn* (discussed below). For discussion of the hymn settings throughout the study, I have chosen in general to include only the text of the first verse.

32 Published with the English sub-heading *Songs of the Irish Gaels*, ed. Máiréad Ní Annagáin and Séamus de Chlanndoiliún (Dublin: Educational Company of Ireland, 1925). A metrical English translation of 'Gile mo chroí' (no. 70 in the collection) was provided, the first verse of which is quoted above.

33 Tomás Ó Canainn and Gearóid Mac an Bhua, *Seán Ó Riada: a shaol agus a shaothar* (Dublin: Gartan, 1993), pp. 135–6.

34 Contained in An tAthair Diarmuid Ó Laoghaire's Ár *bPaidreacha* Dúchais (Baile Átha Cliath: Foilseacháin Ábhair Spioradálta, repr. 1990), no. 197.

35 Ó Canainn (1993), p. 135.

36 Ó Laoghaire, no. 162.

37 Such a version of A *Rí an Domhnaigh* is contained in Mícheál Ó hEidhin's *Cas Amhrán* (Conamara: Cló Iar-Chonnachta, 1990), p. 121.

38 Ní Riain, p. 241.

39 According to Ní Riain, a variant of the tune also appears in an tAthair Pádraig Breathnach's *Raint Amhrán*, p. 80.

40 Seán Ó Riada, *Ó Riada's Farewell* (Claddagh Records, 1971, CC12, track 7).

41 'The air used by Ó Riada is somewhere between that of the song and the jig' (Tomás Ó Canainn, in Harris and Freyer, p. 172). Ó Riada's fascination with these tunes is described in Ó Canainn and Mac an Bhua, p. 135.

42 Tonally relevant examples would include 'Róisín Dubh' and 'An Goirtín Eornan' as transcribed in Ó hEidhin, pp. 37 and 68.

43 Ó Riada's sensitivity to the characterising influence of varying finals within a given modal scheme will be manifested to an even greater degree in the composer's second mass setting, *Aifreann 2*.

44 The only departures from this accompanimental approach occur towards the end of the collection, in hymn nos 10 (partial) and 12 (total).

45 Primary among these could have been a desire to avoid the potentially shrill effect of doubling the male voices up an octave and, perhaps, covering them.

46 'As to the manner of using those instruments which may be admitted with sacred music, we only warn that they be used exclusively to uphold the chant of the words …' (Pope Benedict XIV, from his 1749 encyclical *Annus Qui*, quoted in Hayburn, p. 103).

'Since the singing must always be the chief thing, the organ and the instruments may only sustain and never crush it' (Pope Pius X, *Motu Proprio* (1903), Art. 16, quoted in Hayburn, p. 229).

'The use of musical instruments to accompany the singing can act as a support to the voices, render participation easier, and achieve a deeper union in the assembly' (Vatican II, *Musicam Sacram* (1967), Art. 64, in Flannery, p. 96).

47 This unaccompanied approach is repeated in the course of the immediately succeeding *An phaidir* setting (bar 73).

48 Ó Riada's use of secondary seventh harmony in his accompaniments of Irish traditional music in general is discussed in Adrian Scahill's 'The Knotted Chord: harmonic accompaniment in printed and recorded sources of Irish traditional music', unpublished PhD dissertation, University College Dublin, 2005, pp. 509–11.

49 See for instance bar 4 of the *Iontróid*.

50 Seán Ó Riada, from an interview with Charles Acton in the journal *Éire-Ireland*, vol. 6, no. 1, 1971, p. 109. I am grateful to Dr David C. Wright for directing me to this information.

51 The formal responses/solutions come, as it were, directly from within the tradition itself, given the nature of traditional song and the centuries of contact between melody and symmetrical, strophic textual forms. In encountering strophic texts such as the above, Ó Riada, with his knowledge of the tradition, was unlikely to seek compositional solutions from any other quarter.

52 'I can remember getting a Christmas card from Seán at this time with his newly-composed 'Ár nAthair' reproduced on it. I think he was very proud of it …' (Tomás Ó Canainn, in Harris and Freyer p. 170).

53 See Breandán Ó Madagáin's 'Song for Emotional Release in the Gaelic Tradition' in Gerard Gillen and Harry White (eds), *Irish Musical Studies 2: music and the church* (Dublin: Irish Academic Press, 1993), pp. 254–75.

54 For instance, in the *Catalogue of Hungarian Folksong Types*, ed. Dobszay and Szendrei, they occupy the opening category, entitled, interestingly, 'The Psalmodic Style'.

55 See Breandán Ó Madagáin, *Caointe agus Seancheolta Eile* (Conamara: Cló Iar-Chonnachta, 2005).

56 Quoted in Ó Madagáin, p. 259.

57 I am grateful to my father Vincent O'Keeffe, then proprietor of the Bridge Bar, Portmagee, for this information.

58 'The big songs are performed with passion and involvement, and even in the lighter ones, sung with great heart and spirit, a relish and enjoyment can be heard' (Carolan, p. 2).

59 *Musicam sacram* 61, in Flannery, p. 95.

Chapter 4

1 Tomás Ó Canainn (interview with the author, March 2007) has confirmed that this was the case. Dom Kevin Healy, Choirmaster at Glenstal, later produced a carefully hand-copied transcription of the mass 'from Ó Riada's own MS', in the interests of providing the community with a full and accurate version. A copy of this transcription was kindly provided by Fr Paul Kenny of the Irish Church Music Association.

2 Eilís Cranitch and Tomás Ó Canainn (eds), *Seán Ó Riada: Aifreann 2* (Dublin: Gael Linn, 1979). As an aid to my research, Tomás Ó Canainn supplied me with a copy of the original recording on which this publication was based.

3 *Musicam sacram*, Articles 7, 29 and 30.

4 Harris and Freyer, p. 111.

5 The English-language *Roman Missal* was eventually published in 1974 by ICEL.

6 A final musico-liturgical development in *Aifreann 2* is represented by the inclusion of a chanted introduction to the singing of *An phaidir*.

7 Harris and Freyer, p. 112.

8 Úna Ní Ógáin (ed.), *Dánta Dé* (Dublin: Ó Fallamhain, 1928).

9 Harris and Freyer, p. 111.

10 Interview with the author, 29 July 2004. Under Peadar Ó Riada, *Aifreann 2* has for a long time been the version favoured for regular Sunday liturgical use in Cúil Aodha.

11 Of the remaining three regular strophic texts, two (*Ofráil*, *Iomann Comaoineach*) are in a minor tonality and the final *Iomann Ceilúrtha* leans more towards standard major-mode territory.

12 Apel, p. 308; and Hiley, p. 116. See also Fiona McAlpine: *Tonal Consciousness in the Medieval West* (Bern: Peter Lang, 2008), pp. 313–21.

13 Ní Ógáin, p. 77. Ó Riada selected verse 15 and the concluding verse 19.

14 Petrie, p. xvi.

15 Babb and Palisca, p. 74.

16 *Liber usualis*, 1857, 1859.

17 Ibid., 16–63.

18 This compositional approach reflects also the Gregorian model, which consistently develops the final 'Kyrie' repetition, e.g. *Liber usualis*, 16, 19, 25, etc.

19 The final 'Kyrie' returns on lower *d*', producing a type of melodic mirror image of the opening invocation.

20 The verse 'Ecce panis angelorum' is taken from the Corpus Christi sequence *Lauda Sion* (*Liber usualis*, 945).

21 *Liber usualis*, 408, 846.

22 This passage, in the classic manner of mode 6, is sustained structurally by the third above the tonic, *b*', a pitch which carries many of the accented syllables.

23 See chapter three for a discussion of the use of motifs in the hymn *Ag Críost an síol*.

24 Interview with the author, 29 July 2004.

25 These passages consist of the opening and closing phrases (bar 25 and bars /60–63), and a section strategically positioned towards the middle of the composition (bars 37–42).

26 One possible reading of the evidence might suggest that the composer, responding to the text's opening phrase, sets out joyfully in a mode 6 tonality, but, realising that it will not be strong enough for the whole journey, quickly brings a more robust mode 7 configuration into play.

27 This is the only such treatment of 'glóir' in the *Aifreann 2 Gloria* setting. In the *Ceol an aifrinn* version, three of the four instances of the word received this treatment – the fourth being 'recited' as part of the opening intonation.

28 The open-ended tonal approach on either side of the gospel allows for the possibility, not explicitly referred to in the mass setting, of a chanted gospel, reciting also possibly on *a*'.

29 Harris and Freyer, pp. 111–12.

30 This antiphon, which may be found in the *Antiphonale monasticum*, 123, was adapted and apparently retained over a significant period after Vatican II by the Glenstal community, for regular usage as a 'communal' *Alleluia* setting for mass, where Ó Riada himself is likely to have encountered it. I am indebted to Fr Senan Furlong, Choirmaster at Glenstal, for this information.

31 Dom Jean Claire, pp. 196–211. The theory, in an attempt to understand the 'generating' factors of these orally based repertories, shifts the emphasis from the importance of the final note, as defined in the medieval *octoechos* system, to issues concerning melodic contour and the main structural or 'reciting' note.

32 Dom Daniel Saulnier, *Les Modes Grégoriens* (Solesmes, 1997), p. 132. The antiphons are presented with the concluding melodic formulae of their respective psalm-tones.

33 Cowdery, p. 90.

34 Despite all this, however, when placed back in the overall tonal and aesthetic context of the mass setting, the acclamation remains less than convincing. In this respect it is perhaps worth noting that the *Alleluia* is one of the pieces *not* included in the 1979 Ó Canainn publication of *Aifreann 2*.

35 Isaiah 52:7.

36 Commovisti, mode 8 Tract, *Liber usualis*, 507.

37 Bar 81c, p. 117.

38 Saulnier (1997), p. 93.

39 Ó Riada's musical linking of dialogic and litanic sections has already been noted in the tonal summary of *Ceol an aifrinn* (p. 91).

40 *Liber usualis*, 63.

41 The only comparable example in the mass is the motivically unified triple litany 'Molaimid Thú, Móraimid Thú, Adhraimid Thú' from the *Gloria* (bars 30–32), which is, however, tonally more stable by virtue of its under- and over-auxiliary melodic movement.

42 This declamatory ending to the *Sanctus*, however, is the only clearly recognisable point of contact with his earlier *Ceol an aifrinn* setting.

43 A practice maintained in over three quarters of the *Liber usualis* settings.

44 Prior to Vatican II, the eucharistic prayer was delivered in silence from the Sanctus onwards and featured no such congregational interpolations.

45 Many recent vernacular settings of this proclamation tend to opt for a triumphant rather than an 'expectant' musical ending.

46 *General Instruction of the Roman Missal* (*GIRM*) 55 (h), *The Roman Missal* (Alcester and Dublin: Goodliffe Neale, 1974), p. xxxii.

47 *Missale romanum* (Vatican City: Typis Polyglottis Vaticanis, 1970).

48 Certainly not to the extent of, for instance, the *Sanctus*, which marked a significant conceptual departure from his earlier setting of the text.

49 The sections are divided up as follows: A (bars 109–116); B (bars 116–122); A (bars 123–128).

50 A further example of the influence, within a prose context, of *number* on *form*.

51 As Ó Canainn (1978), p. 33, states: 'The seventh is by far the most commonly inflected note [in Irish music] ...'.

52 Ó Riada repeats the final five-syllable refrain line 'Ó a Shlánaitheoir', giving more rounded proportions of 8.8.8.8.10.

53 For example, the popular love song 'Pé in Éirinn í' (Ó hEidhin, p. 39).

54 Breathnach, p. 10.

55 Albert Lord (1960) treats the question in detail. The Parry–Lord concept of orally derived 'thrift' is explored more fully in chapter six.

56 This eighth-century native hymn, attributed to Dallan Forgaill, is today better known in its English version 'Be thou my vision', translated by Mary Byrne and versified by Eleanor Hull.

57 In the Roman tradition there is no significant precedent for the use of a concluding hymn at the end of mass. In *Ceol an aifrinn*, Ó Riada effectively designated the recessional hymn as optional.

58 Acton (1971), p. 111.

59 Richard Henebry, A *Handbook of Irish Music* (Cork: Cork University Press, 1928), p. 70. This publication follows on from his 1903 study entitled *Irish Music: being an examination of the matter of scales, modes and keys, with practical instruction* (Dublin: An Cló-Chumann, 1903). Henebry's identification of *doh*, *ray*, *soh* and *lah* as the principal modes of Irish music is the concept which still holds the widest currency. See Breathnach, p. 12, Ó Canainn, p. 27, and Máire Ní Chathasaigh's entry 'Modes' in Vallely (ed.), *Companion to Irish Traditional Music*, p. 243.

60 Ó Canainn and Mac an Bhua, p. 136.

61 Aloys Fleischmann in the Introduction (p. xxxv) to his monumental *Sources of Irish Traditional Music c. 1600–1855* (New York: Garland, 1998) attests to the existence in the tradition of bi-modal tunes.

62 See, for example, Samuel Bayard, 'Aspects of Melodic Kinship and Variation in British-American Folk-Tunes', in *Papers Read at the International Congress of Musicology 1939* (1944).

63 These are included in Cowdery, Appendix B, pp. 169–80.

64 Ibid., p. 131.

65 Reproduced (with permission of the author) from Cowdery, p. 131.

66 Henebry (1928), p. 70.

Chapter 5

1 Composer, performer, director of Cór Chúil Aodha and Cór Ban Chúil Aodha. B.Mus graduate of UCC (1977). In 2007, was awarded the TG4 Gradam Ceoil for his compositional contribution to traditional Irish music. His instrumental compositions feature imaginative re-workings (*The Blackbird*, unpublished), original compositions on traditional structures (*Spórt*, 1995) and the exploration of potentially new melodic models (*Fiach*, 1996). Vocal composition on secular texts range from the unison *Bóthar na síocháin* (1996) to the large-scale multi-voiced choral setting of *Caoineadh Airt Uí Laoghaire* (2003). Has also composed incidental music for both film and theatre. His most significant body of music is, however, liturgical, and it includes a large (mainly unpublished) body of Irish-language psalm and hymn settings, as well as settings of the mass parts and other key texts of the Roman rite. See 'Ó Riada, Peadar' in White and Boydell, p. 803.

2 From page 5 of *Aifreann Eoin na Croise*, the mass booklet from the first performance.

3 By choice rather than by necessity – Peadar Ó Riada is, in fact, classically trained, having achieved his BMus. in UCC under Prof. Aloys Fleischmann.

4 The celebration took place on 14 December 1990.

5 Not included as part of Ó Riada's score are the hymn *Cé dorcha an oíche* and other supplementary texts performed on the night. While *Cé dorcha an oíche* is in itself an interesting setting of a John of the Cross text, it lies well outside the stylistic musical boundaries of the mass setting and so will not be included as part of this study.

6 This setting of the prayer of the faithful is a pre-existing composition by Peadar Ó Riada, which he integrated into the commission.

7 The memorial acclamation setting is that of Seán Ó Riada's *Aifreann 2*.

8 Interview with the author, 14 July 2006.

9 A copy of this unofficial 'in-house' cassette recording was first given to me by Ronan McDonagh in early 1992. A recent recording of the mass, sung bu Cor Chúil Aodha is available on Peadar Ó Riada's *Naomh Gobnait* (CD, POR 015, 2012)

10 That this preference for three over two may be related to the intrinsic numerical qualities of the Irish language is suggested by the following quote from Virginia S. Blankenhorn: 'The results of our survey indicate that the Irish poets have, over the centuries, largely preferred triple rhythmic patterns to duple ones' (Blankenhorn, p. 75).

11 Peadar Ó Riada's compositional method will be specifically discussed in the final chapter of the thesis.

12 A standard practice, for instance, in the chant settings of the *Liber usualis*.

13 In relation to the early sequence, Stevens, p. 90, observes that the relationship between text and melody 'is syllabic (its basis is number in its most literal sense); and it is structural (words and music work together line by line, strophe by strophe)'. Again, in relation to the *lai-planctus*: 'The form of the melody is the form of the poem; the shape of the musical strophe coincides with the metrical; the musical phrase is the poetic line; each note or short note-group has its corresponding syllable' (p. 129).

14 Email correspondence with the author, 27 March 2006. The 'phrases and thoughts' which the composer overlays on the monotone chanting of 'An marnabh', and which themselves constitute an imposing musico-textual structure, will form the primary focus of the analysis which follows.

15 The English translations of *Aifreann Eoin na Croise* are those prepared by Cúil Aodha poet and writer Dónal Ó Liatháin for the original mass booklet, adapted by the author where necessary to supply a more literal realisation.

16 See note 2 above.

17 In his 1909 essay 'Epische Gesetze der Volksdichtung' ('Epic Laws of Folk Narrative'), reprinted in translation for Alan Dundes' *The Study of Folklore* (New Jersey: Prentice-Hall, 1965), Axel Olrik has the following to say concerning the *Law of Opening* (*das Gesetz des Einganges*) and the *Law of Closing* (*das Gesetz des Abschlusses*) of the folk epic or *Sage*: 'The *Sage* begins by moving from calm to excitement, and … ends by moving from excitement to calm' (p. 132).

18 From page 5 of *Aifreann Eoin na Croise*, the mass booklet from the first performance.

19 Dundes, pp. 132–3, described by Olrik as the *Law of Three* (*das Gesetz der Dreisahl)*.

20 *dc#c#* and *g#aa*.

21 These are supported by a sparsely textured keyboard accompaniment which mainly follows the melody in thirds and sixths over an A-drone, notably avoiding the leading note in any other part but the melody.

22 This *g* may be viewed within the context of a broader structural descent outlined by the distinctive sequence *a-g-f#-e* (bars 10–15).

23 Ó Riada again appears to draw on Olrik's 'super-organic' *Law of Three*, and these closing repetitions combine with the triple-litany opening to produce a ternary-type prayer structure. After the dramatic build-up of the main part of the prayer, the concluding, non developmental 'simple repetitions' recall Olrik's *Law of Closing*,

where 'the *Sage* ends by moving from excitement to calm' (p. 123). The use of litanic textual and musical repetition as an effective means of releasing musical tension is a characteristic feature of the religiously inspired 'epic'-style compositions of the contemporary Polish composer, Gorecki. See for instance his *O domina nostra*, op. 55 for solo voice and organ (Krackow: PWM, 1994).

24 A similar aesthetic informs Guido d'Arezzo's views on the structural composition of monophonic music: 'Also note that when a neume traverses a certain range or contour by leaping down from high notes, another neume may respond similarly in an opposite direction from low notes, as happens when we look for our likeness confronting us in a well' (Babb and Palisca, p. 71).

25 Ibid., p. 76.

26 This musico-textual crossweave effect is inherent in traditional ballad/song quatrains which use an ABBA melodic form to span the natural divide between two usually self-sufficient couplets. Commenting on the effectiveness of such a combination in relation to couplet *rhymes* in the ballad 'Anne Jane Thornton', as sung by Robert Butcher, Hugh Shields says: 'The melody is organized symmetrically in its phrases (ABBA) so that musical repetition *contrasts agreeably* [my italics] with the repetition of couplet rhymes (*aabb*)' (p. 85).

27 The presence of deliberately rising melodic 'questings' has already been noted in the second prayer where the extra ground was gained more elegantly and in keeping with a traditional aesthetic, and in the third prayer where the ascent was more relentlessly steep. The almost brutal nature of the ascent which dramatically carries the main part of this final litany, and which in doing so forges yet another thematic connection with the preceding prayers, prompts the following question: to what extent is the instrumental keyboard, with its clearly visual succession of notes rising in pitch from left to right, influential in fashioning the melodic shapes? Certainly the musical responses to this litany seem to owe more to an independent visual or even mechanistic model than anything that would emerge naturally from composition on the voice itself.

28 This structural fluctuation between tonic and subdominant tonalities in the context of a large-scale textual canvas recalls the bi-modality identified earlier in Seán Ó Riada's *Aifreann 2*.

29 When questioned about the use of this extremely low tessitura, Ó Riada referred to its 'relaxing' and 'preparatory' effects on participants within a liturgical context (interview with the author, 12 June 2007).

30 See note 22.

31 The published version of *Aifreann 2* contains a psalm setting, not by Seán Ó Riada, but by the editor Tomás Ó Canainn.

32 Though not *metrically*. The Vulgate Latin translations of the Hebrew psalms may be described as 'lyrical prose', a phrase used by Crocker, 10, and a description which accurately characterises the nature of the Irish vernacular version given above. See also Shiloah (2006), p. 19, on the non-metrical, 'floating' nature of Hebrew psalmody.

33 The parallelism and asymmetricality which tend to characterise Hebrew psalmody are discussed in Norman Gottwald's *The Hebrew Bible: a socio-literary introduction* (Philadelphia: Fortress Press, 1985), pp. 522–5.

34 Modifiable, by means of a *flex*, to accommodate frequent irregularities in the textual structure. See *Liber usualis*, 113.

35 Compare bars 47 (*Salm 139*) and 36 (*Admhaím do Dhia mhóir*).

36 Finnegan, pp. 98–109.

37 Shields, p. 33.

38 Lord, p. 54.

39 In a reference to his method of composing, Ó Riada described his approach as 'a linear development' (interview with the author, 29 July 2004).

40 This method of working was publicly demonstrated at a liturgical composition seminar which Ó Riada gave in Cúil Aodha in May 2006.

41 Emma Hornby, *Gregorian and Old Roman Eighth-Mode Tracts* (Aldershot: Ashgate, 2002), p. 207.

42 A repetition of the cadential phrase which concluded the fourth prayer of the *Opening Chant* – compare bars 51 and 23.

43 He was genuinely surprised when I informed him in May 2006 of the existence of an *Alleluia* composed by his father for *Aifreann 2*.

44 *Iubilate Deo* (London: Catholic Truth Society, 1974), p. 15.

45 Interview with the author, 29 July 2004.

46 Samuel Bayard, describing compositional processes of folk music in general, refers to 'the continual use of closely related melodic formulae of progression and cadence … now appearing side by side in a regular order of succession, now exchanging places' (Samuel Bayard, p. 126, as quoted in Cowdery, p. 83).

47 The cadential motif which carries these closing 'Aililiúia's is the same motif which concluded both *Bronnaim m'anam ort* (bar 23) and the verse melody of *Salm 139* (bar 51).

48 Interview with the author, 12 June 2007. The above passage bears a striking resemblance to the following quotation from the ninth-century musical theorist Aurelian of Réôme concerning the liturgical purpose of the text: 'The Alleluia … is very fittingly sung before the Gospel, that the minds of the faithful may be prepared by this song for the reception of the words of salvation' (*Aurelianus Reomensis: musica disciplina*, ed. Lawrence Gushee, CSM, p. xxi (1975)).

49 As already observed (see note 6), this setting pre-existed the commission.

50 For example, the responsorial 'Alleluia omnes gentes' associated with Ascension (*Graduale simplex* (Rome: Libreria Editrice Vaticana, 1975), p. 179) and the standard office-based form of the communal short responsory (e.g. *Liber usualis*, 269), which avoids slavish repetition in favour of a more engaging structure. Ó Riada's approach may be said to build on the more challenging and ultimately 'en-nobling' responses provided for the assembly by Seán Ó Riada in the priest–people dialogues of his *Aifreann 2* setting.

51 Peadar Ó Riada's approach to accompanying presidential cantillation of prayers and dialogues is, he says, the result of years of coaxing priests to chant their allotted portions of the mass. He usually suggests a monotone chanting, around which he builds a very stable, controlled, yet enabling harmonic context, along the lines provided above.

52 This musical 'echo' was already noted in our discussion of Seán Ó Riada's *Aifreann 2*, where the same motif was used to link the opening 'Is *Nao*fa' and our now 'missing' phrase, 'sna *har*da', which also shares the same phonic characteristics.

53 I have noted it in the unpublished melodies of his hymn to St Patrick, 'A Phádraig aspail, príomháidh Gael' and a recent setting of Psalm 62, 'Tá iota tarta ar m'anam liom'. The device may also be observed in Seán Ó Riada's *Ceol an aifrinn* setting of *A Rí an Domhnaigh* (bar 153).

54 Interview with the author, 12 June 2007. Seán Ó Riada with his direction 'Curfá arís, dhá uair' at the end of *A Íosa bháin* fashioned a conclusion to the hymn which featured a quadruple repetition of the final phrase 'Ó a Shlánaitheoir'.

55 Literally, 'Great Amen', following a concept strongly promoted by post-conciliar liturgists, which encouraged substantial congregational involvement at this concluding moment of the Eucharistic Prayer. See, for example, Margaret Daly (ed.), *Alleluia! Amen!* (Dublin: Veritas, 1978), p. 16.

56 We recall the ninth-century *De harmonica*'s tetrachordal interpretation of the Boethian two-octave scale (chapter two). Ó Riada's instinctive awareness of these elemental musical realities demonstrates to what extent the diatonic scale sets the tonal landscape for his work.

57 These developments, which focused mainly on priest–people dialogues, included settings of the acclamations at the gospel, memorial acclamation, eucharistic prayer doxology and the Alleluia.

58 The full, official missal text for this acclamation runs as follows: 'Óir is leatsa an ríocht agus an chumhacht *agus an ghlóir* trí shaol na saol.' The omission, according to Ó Riada (interview with the author, 12 June 2007), was inadvertent.

59 The only significant departure is the A-based recitation of the Ár nAthair, the accompaniment of which, however, still keeps alive the possibility of a *D* tonality.

60 Saulnier, p. 93.

61 Email correspondence with the author, 27 March 2006.

62 The underpinning of A at the beginning and throughout much of this final substantial movement of the mass setting is not without some architectural significance. In one sense the return to a bass A may be viewed as a 'return to the source' of the whole mass setting, in that A provides the basis of the entire and very substantial *Opening Chant*. Yet, in another sense the full musical unfolding of *An cosán draíochta* may be said to tonally counterbalance the opening movement. The *Opening Chant*, while occasionally adverting to the subdominant (in its frequent use of *g*-natural and in one clear, if brief, tonal shift towards *D* at the beginning of *Admhaím do Dhia mhóir*) is melodically oriented primarily towards the dominant *E*. In *An cosán draíochta*, as we shall see, the A-based tonal dynamic ultimately turns towards *D*. In harmonic terms a succinct summary might run as follows: Opening movement, tonic to dominant; Closing movement, dominant to tonic. In melodic terms we are brought back to the central mode 7 question of Seán Ó Riada's *Aifreann 2* and the contending of the fifth and fourth degrees above a foundational pitch.

63 Thus providing a further example of the ABBA (music) / *abab* (text) 'crossweave' observed earlier in the *Opening Chant*.

64 This type of melodic development may be seen, for instance, in 'An goirtín eornan' (Phrase 1 *doh-mi-soh*; Phrase 2 *mi-soh-doh'*; Phrase 3 *mi-soh-doh'*; Phrase 4 *doh-mi-soh*) and the more developed melodic form of 'An mhaighdean mhara' (*soh-doh'*; *doh'-mi'*; *mi'-soh'*; *mi-soh*). Notated versions may be found in Ó Canainn (1995), p. 91.

65 The phrase is not just tonally cadential, but also, in traditional Irish terms, thematically cadential: it has fulfilled this function three times already in the mass – at bars 23, 51 and 54.

66 A description frequently used by the composer himself.

Chapter 6

1 William Drabkin, 'Motif', in Stanley Sadie (ed.), *The New Grove Dictionary of Music and Musicians*, xvii (London: Macmillan, 2001), pp. 227–8.

2 Jeffery, p. 92.

3 Lord, p. 4.

4 Jeffery, p. 92.

5 Ibid., p. 96.

6 Though, as we shall see, the *extent* and *distribution* of recurrence also has a bearing on the issue.

7 Karp, p. 288.

8 Babb and Palisca, p. 71.

9 *Note on the musical score*: For purposes of clarity, I have adopted a stemless, chant-type notation, using only short and long note values. Omitted from the analysis are the two pre-existing pieces, *Guí an phobail* and *Rúndiamhair an chreidimh*.

10 Interview with the author, 29 July 2004. A melodic version is contained in Ó Canainn (1995), p. 54.

11 Published as the title track of the composer's first recorded collection of liturgical music *Go mBeannaítear Duit: ceol ó shéipéal Chúil Aodha* (Cassette Gael Linn, CEFC 125, 1987).

12 The 8–7–5 progression characterises traditional airs such as 'Port na bpúcaí' (Ó Canainn (1995), p. 60), 'Róisín dubh' (Joe Heaney's version, quoted in Cowdery, p. 171) and 'An poc ar buile' (see page 96). Ó Canainn (1978), p. 34, singles it out as a characteristic 'pattern' and Fleischmann, p. xxxii, identifies it as part of a common 'mode-type'. The 8–7–5 motif appears throughout the mass settings of Seóirse Bodley (*Three Congregational Masses*, ed. Lorraine Byrne, Carysfort Press, 2005), which are directed towards congregations with a 'knowledge of Irish musical style' (p. xiii).

13 Leo Treitler, in his seminal article 'Homer and Gregory: the transmission of epic poetry and plainchant' (*The Musical Quarterly*, vol. 60, July 1974, p. 352), uses this term to describe particular sequences of directional changes around specific pitches, thus focusing on the generative compositional potential of such systems, in contrast with the concept, at the other end of the analytical spectrum, of fixed, recurring motivic configurations.

14 A version of it completes a two-part melodic formula traditionally used to carry the extended text of the Ossianic *Laoi na mná móire*. The formula is quoted in Breathnach, p. 26.

15 The dramatic instance of a motivic 'breakthrough' at the end of *A Uain Dé*, adverted to in the preceding chapter, will be discussed in the next section of this chapter.

16 Babb and Palisca, p. 72.

17 This is due mainly to the extended *Opening Chant*, which accounts for nearly half of the total content.

18 Lord, p. 47.

19 I estimate that of the newly composed material under discussion, approximately 7.5% could be described as 'non-formulaic'.

20 Lord, p. 43.

21 'They will express the names of the actors, the main actions, time and place' (ibid., p. 34).

22 Ibid., p. 4.

23 Ibid., p. 5.

24 Ibid., p. 54.

25 Ibid., p. 95.

26 Karp, p. 60. See also Treitler (1974), p. 345: 'A salient detail may be common to two or more themes or streams of interest, and it may serve as a crossing point between them. In that way the theme originally presented may be left and another entered.'

27 Paulo Ferretti, *Estetica gregoriana ossia trattato delle forme musicali del canto gregoriano* (Rome: Pontificio Istituto di Musica Sacra, 1934).

28 Geoffrey Chew, James McKinnon, 'Centonisation', in Stanley Sadie (ed.), *NG*, v (London: Macmillan 2001), pp. 356–7.

29 Apel, p. 316.

30 Karp, p. 134.

31 Prou, p. 545.

32 Apel, p. 363.

33 Lord, p. 50.

34 Milman Parry, 'Studies in the Epic Technique of Oral Verse-Making. 1. Homer and Homeric Style', *Harvard Studies in Classical Philology*, vol. 41, 1930, pp. 73–147.

35 Nowacki (1980), p. 299.

36 Edward Nowacki, 'The Gregorian Office Antiphons and the Comparative Method', *Journal of Musicology*, vol. 4, 1985–1986, p. 243.

37 Leo Treitler, *With Voice and Pen: coming to know medieval song and how it was made* (New York: Oxford University Press, 2003), p. 151.

38 Bohlman, p. 16.

39 Ibid., pp. 16–17.

40 Ó Canainn (1978), p. 34.

41 Cowdery, p. 88.

42 Ibid., p. 90.

43 Bertrand Bronson, *The Ballad as Song* (Berkeley: University of California Press 1969), p. 141, quoted in Cowdery, p. 85.

44 Ibid., pp. 92–3.

45 Nowacki (1980), p. 312.

46 Vatican II, *Sacrosanctum concilium* 112, Flannery, p. 31.

47 Jeffery, pp. 92, 96.

48 Contrast bars 4, 33 and the closing phrase of bar 41, with bars 39, 65 and the opening of 41. The repetitions of the equally accented 'A-men' syllables (bar 76) mark a middle way between these two alternatives.

49 Apel, p. 260.

50 See the opening lines (page 45) of Seán Ó Riada's *Is Beannaithe Tigh Dé* (*Ceol an aifrinn*) for a similar musico-rhetorical treatment of this word.

51 Apel, pp. 316–17.

52 A similar set of constraints operate in the case of the chant genre of the gradual (ibid., pp. 344–63).

53 See Apel, p. 403, for a representative table.

54 Rebecca Maloy, 'The Offertory Chant: aspects of chronology and transmission', unpublished PhD disseration, Cincinnati University, 2001.

55 As summarised by her tutor, Edward Nowacki, in his paper 'Linguistic Perspectives in the Analysis of Plainchant' given at the Irish World Music Centre, University of Limerick in March 2004.

56 Stevens, pp. 98–9.

57 Ibid., p. 105.

58 Ibid., p. 77: 'The truths about "number" stand firm; I will not reiterate the arguments for believing that under the encrustations this is "syllabic melody" still and belongs to the centuries-old tradition of song-making in which counting your syllables, balancing your lines, weaving an harmonious fabric of units, was the all-important thing.'

59 Treitler (2003), p. 26. See also Apel, p. 363.

60 *Liber usualis*, 37.

61 Lord, p. 47.

62 Cowdery, p. 85. See the adaptation of motif *c*, bars 3, 4, and 10.

63 Among the rest of the corpus of larger-scale mass ordinary settings, only Credo III (*Liber usualis*, 68), also considered to be a later setting, displays similar compositional characteristics. It is distinguished, however, by a greater amount of thematically 'free' material and by a greater degree of motivic variation than is evident in either of the above compositions.

64 Stevens' 'non-relationship' concept has to be seen within its proper context, implicit in the pages of *Words and Music*, as a blow for freedom from the narrow confines of received musicological notions concerning the nature of word/music aesthetics originating in the Renaissance. In no sense is he suggesting that in medieval song and chant, melody has an ambivalent, neutral, 'non-effect' on the words, and indeed the many examples he quotes demonstrate ample evidence of a positive, vigorous and vivifying relationship, one which we have seen replicated in the compositions of *Aifreann Eoin na Croise*.

65 Stevens, p. 154.

66 Lord, pp. 35–6.

67 Treitler (2003), p. 134.

68 Ibid., p. 45.

69 Lord, p. 30.

70 Ibid., p. 66. We are reminded here of the 'characteristic expressions' of the 'spirit' and 'traditions' of particular cultures. (Vatican II, *Musicam sacram* 61, in Flannery, p. 95).

71 Treitler (2003), p. 137.

72 Interview with the author, 6 August 2004. Loch Uí Bhogaigh, a lake situated below Cúil Aodha parish church, retains for locals strong resonances of an ancient culture pre-dating the arrival of Christianity to the area.

73 Interview with the author, 6 August 2004.

74 Prou, p. 545.

Chapter 7

1 As already noted (see chapter one, note 6), the relevant passage from *Sacrosanctum concilium* includes the word 'sacred' (i.e. 'a combination of sacred music and words'). The concept of a 'sacred' music (i.e. a musical language which is inherently sacred) has been losing ground in recent decades – see Michael Joncas' survey of Catholic Church music legislation and scholarly reflection, *From Sacred Song to Ritual Music: twentieth century understandings of Roman Catholic worship music* (Collegeville, MN: The Liturgical Press, 1997), and Gerard Gillen's more recent treatment of the question in 'Towards a Definition of "Good" Liturgical Music' (included in Helen Phelan's *Anáil Dé – The Breath of God: music, ritual and spirituality* (Dublin: Veritas, 2001)). Gillen's article (pp. 189–200) traces the origins of the concept of a 'sacred' musical style and reflects on some of the reasons why it has become increasingly difficult to sustain, and Joncas' survey concludes: 'while "holiness" remains a prime desideratum in Roman rite worship music, this holiness is increasingly conceptualized functionally rather than ontologically' (p. 71). More recently, the introduction to Christopher Page's magisterial study *The Christian West and Its Singers: the first thousand years* (Yale, 2012), notes on its opening page 'the want of any suggestion in the first three centuries of the churches that it was considered essential to define a distinctively Christian musical idiom'.

2 The motivic analysis of *Aifreann Eoin na Croise* brought this process even further, revealing a freedom of association between music and textual *syntax* and *accent*, the latter providing clear aesthetic links with the medieval repertory of prose sequences.

3 Stevens, p. 40.

4 'If you then fill in the gaps, space out the constricted places, draw together the overextended, and broaden the overcondensed, you will make a unified, polished work' (*Micrologus*, in Babb & Palisca, p. 76).

5 John Ainslie (ed.), *The Simple Gradual for Sundays and Holy Days* (London: Chapman, 1970).

6 The most popular complete collection of liturgical psalmody in use in this country, Fintan O'Carroll's *Responsorial Psalms for Sundays and Feast Days* (published by the Irish Church Music Association in 1983 and re-published by Veritas in 2006) reflects many of the principles established by Gelineau.

7 Published in the collection *Ancient Promise* (Dublin: Fuaimlaoi, 2011). See also his settings of Psalm 138 (*In caelo* (Dublin: Veritas, 1999), no. 39) and Psalm 83 (*Feasts and Seasons* (Maynooth: St Patrick's College, 2003), no. 2).

8 Contained in the publication *Music to Honour God's Name* (Dublin: Veritas, 2000). This compositional principle is also applied to McDonagh's version of *An Ghlóir* (*Feasts and Seasons*, no. 6) providing a relatively rare example of a successfully through-composed vernacular setting of the Gloria text.

9 In Latin, 'cultus mentalis'.

10 'The whole plan of singing in musical modes should be constituted not to give empty pleasure to the ear, but in such a way that the words may be clearly understood by all …' (Council of Trent, Canon 8, quoted in Hayburn, p. 27).

11 Pius X, *Tra le sollecitudini* (1903), Art. 9, ibid., 227. A theme revisited in contemporary papal reflections on liturgical music: see Article 5 of John Paul II's 2003 *Chirograph on Sacred Music*, and Benedict XVI's *Liturgiam Authenticam*, Article 60.

12 See, for instance, all of the prize-winning Sanctus and Gloria settings contained in the publication *I Sing for Joy: music from the RTÉ Radio One church music competitions* (Dublin: Columba Press, 2006). My survey 'Singing the Mass: mass composition in Ireland since Vatican II', in Liam Tracey and Thomas Whelan (eds), *Serving Liturgical Renewal: pastoral and liturgical questions* (Veritas: Dublin, 2015), charts some of the main compositional trends in this country over the past five decades.

13 In fact, there exists the real possibility that it may in the long run alienate them, not simply because it unnecessarily lengthens the ritual moment (a responsorial Gloria, for instance, can end up taking two-and-a-half times the length of a through-composed one), but because, ultimately, the form of the piece is not felt to correspond with its liturgical function.

14 Joseph Gelineau, *Liturgical Assembly, Liturgical Song* (Oregon: Pastoral Press, 2002), p. 84.

15 *Sacrosanctum concilium* 23, quoted in *Musicam sacram*, Art. 59, under the heading 'Preparing Melodies for Vernacular Texts'. Flannery, p. 95.

16 Acton (1971), p. 112.

17 The Carmelite Church of St Teresa's, Clarendon Street, Dublin.

18 Commissioned and published by the Music Panel of the Irish Commission for Liturgy (Dublin, 1977).

19 Commissioned and published by the Music Panel of the Irish Commission for Liturgy (Dublin, 1976).

20 Nowacki (1980), p. 337.

21 The 'thriftiness' of both these compositions, guided, it would appear, by principles of orality and memorisation, has rendered them particularly successful as practical, congregation-oriented, through-composed settings of the Gloria. A more recent application of these compositional principles may be observed in the Gloria and Apostles' Creed from the author's congregational *Mass of Saint Mel* (2015).

22 This clearly understated approach to the 'Hosanna' sections has an illustrious predecessor in the earliest-known Roman setting of the Sanctus, that of Mass XVIII.

23 Babb and Palisca, p. 74.

24 To the Gloria and Sanctus discussed above could be added the two settings provided by the composer for the memorial acclamation. Bodley's congregational settings were proposed as key models for younger composers to emulate in a 2009 document, *Music for the New Order of Mass: guidelines for composers*, produced by the Irish Episcopal Conference's Advisory Committee on Church Music as part of the preparation for the Third Edition of the *Roman Missal*.

25 McKinnon's 1986 survey of musical references in early Christian sources cites many passages referring to the selection of sung texts appropriate to (a) the time of day, and (b) the specific part of the celebration.

26 Josef A. Jungmann, *The Mass of the Roman Rite: its origins and development* (London: Burns & Oates, 1959), p. 214.

27 László Dobszay, *The Bugnini-Liturgy and the Reform of the Reform*, Musicae Sacrae Meletemata, vol. 5 (Hungary: Front Royal VA, 2003), pp. 97–8.

28 Professor Dobszay (1935–2011), a founder of the international chant study group Cantus Planus, and founder-director of the international chant ensemble Schola Hungarica, was also head of church music at the Liszt Ferenc Music University in Budapest.

29 Margaret Daly-Denton, 'Psalmody as "Word of Christ"', in Kathleen Hughes (ed.), *Finding Voice to Give God Praise: essays in the many languages of the liturgy* (Collegeville, MN: The Liturgical Press, 1998), pp. 80–1.

30 *Musicam sacram*, 56, Flannery, p. 94.

31 I became aware of this when I addressed a gathering of the Panel of Monastic Musicians of England, Scotland, Wales and Ireland at their annual meeting of 2002, held at the Cistercian Abbey of Roscrea. Over the past fifteen years, however, it has enjoyed a notable revival worldwide among English-speaking church musicians seeking to reconnect with the textual richness of the church's musical tradition.

32 Published at St Mary's Press, Wantage.

33 Bruce E. Ford, *An American Gradual: chants of the proper of the mass adapted to English words* (Hopkinsville, KY: St James Music Press, 2001).

34 Paul F. Ford, *By Flowing Waters: chant for the liturgy* (Collegeville, MN: The Liturgical Press, 1999).

35 *Graduale simplex* published principally in response to Vatican II's *Sacrosanctum concilium* decree that 'an edition [of mass propers] be prepared containing melodies suitable for use in smaller churches' (Art. 117).

36 Ford (1999), p. xi.

37 Ibid., p. xvi.

38 In the course of the analyses which formed part of this study, I identified only two occasions, the *Alleluia* and *Sanctus*-opening of Seán Ó Riada's *Aifreann 2*, when the composer's efforts seemed less than convincing. Both of these were judged to be the result of undue and unnecessary deference to the Gregorian *melodic* tradition.

39 Nowacki (1980), p. 337.

40 It seems reasonable to suggest, then, that if we are going to speak of a genuine 'vernacular chant', it is imperative that (a) the concept be liberated from the very narrow confines of the English-language pastiche tradition stretching back to Palmer's 1926 publication, and be re-defined according to the broader concept of *sung prose* advanced in this study; and (b) that we should expect from any musico-liturgical project so termed, the same artistic quality and generative potential which characterise the Latin-based Gregorian and Old-Roman chant traditions.

41 Harry White, 'Church Music and Musicology in Ireland: an afterword', in Gillen and White (eds), *Irish Musical Studies Volume 2: music and the church* (Dublin: Irish Academic Press, 1993), p. 335.

42 Lord, pp. 147, 150–1.

43 Taking the carefully honed keyboard accompaniments of *Aifreann Eoin na Croise* as but one pertinent example.

44 For example, his reworking of the well-known tune *The Blackbird*, which has been described by traditional musician Tony McMahon as 'innovative yet totally organic'. Even more striking is his composition *Fiach* (opening track of the CD *Peadar Ó Riada: winds – gentle whisper*, Bar/None Records, 1995) which forges motivic elements from the polka-tune tradition into a six-quaver pattern in which a rhythmic re-framing from 3/4 to 6/8 'clicks in' almost imperceptibly halfway through an extremely minimalistic texture, and, before the listener is even aware of it, the entire rhythmic landscape has changed. This genuinely innovative use of the hemiola contrasts markedly with the clichéd and oft-times forced imposition of the device by contemporary traditional instrumental performers onto the 6/8 patterns of jig tunes. Ó Riada's achievement with *Fiach* has been to create from a traditional language a radically new and engaging melodic form, capable of two independent rhythmical 'readings'.

45 Lord, p. 130.

46 Seán Ó Riada, who came to the tradition significantly later in life, would spend less than a decade of intense involvement with, and total immersion in, that tradition.

47 Lord, pp. 31–2. This description of the oral composer finds a strong echo in the following observation of pre-eminent traditional Irish musician Martin Hayes on Peadar Ó Riada's compositional method: 'I think he has internalised the structures of the music and the richness of all its phrases and I think he allows it to be reformulated in him in some way' (RTÉ television documentary *3Triúr: In Search of Musical Form* (first broadcast on Tuesday, 6, September 2016).

48 Cowdery, p. 93. The point is emphasised strongly by McKean in the introduction (p. xxii) to his study of Ian MacNeacail, the Hebridean song-maker: 'In recording MacNeacail, I have had the chance of which many folklorists only dream: to interview and write about a person who is not only a great tradition-bearer, but who also creates from within a strong tradition.' An even greater distance, it would seem, separates scholars of western plainchant from the wellsprings of their chosen discipline, as is evidenced by the following excerpt from Shai Burstyn's review of Peter Jeffery's 1992 study *Re-Envisioning Past Musical Cultures: ethnomusicology in the study of Gregorian chant*: 'A case of observable oral practice indisputably supporting his theory is surely every chant scholar's dream' (in *Plainsong and Medieval Music*, vol. 3, part 2, October 1994, p. 210). The description which follows in the pages of this study of actual oral liturgical composition 'from within a strong tradition' presents, I believe, a significant distillation and realisation of the 'dreams' of both disciplines.

49 *Cúrsa ar Cheol agus Searmanasaí Eaglasta*, 5–7 May 2006, organised under the auspices of Iontaoibheas Fódhla, a trust established in order to continue the work begun by Seán Ó Riada in the promotion of so many aspects of Irish culture.

50 The interview took place on 29 July 2004.

51 The fundamental image of the liturgical composer as 'reader' of the liturgical text is implicit in the following passage from Theodore Karp: 'Thus the most basic task of the "reader" is to divide the text appropriately into phrases, sentences and main divisions, and to communicate these divisions to the assembled congregation' (Karp, p. 25).

52 Interview with the author, 29 July 2004. This description of the process corresponds with Lord, pp. 44–5: '… in speaking of "creating" phrases … we do not intend to

convey the idea that the singer [of tales] *seeks originality* or fineness of expression. *He seeks expression of the idea under stress of performance* [my italics] … If the singer knows a ready-made phrase and thinks of it, he uses it without hesitation, but he has, as we have seen, a method of making phrases when he does not know one or cannot remember one.'

53 Presumably because, in the Irish language liturgies of Cúil Aodha, there was never any occasion to do so. It is important to remember, however, that the general song tradition of Cúil Aodha includes a significant portion of high-quality English-language compositions.

54 The layout mirrors his phrase-by-phrase approach to the text, and the pause marks were additional practical points of repose for the composer as he considered the next portion of the text.

55 At this point Ó Riada presented the option of a concluding triple repetition of the final phrase 'near to you, my God' (See chapter five, note 54).

56 In oral cultures, as Regina Randhofer states, 'thinking and expression are one single process' (Randhofer (2004)).

57 '… that the phrases be of the same length, like lines of verse, and be sometimes repeated, either the same or modified by some change, even though slight, and, if they are particularly beautiful, be duplicated, with their "parts" not too diverse: and let those occasional phrases that are the same be varied as to intervals [*per modos*], or, if they retain the same intervals, let them be heard transposed higher or lower. Also a neume, turning back on itself, may return the same way it came and by the same steps' (Babb and Palisca, p. 71).

58 He was equally happy with either a melodic ascent or a descent towards this word.

59 This aptness of expression within a living, developing and ultimately convincing melodic structure puts us in mind, one final time, of Nowacki's Old Roman cantor and of that 'command of tonal syntax … so pliable that he could always declaim a text in a manner that was at once unique and idiomatic, innovative and traditional' (Nowacki (1980), p. 32).

60 The alternation of these structural notes between tonic (taken in this case to be the drone), fourth and fifth degrees distils for one final time in this study the elemental nature of these pitches.

61 Babb and Palisca, p. 76.

62 Treitler (1974), pp. 346–7.

63 Lord, p. 220.

64 These were, in chronological order, the *psaltes*, schola cantorum, choir, cantoratus and cantor-organist.

65 A representative sample of the repertoire has been captured on the CD recordings *Go mBeannaítear Duit: ceol ó shéipéal Chúil Aodha* (Gael Linn, CEFCD 125, 2009) and *Naomh Gobnait* (POR 015, 2012).

BIBLIOGRAPHY

Acton, Charles, 'Interview with Seán Ó Riada', *Éire-Ireland*, vol. 6, no. 1, 1971, pp. 106–115

Acton, Charles, 'I gCuimhne Sheáin Uí Riada', *Éire-Ireland*, vol. 6, no. 4, 1971, pp. 3–5

Adams, John, *Harmonielehre* (New York: AMP, 1985)

Ainslie, John (ed.), *The Simple Gradual for Sundays and Holy Days* (London: Chapman, 1970)

An Leabhar Aifrinn (Maigh Nuad: An Sagart, 1973)

Antiphonale Monasticum (Tournai: Desclée, 1934)

Antiphonale Sacrosanctae Romanae Ecclesiae pro Diurnis Horis (Paris: Desclée, 1924)

Apel, Willi, *Gregorian Chant* (Bloomington: Indiana University Press, 1958)

Aubrey, Elisabeth, *The Music of the Troubadours* (Bloomington: Indiana University Press, 1996)

Babb, Warren and Palisca, Claude (eds), *Hucbald, Guido and John on Music: three medieval treatises* (New Haven: Yale University Press, 1978)

Bayard, Samuel, 'Aspects of Melodic Kinship and Variation in British-American Folk-Tunes', *Papers read at the International Congress of Musicology*, 1939 (1944), pp. 122–129

Blankenhorn, Virginia S., *Irish Song-Craft and Metrical Practice since 1600* (New York: Edwin Mellen Press, 2003)

Bodley, Seóirse, 'Technique and Structure in Sean-Nós Singing', *Irish Folk Music Studies*, vol. 1, 1972–1973, pp. 44–53

Bodley, Seóirse, *Three Congregational Masses*, ed. Lorraine Byrne (Dublin: Carysfort Press, 2005)

Bohlman, Philip, *The Study of Folk Music in the Modern World* (Indianapolis: Indiana University Press, 1988)

Bomm, Urbanus, *Der Wechsel der Modalitätbestimmung in der Tradition der Messgesängeim IX. bis XIII. Jahrhundert und sein Einfluss auf die Tradition ihrer Melodien* (diss., Göttingen, 1928; Einsiedeln, 1929)

Bradshaw, Paul, *The New SCM Dictionary of Liturgy and Worship* (London: SCM Press, 2002)

Bradshaw, Paul and Johnson, Maxwell E. *The Eucharistic Liturgies* (Collegeville: Liturgical Press, 2012)

Breathnach, Breandán, *Folk Music and Dances of Ireland* (Dublin and Cork: Mercier Press, 1971)

Breathnach, Breandán, 'Ireland II: Folk Music', in Sadie, Stanley (ed.), *The New Grove Dictionary of Music and Musicians*, ix (London: Macmillan, 1980), pp. 316–325

Breathnach, Pádraig, *Raint Amhrán* (Baile Átha Cliath, 1916–17)

Bronson, Bertrand, *The Ballad as Song* (Berkeley: University of California Press, 1969)

Brunner, Horst, 'Ton' (i), in Sadie, Stanley (ed.), *The New Grove Dictionary of Music and Musicians*, xix (London: Macmillan, 1980), pp. 49–50

Bunting, Edward, *A General Collection of the Ancient Music of Ireland* (London: 1809), contained in *The Ancient Music of Ireland: the Bunting collections* (Dublin: Waltons, 2002)

Burstyn, Shai, Review of P. Jeffery, *Re-Envisioning Past Musical Cultures: ethnomusicology in the study of Gregorian chant* (Chicago: University of Chicago Press, 1992), *Plainsong and Medieval Music*, vol. 3, part 2 (October 1994), pp. 207–212

Cantus Planus 1990: International Musicological Society Study Group 'Cantus Planus', Papers read at the Third Meeting, Tihany, Hungary, 19–24 September 1988, ed. László Dobszay, Péter Halász, János Mezei and Gábor Prószéky (Budapest, 1990)

Cardine, Eugène, *Gregorian Semiology* (Solesmes, 1982)

Carolan, Nicholas, 'Songs of Múscraí', *Ceol Tíre*, vol. 12, 1978, pp. 2–3

Chambers Twentieth Century Dictionary, ed. A.M. Macdonald (Edinburgh: Chambers, 1972)

Chambers, G.B., *Folksong – Plainsong: a study in origins and musical relationships*, 2nd edition (London: The Merlin Press, 1972)

Chew, Geoffrey and McKinnon, James, 'Centonisation', in Sadie, Stanley (ed.), *The New Grove Dictionary of Music and Musicians*, v (London: Macmillan, 2001), pp. 356–357

Claire, Dom Jean, 'L'évolution Modale dans les Repertoires Liturgiques Occidentaux', *Revue Grégorienne*, 40, 1962, pp. 196–211 and 229–245

Connolly, Thomas, 'Introits and Archetypes: some archaisms of the Old Roman chant', *Journal of the American Musicological Society*, 25, 1972, pp. 157–174

Connolly, Thomas, 'The Gradual of S. Cecilia in Trastevere and the Old Roman Tradition', *JAMS*, 28, 1975, pp. 413–458

Cowdery, James, *The Melodic Tradition of Ireland* (Kent, OH: Kent State University Press, 1990)

Crocker, Richard, Review of J. Stevens, *Words and Music in the Middle Ages: song, narrative, dance and drama, 1050–1350* (Cambridge: Cambridge University Press, 1986) in *Music and Letters* vol. 68, no.4 (October 1987), 364–366

Crocker, Richard, *An Introduction to Gregorian Chant* (New Haven: Yale University Press, 2000)

Daly, Margaret (ed.), *Alleluia! Amen!* (Dublin: Veritas, 1978)

Daly-Denton, Margaret, 'Psalmody as "Word of Christ"', in Hughes, Kathleen (ed.), *Finding Voice to Give God Praise: Essays in the Many Languages of the Liturgy* (Collegeville, MN: The Liturgical Press, 1998), pp. 73–86

Deiss, Lucien, *Spirit and Song of the New Liturgy* (Cincinnati: World Library Publications, 1976)

Deiss, Lucien, *Visions of Liturgy and Music for a New Century* (Collegeville, MN: The Liturgical Press, 1996)

De Noraidh, Liam, *Ceol ón Mumhain* (Dublin: An Clócomhar, 1965)

Devine, Patrick and White, Harry (eds), *Irish Musical Studies 4: The Maynooth International Musicological Conference 1995: Selected Proceedings Part One* (Dublin: Four Courts Press, 1996)

Devine, Patrick, and White, Harry (eds), *Irish Musical Studies 5: The Maynooth International Musicological Conference 1995: Selected Proceedings Part Two* (Dublin: Four Courts Press, 1996)

Dix, Gregory, *The Shape of the Liturgy* (London: Adam & Charles Black, 1975)

Dobszay, László, 'Experiences in the Musical Classification of Antiphons', *Cantus Planus 1990*, pp. 143–156

Dobszay, László and Szendrei, Janka (eds), *Catalogue of Hungarian Folksong Types* (Budapest: Institute for Musicology of the Hungarian Academy of Sciences, 1992)

Dobszay, László, *The Bugnini-Liturgy and the Reform of the Reform*, Musicae Sacrae Meletemata, vol. 5 (Budapest: Front Royal VA, 2003)

Dobszay, László, *The Antiphon* (Budapest: Hungarian Academy of Sciences – Liszt Ferenc Music Academy Church Music Research Group and Hungarian Church Music Association, 2006)

Drabkin, William, 'Motif', *The New Grove Dictionary of Music and Musicians*, xvii, ed. Sadie, Stanley (London: Macmillan, 2001), pp. 227–228

Dundes, Alan, *The Study of Folklore* (New Jersey: Prentice-Hall, 1965)

Fellerer, Karl Gustav, *The History of Catholic Church Music*, trans. Francis A. Brunner (Baltimore: Helicon, 1961)

Ferreira, Manuel Pedro, 'Music at Cluny: the tradition of Gregorian chant for the proper of the mass. Melodic variants and microtonal nuances', unpublished PhD diss., Princeton, 1997

Ferretti, Paulo, *Estetica Gregoriana Ossia Trattato delle Forme Musicali del Canto Gregoriano* (Rome: Libreria Editrice Vaticana, 1934)

Finnegan, Ruth, *Oral Poetry: its nature, significance and social context* (Cambridge: Cambridge University Press, 1980)

Flannery, Austin (ed.), *Vatican Council II: the conciliar and post-conciliar documents*, revised edition (New York: Costello Publishing Company, 1988)

Fleischmann, Aloys, *Sources of Irish Traditional Music c. 1600–1855, volumes I and II* (New York: Garland, 1998)

Foley, Edward, *Age to Age* (Chicago: Liturgical Training Publications, 1991)

Foley, Edward, *Ritual Music: studies in liturgical musicology* (Beltsville, MD: Pastoral Press, 1995)

Ford, Bruce E., *An American Gradual: chants of the proper of the mass adapted to English words* (Hopkinsville, KY: St James Music Press, 2001)

Ford, Paul F., *By Flowing Waters: chant for the liturgy* (Collegeville, MN: The Liturgical Press, 1999)

Fránk, István, *Répertoire Métrique de la Poésie des Troubadours*, Bibliothèque de L'École des Hautes Études, 303 and 308 (Paris, 1953 and 1957)

Freeman, A. Martin, 'Irish Folk Songs', *Journal of the Folk Song Society*, part 6, no. 23 (January 1920), iii–xxviii, pp. 95–205; no. 24 (January 1921), pp. 205–266; no. 25 (September 1921), pp. [265]–342

Funk, Virgil (ed.), *Music in Catholic Worship: the NPM commentary* (Washington, DC: NAPM, 1982)

Gelineau, Joseph, *Voices and Instruments in Christian Worship*, trans. Clifford Howell (Collegeville, MN: The Liturgical Press, 1964)

Gelineau, Joseph, *Liturgical Assembly, Liturgical Song* (Portland: Pastoral Press, 2002)

Georgiades, Thrasybulos, *Music and Language: the rise of western music as exemplified in the settings of the mass* (Cambridge: Cambridge University Press, 1982)

General Instruction of the Roman Missal, from *The Roman Missal* (Alcester and Dublin: Goodliffe Neale, 1974)

Gilchrist, Annie, 'A Note on the Modal System of Gaelic Tunes', *JFSS*, vol. 4, 1910–1913, p. 150

Gilchrist, Annie, 'Lambkin: a study in evolution', *Journal of the English Folk Dance and Song Society*, vol. 1, 1932, pp. 1–17

Gillen, Gerard, 'Towards a Definition of "Good" Liturgical Music', in Phelan, Helen (ed.), *Anáil Dé: the breath of God. Music, ritual and spirituality* (Dublin: Veritas, 2001), pp. 189–200

Gillen, Gerard and Johnstone, Andrew (eds), *Irish Musical Studies 6: a historical anthology of Irish church music* (Dublin: Four Courts Press, 2001)

Gillen, Gerard and White, Harry (eds), *Irish Musical Studies 2: music and the church* (Dublin: Irish Academic Press, 1993)

Gillen, Gerard and White, Harry (eds), *Irish Musical Studies 3: music and Irish cultural history* (Dublin: Irish Academic Press, 1995)

Gorecki, Henryk, *O Domina Nostra*, op. 55 for solo voice and organ (Krackow: PWM, 1994)

Gottwald, Norman, *The Hebrew Bible: a socio-literary introduction* (Philadelphia: Fortress Press, 1985)

Graduale Simplex (Rome: Libreria Editrice Vaticana, 1975)

Graduale Triplex (Solesmes, 1974)

Gushee, Lawrence (ed.), *Aurelianus Reomensis: musica disciplina*, CSM, xxi, 1975

Gwynn, Aubrey, *Anglo-Irish Church Life, Fourteenth and Fifteenth Centuries* (Dublin, 1968)

Harper Collins Study Bible: new revised standard version (New York: Harper Collins, 1993)

Harris, Bernard and Freyer, Grattan (eds), *The Achievement of Seán Ó Riada* (Ballina: The Irish Humanities Centre, 1981)

Hayburn, Robert F., *Papal Legislation on Sacred Music 95 AD to 1977 AD* (Collegeville, MN: The Liturgical Press, 1979)

Heartz, Daniel and Wade, Bonnie (eds), *International Musicological Society: report of the twelfth congress, Berkeley 1977* (Kassel: Bärenreiter 1981)

Hegarty, Patricia and Nugent, Mary (eds), *Music to Honour God's Name* (Dublin: Veritas, 2000)

Henebry, Richard, *Irish Music: being an examination of the matter of scales, modes and keys, with practical instruction* (Dublin: An Cló-Chumann, 1903)

Henebry, Richard, *A Handbook of Irish Music* (Cork: Cork University Press, 1928)

Hennigan, Julie, 'Sean-nós', in Vallely, Fintan (ed.), *The Companion to Irish Traditional Music* (Cork: Cork University Press, 1999), pp. 336–339

Hiley, David, *Western Plainchant: a handbook* (Oxford: Clarendon Press, 1993)

Hiley, David, Review of P. Jeffrey, *Re-Envisioning Past Musical Cultures: ethnomusicology in the study of Gregorian chant* (Chicago: Chicago University Press, 1992), *Early Music History*, vol. 13, 1994, pp. 276–277

Hornby, Emma, *Gregorian and Old Roman Eighth-Mode Tracts* (Aldershot: Ashgate, 2002)

Hornby, Emma, 'Ways in Which the Second-Mode Tracts Function as "Readings" of Their Texts', paper read at *Cantus Planus 2004* (12th Meeting of the IMS, Lillafüred, Hungary)

Hucke, Helmut, 'Towards a New Historical View of Gregorian Chant', *JAMS*, 33, 1980, pp. 437–467

Huglo, Michel, *Les Tonaires: inventaire, analyse, comparaison* (Paris: Heugel, 1971)

Huglo, Michel, *Chant Grégorien et Musique* Médiévale (Aldershot: Ashgate, 2005), as part of the Variorum Collected Studies Series – CS814

Huijbers, Bernard, *The Performing Audience: six and a half essays on music and song in the liturgy*, trans. Ray Noll *et al.* (Phoenix: North American Liturgy Resources, 1980)

Iubilate Deo (London: Catholic Truth Society, 1974)

Jeffery, Peter, *Re-Envisioning Past Musical Cultures: ethnomusicology in the study of Gregorian chant* (Chicago: University of Chicago Press, 1992)

Joncas, Jan Michael, *From Sacred Song to Ritual Music: twentieth-century understandings of Roman Catholic worship music* (Collegeville, MN: The Liturgical Press, 1997)

Jones, Cheslyn, Wainwright, Geoffrey and Yarnold, Edward, *The Study of Liturgy* (New York: Oxford University Press, 1978)

Jones, Paddy, 'Ag Críost an Síol', *Intercom*, November 2009, p. 33

Jungmann, Josef A., *The Mass of the Roman Rite: its origins and development* (London: Burns & Oates, 1959)

Karp, Theodore, *Aspects of Orality and Formularity in Gregorian Chant* (Evanston, IL: Northwestern University Press, 1998)

Kenny, Paul and Curtin, Mary (eds), *I Sing for Joy: music from the RTÉ Radio One church music competitions* (Dublin: Columba Press, 2006)

Lawton, Liam (ed.), *In Caelo* (Dublin: Veritas, 1999)

Leaver, Robin A. and Zimmermann, J. (eds), *Liturgy and Music: lifetime learning* (Collegeville, MN: The Liturgical Press, 1998)

Levy, Kenneth, 'Charlemagne's Archetype of Gregorian Chant', *JAMS*, 40, 1987, pp. 1–30

Liber Cantualis (Tournai: Desclée, 1978)

Liber Usualis (Tournai: Desclée, 1938)

Lord, Alfred B., *The Singer of Tales* (Cambridge, MA: Harvard University Press, 1960)

Lutolf, Max (ed.), *Das Graduale von Santa Cecilia in Trastevere* (Cod. Bodmer 74), 2 vols (Cologne: Music Library Association, 1987)

Mac Con Iomaire, Liam, 'Sean-nós', in Vallely, Fintan (ed.), *The Companion to Irish Traditional Music* (Cork: Cork University Press, 1999), p. 336

Maloy, Rebecca, 'The Offertory Chant: aspects of chronology and transmission', unpublished PhD dissertation, Cincinnati University, 2001

Mascarenas, Oscar, 'Ornamental Procedures in Gregorian Chant: a syntactic study of the quilisma and oriscus', paper read at *Cantus Planus 2004* (12th Meeting of the IMS, Lillafüred, Hungary)

Mazza, Enrico, *The Celebration of the Eucharist: the origin of the rite and the development of its interpretation* (Collegeville, MN: 1998)

McAlpine, Fiona, *Tonal Consciousness in the Medieval West*, Varia Musicologica 10 (Bern: Peter Lang, 2008)

McDonagh, Ronan, *Ancient Promise* (Dublin: Fuaimlaoi, 2011)

McDonnell, Paul, 'Ó Riada at Glenstal Abbey', in Harris, Bernard and Freyer, Grattan (eds), *The Achievement of Seán Ó Riada* (Ballina: The Irish Humanities Centre, 1981), pp. 110–120

McDonnell, Paul, 'Music: a supplement to *The Furrow*', no. 1, summer 1968 (*The Furrow*, vol. 19, nos 8/9)

McFarland, Jason, *Announcing the Feast: the entrance song in the mass of the Roman Rite* (Collegeville, MN: Liturgical Press, 2012)

McGee, Timothy, 'Music, Rhetoric and the Emperor's New Clothes', in Haines, John, Rosenfeld, Randall and Hughes, Andrew (eds), *Music and Medieval Manuscripts: paleography and performance. Essays dedicated to Andrew Hughes* (Aldershot: Ashgate, 2004)

McKean, Thomas A., *Hebridean Song-Maker: Iain MacNeacail of the Isle of Skye* (Edinburgh: Polygon, 1997)

McKinnon, James, *Music in Early Christian Literature* (Cambridge: Cambridge University Press, 1987)

McKinnon, James, *The Advent Project: the later-seventh-century creation of the Roman mass proper* (Berkeley: University of California Press, 2000)

Missale Romanum (Rome: Typis Polyglottis Vaticanis, 1970)

Mocquereau, André, *Le Nombre Musical Grégorien ou Rhythmique Grégorienne*, 2 vols (Rome and Tournai: Desclée, 1908–1927)

Murphy, Gerard, *Ossianic Lore* (Dublin: At The Sign of the Three Candles, 1955)

Ní Annagáin, Máiréad and de Chlanndoilún, Séamus (eds), *Londubh an Chairn: songs of the Irish Gaels* (Dublin: The Educational Company of Ireland, 1925)

Ní Chathasaigh, Máire, 'Modes', in Vallely, Fintan (ed.), *The Companion to Irish Traditional Music* (Cork: Cork University Press, 1999), p. 243

Ní Ógáin, Úna (ed.), *Dánta Dé* (Dublin: Ó Fallamhain, 1928)

Ní Riain, Nóirín, 'The Nature and Classification of Traditional Religious Songs', in Gillen, Gerard and White, Harry (eds), *Irish Musical Studies 2: music and the church* (Dublin: Irish Academic Press, 1993), pp. 191–196

Nowacki, Edward, 'Studies on the Office Antiphons of the Old Roman Manuscript', unpublished PhD dissertation, Brandeis University, 1980

Nowacki, Edward, 'The Syntactical Analysis of Plainchant', in Heartz, Daniel and Wave, Bonnie (eds), *International Musicological Society: report of the Twelfth Congress, Berkeley 1977* (Kassel: Bärenreiter 1981), pp. 191–201

Nowacki, Edward, 'The Gregorian Office Antiphons and the Comparative Method', *Journal of Musicology*, vol. 4, 1985–1986, pp. 243–275

Nowacki, Edward, 'Linguistic Perspectives in the Analysis of Plainchant', paper read at the Irish World Music Centre, University of Limerick, March 2004

Ó Baoill, Seán, *The Irish Song Tradition* (Dublin: Gilbert Dalton, 1976)

Ó Canainn, Tomás, *Traditional Music in Ireland* (London: Routledge & Kegan Paul, 1978)

Ó Canainn, Tomás, *Traditional Slow Airs of Ireland* (Cork: Ossian Press, 1995)

Ó Canainn, Tomás, *Seán Ó Riada: his life and work* (Cork: The Collins Press, 2003)

Ó Canainn, Tomás, 'In the West Cork Gaeltacht', in Harris, Bernard and Freyer, Grattan (eds), *The Achievement of Seán Ó Riada* (Ballina: The Irish Humanities Centre, 1981), pp. 166–181

Ó Canainn, Tomás and Mac an Bhua, Gearóid, *Seán Ó Riada: a shaol agus a shaothar* (Dublin: Gartan, 1993)

O'Carroll, Fintan, *Mass of the Immaculate Conception* (Dublin: Irish Commission for Liturgy, 1977)

O'Carroll, Fintan, *Responsorial Psalms for Sundays and Major Feast Days* (Dublin: Irish Church Music Association, 1983)

Ó Cróinín, Dáibhí, *The Songs of Elisabeth Cronin, Traditional Singer* (Dublin: Four Courts Press, 2000)

Ó hEidhin, Mícheál, *Cas Amhrán* (Conamara: Cló Iar-Chonnachta, 1990)

Ó Fiannachta, Pádraig and Forristal, Desmond (eds), *Saltair: prayers from the Irish tradition* (Dublin: Columba Press, 1988)

O'Keeffe, John (ed.), *Feasts and Seasons* (Maynooth: St Patrick's College, 2003)

O'Keeffe, John, *Mass of Saint Mel* (Galway: Tela Design, 2015)

O'Keeffe, John, 'Singing the Mass: mass composition in Ireland since Vatican II', in Tracey, Liam and Whelan, Thomas (eds), *Serving Liturgical Renewal: pastoral and liturgical questions* (Veritas: Dublin, 2015), pp. 70–80

O'Keeffe, John, 'Ó Riada's *Ár nAthair*', in Ryan, Salvador and Leahy, Brendan (eds), *Treasures of Irish Christianity*, (Dublin: Veritas, 2012), pp. 229–233

Ó Laoghaire, An tAthair Diarmuid, *Ár bPaidreacha Dúchais* (Baile Átha Cliath: Foilseacháin Ábhair Spioradálta, repr. 1990)

Ó Madagáin, Breandán, 'Song for Emotional Release in the Gaelic Tradition', in Gillen, Gerard and White, Harry (eds), *Irish Musical Studies 2: music and the church* (Dublin: Irish Academic Press, 1993), pp. 254–275

Ó Madagáin, Breandán, *Caointe agus Seancheolta Eile* (Conamara: Cló Iar-Chonnachta, 2005)

Ó Riada, Peadar, *Go mBeannaítear Duit: ceol ó shéipéal Chúil Aodha* (Cassette, Gael Linn, CEFC 125, 1987)

Ó Riada, Peadar, *Aifreann Eoin na Croise* (Mass booklet from first performance at St Teresa's, Clarendon St, Dublin, 1991)

Ó Riada, Peadar, *Peadar Ó Riada: winds – gentle whisper* (CD, Bar/None Records, 1995)

Ó Riada, Peadar, *Naomh Gobnait* (CD, POR 015, 2012) (Includes *Aifreann Eoin na Croise*)

Ó Riada, Seán, *Ceol an Aifrinn mar a Chantar i nGaeltacht Chúil Aodha* (Baile Átha Cliath: An Clóchomhar Teoranta, 1971)

Ó Riada, Seán, *Ó Riada's Farewell* (Claddagh Records, 1971, CC12)

Ó Riada, Seán, *Aifreann 2*, ed. Eilís Cranitch and Tomás Ó Canainn (Dublin: Gael Linn, 1979)

Ó Riada, Seán, *Seán Ó Riada: Ceol an Aifrinn & Aifreann 2* (CD, Gael Linn in association with Oidhreacht an Riadaigh, with sleeve notes by Peadar Ó Riada, Ó Riada CD02, 2005)

Ó Riada, Seán, *Our Musical Heritage* (Mountrath: The Dolmen Press, 1982)

Ó Riada, Seán: *Aifreann 2* (manuscript transcription by Dom Kevin Healy, Glenstal Abbey)

O'Sullivan, Donal, *Songs of the Irish* (Dublin: Browne & Nolan, 1960)

Ó Tuama, Seán, *An Grá in Amhráin na nDaoine* (Dublin, 1960)

Page, Christopher, *The Christian West and Its Singers: the first thousand years* (Yale: An Clóchomhar, New Haven: University Press, 2012)

Palmer, Rev. George Herbert, *The Diurnal Noted from the Salisbury Use* (Wantage: St Mary's Press, 1926)

Palmer, Rev. George Herbert, *The Order of Vespers throughout the Year* (Wantage: St Mary's Press, 1947)

Parry, Milman, 'Studies in the Epic Technique of Oral Verse-Making. 1. Homer and Homeric Style', *Harvard Studies in Classical Philology*, 41, 1930, pp. 73–147

Péres, Marcel and Cheyronnaud, Jacques, *Les Voix du Plain-chant* (Paris: Desclée de Brouwer, 2001)

Petrie, George, *The Petrie Collection of the Ancient Music of Ireland* (Dublin: Gill, 1855, repr. Aldershot: The Scolar Press, 1978)

Phelan, Helen, 'Laus Perennis: the emergence of a theology of music with reference to post-Vatican II Irish Catholicism', unpublished PhD dissertation, University of Limerick, 2000

Phelan, Helen (ed.), *Anáil Dé: the breath of God. Music, ritual and spirituality* (Dublin: Veritas, 2001)

Powers, Harold, 'Mode', in Sadie, Stanley (ed.), *The New Grove Dictionary of Music and Musicians*, xii (London: Macmillan, 1980), pp. 376–450

Prassl, Franz Karl, 'Erste Spuren des "Germanischen Choraldialekts" in Codex Einsiedeln 121 und in St Galler Handschriften', paper read at *Cantus Planus 2004* (12th Meeting of the IMS, Lillafüred, Hungary)

Prou, Dom Jean, OSB, 'Gregorian Chant in the Spirituality of the Church', paper given at the 1983 International Symposium on Gregorian Chant held in Washington DC, in *Jubilus Review*, vol. 4, no. 4, 1987, pp. 539–547

Quasten, Johannes, *Music and Worship in Pagan and Christian Antiquity*, trans. Boniface Ramsey (Washington, DC: NAPM, 1983)

Quinn, Bob, 'Sean-nós', in Vallely, Fintan (ed.), *The Companion to Irish Traditional Music* (Cork: Cork University Press, 1999), pp. 339–345

Randhofer, Regina, 'Oral versus Written: structural differences in Jewish and Christian psalms', paper read at *Cantus Planus 2004* (12th Meeting of the IMS, Lillafüred, Hungary)

Ruff, Anthony, *Sacred Music and Liturgical Reform: treasures and transformations* (Chicago: Hillenbrand, 2007)

Ryan, Joseph, 'Assertions of Distinction: the modal debate in Irish music' in Gillen, Gerard and White, Harry (eds), *Irish Musical Studies 2: music and the church* (Dublin: Irish Academic Press, 1993), pp. 62–77

Sachs, Curt, *The Wellsprings of Music*, ed. Jaap Kunst (The Hague: Martinus Nijhoff; repr. New York: Da Capo Press, 1977)

Sandon, Nick, *The Use of Salisbury: the ordinary of the mass* (Lustleigh: Antico, 1984)

Sandon, Nick, *The Use of Salisbury 2: the proper of the mass* (Lustleigh: Antico, 1986)

Sandon, Nick, *The Use of Salisbury 3: the proper of the mass from Septuagesima to Palm Sunday* (Lustleigh: Antico, 1991)

Saulnier, Daniel (ed.), *Requirentes Modos Musicos: mélanges offerts à Dom Jean Claire, maître de choeur* (Solesmes, 1995)

Saulnier, Dom Daniel, *Les Modes Grégoriens* (Solesmes, 1997)

Scahill, Adrian, 'The Knotted Chord: harmonic accompaniment in printed and recorded sources of Irish traditional music', unpublished PhD dissertation, University College Dublin, 2005

Seasoltz, Kevin, *New Liturgy, New Laws* (Collegeville, MN: The Liturgical Press, 1980)

Shields, Hugh, *Narrative Singing in Ireland: lays, ballads, come-all-yes and other songs* (Dublin: Irish Academic Press, 1993)

Shiloah, Amnon, 'The Viewpoints of two Medieval Jewish Philosophers on Music and Its Relation to the Old Testament and Cantillation', *Cantus Planus Lillafüred/Hungary, 2004: papers read at the 12th meeting of the IMS Study Group* (Budapest: Institute for Musicology of the Hungarian Academy of Sciences, 2006), pp. 9–23

Snow, Robert, 'The Old-Roman Chant', in Apel, Willi, *Gregorian Chant* (Bloomington: Indiana University Press, 1958), pp. 484–505

Stevens, John, *Words and Music in the Middle Ages: song, narrative, dance and drama, 1050–1350* (Cambridge: Cambridge University Press, 1986)

Strunk, Oliver, *Source Readings in Musical History*

Szendrei, Janka and Hiley, David (eds), *Laborare Fratres in Unum: fetschrift László Dobszayzum 60. Geburtstag* (Hildesheim and Zürich: Weidmann, 1995)

The Roman Missal (Alcester and Dublin: Goodliffe Neale, 1974)

The Roman Missal (Dublin: Veritas, 2011)

Tietze, Christoph, 'The Use of Old Latin in the Non-Psalmic Introit Texts', paper read at *Cantus Planus 2004*, 12th Meeting of the IMS, Lillafüred, Hungary

Tracey, Liam and Whelan, Thomas, *Serving Liturgical Renewal: pastoral and liturgical questions* (Veritas: Dublin, 2015)

Treitler, Leo, 'Homer and Gregory: the transmission of epic poetry and plainchant', *The Musical Quarterly*, vol. 60, July 1974, pp. 333–372

Treitler, Leo, '"Centonate Chant": Übles Flickwerk or *E pluribus unus?*', JAMS, 28, Spring 1975), pp. 1–23

Treitler, Leo, *With Voice and Pen: coming to know medieval song and how it was made* (New York: Oxford University Press, 2003)

Ua Duinnín, Mícheál, *An Duinníneach: amhráin sean-nóis le Mícheál Ua Duinnín* (CD, Comhchoiste Ghaeltacht Uíbh Ráthaigh, 2004)

Vallely, Fintan (ed.), *The Companion to Irish Traditional Music* (Cork: Cork University Press, 1999)

Van Betteray, Dirk, 'Liqueszenzenals Schlüssel zur Textinterpretation: eine semiologische Untersuchung an St Galler Quellen', paper read at *Cantus Planus 2004*, 12th meeting of the IMS, Lillafüred, Hungary

White, Harry, 'Church Music and Musicology in Ireland: an afterword', in Gillen, Gerard and White, Harry (eds), *Irish Musical Studies, Volume 2: music and the church* (Dublin: Irish Academic Press, 1993), pp. 333–339

White, Harry and Boydell, Barra (eds), *The Encyclopaedia of Music in Ireland* (Dublin: University College Dublin Press, 2013)

Winter, Miriam Therese, *Why Sing? Toward a Theology of Catholic Church Music* (Washington DC: The Pastoral Press, 1984)

Yudkin, Jeremy, *Music in Medieval Europe* (Englewood, NJ: Prentice Hall, 1989

INDEX

The accompanying disc contains sung solo illustrations of the various mass movements. To access the authentic choral versions, readers are directed to the original Ó Riada/Cór Chúil Aodha recordings of all three masses, available through the following website: **www.peadaroriada.ie**

The Masses of Seán and Peadar Ó Riada

TRACK LISTING

Ceol an aifrinn

1. Iontróid (Example 3.1)
2. Kyrie eleison (3.3)
3. An ghlóir (Example 3.5)
4. An phreafáid (3.10)
5. Sanctus (3.13)
6. An phaidir (3.14)
7. Agnus Dei (3.18)
8. Ag Críost an síol (3.20)
9. Gile mo chroí (3.21)
10. Réir Dé go ndeineam (3.23)
11. Bí a Íosa im chroíse (3.24)
12. A Rí an Domhnaigh (3.25)

Aifreann 2

13. Iontróid (4.2)
14. Kyrie (4.3)
15. Gloria (4.5)
16. Alleluia (4.12)
17. Roimh an soiscéal/
Ag deireadh an tsoiscéil (4.12)
18. An phreafáid (4.17)
19. Sanctus (Example 4.19)
20. Tar éis an choisreacadh (4.21)
21. Deireadh an phaidir eochairistigh (4.23)
22. An phaidir (4.25)
23. Agnus Dei (4.34)
24. A Íosa bháin (4.38)
25. Gurab Tú mo bhoile (4.40)
26. Beannaigh sinn, a Athair (4.41)

Aifreann Eoin na Croise

27. Go mbeannaíthear duit (5.1)
28. Umhlaím duit (5.2)
29. Im' chroí 'tá'n t-olc (5.3)
30. Bronnaim m'anam ort (5.4)
31. Admhaím do Dhia mhóir (5.5)
32. Salm 139 (5.6)
33. Aililiúia (5.9)
34. Guí an phobail (5.10)
35. Is naofa (5.11)
36. Rúndiamhair an chreidimh (5.13)
37. Is tríd/ Amen mór (5.14)
38. Ar nAthair/ Síocháin (5.15)
39. A Uain Dé (5.16)
40. An cosán draíochta (5.19)